CW00400620

# MODERN LEGAL STUDIES

# CONSTRUCTIVE TRUSTS

AUSTRALIA AND NEW ZEALAND
The Law Book Company Ltd.
Sydney : Melbourne : Perth

CANADA AND U.S.A.
The Carswell Company Ltd.
Agincourt, Ontario

INDIA
N. M. Tripathi Private Ltd.
Bombay
*and*
Eastern Law House Private Ltd.
Calcutta and Delhi
M.P.P. House
Bangalore

ISRAEL
Steimatzky's Agency Ltd.
Jerusalem : Tel Aviv : Haifa

MALAYSIA : SINGAPORE : BRUNEI
Malayan Law Journal (Pte.) Ltd.
Singapore and Kuala Lumpur

PAKISTAN
Pakistan Law House
Karachi

# MODERN LEGAL STUDIES

# CONSTRUCTIVE TRUSTS

by

**A. J. OAKLEY**, M.A., LL.B.,
*Fellow of Trinity Hall, Cambridge*
*Lecturer in Law in the University of Cambridge*

## SECOND EDITION

LONDON
SWEET & MAXWELL
1987

First edition    1978
Second edition    1987


Published by
Sweet & Maxwell Limited of
11 New Fetter Lane, London.
Computerset by Promenade Graphics Limited, Cheltenham.
Printed in Great Britain by
Adlard & Son Ltd The Garden City Press,
Letchworth, Herts.

**British Library Cataloguing in Publication Data**
Oakley, A.J.
    Constructive trusts.—2nd ed.—(Modern
    Legal Studies).
    1. Trusts and trustees—England
    I. Title   II. Series
    344.2065'9        KD1925


ISBN 0–421–34740–6
ISBN 0–421–34750–3 Pbk

# PREFACE

The study of constructive trusts has always formed a small but important part of courses on the law of trusts and on conveyancing. During the last 20 years, however, constructive trusts have been the subject of more judicial discussion than in any other comparable period this century. As a result of the interest which has thus been generated, much greater attention has been given to the study of constructive trusts in degree courses on equity and trusts and this area of the law has become an important part of courses on the law of restitution and on family law. As yet, however, this increased emphasis has not been paralleled in the standard texts and it is in the hope of filling this gap that this monograph has been written.

This book has obviously been written primarily for those studying the law of trusts and conveyancing but I hope that it will also be of interest both to those studying the other subjects to which constructive trusts have become relevant and to academics and practitioners. One of the more unexpected developments of the last 20 years has been the diversity of the areas in which the possibility of the imposition of a constructive trust has been raised and it is hoped that this book will be of assistance to practitioners who are suddenly confronted with such a possibility. I have deliberately set out to write a book on the English law relating to constructive trusts and thus this work does not in any way purport to be a comparative study of its subject matter. I have, however, discussed authorities from other common law jurisdictions where I have felt that English law has something to learn from their attitudes and approach.

The format of this second edition has remained essentially the same as that of the first edition, although each of the first four chapters has been rewritten to take account of the many important decided cases and the considerable quantity of academic writing that have appeared in the years that have passed since the publication of the first edition. The law has been stated from the sources which were available to me on December 1, 1986.

I would like to thank those of my colleagues and former colleagues with whom I have discussed the subject matter of this book for the benefit of their ideas and criticisms and in particular I would like to acknowledge with deep gratitude the assistance given by my former colleague, Mr. J. D. R. Adams, now Registrar of the Court of Appeal, in the preparation of the first edition. I would also like to thank all those who reviewed the first edition or wrote to me about its contents—all their comments were very greatly appreciated, whether or not they have actually been incorporated into this second edition. I would also like to acknowledge my indebtedness to the published work of Professor Gareth Jones, Downing Professor of the Laws of England in the University of Cambridge, Professor D. W. M. Waters, Professor of Law at McGill University, and Dr. P. D. Finn, Reader in Law at the Australian National University. Finally, I would like to thank the Publishers for inviting me to prepare this further edition and for the patience which they have displayed while awaiting the manuscript.

January 1, 1987                                           A. J. Oakley
Trinity Hall,
Cambridge.

# OTHER BOOKS IN THE SERIES

# CONTENTS

# TABLE OF CASES

# TABLE OF STATUTES

# Chapter 1

## INTRODUCTION

### The nature of constructive trusts

Constructive trusts arise by operation of law. Unlike all other trusts, a constructive trust is imposed by the court as a result of the conduct of the trustee and therefore arises quite independently of the intention of any of the parties.[1]

Trusts are generally described as relationships in respect of property under which one person, known as a trustee, is obliged to deal with property vested in him for the benefit of another person, known as a beneficiary. Consequently, when property is declared to be the subject matter of a constructive trust, the imposition of that trust necessarily confers on the beneficiary proprietary rights in the subject matter of the constructive trust. However, quite apart from these proprietary rights, the imposition of a constructive trust also produces liabilities of a personal nature for the constructive trustee; he will be subject to the liability which is imposed on every trustee to account personally to his beneficiary for his actions as trustee. Thus, when property is declared to be the subject-matter of a constructive trust, the imposition of that trust produces liabilities both of a proprietary and of a personal nature for the constructive trustee. The precise nature of these two liabilities and the circumstances in which it will be advantageous for the beneficiary to rely on either or both will be discussed in the next section of this chapter.

It might be expected to follow from the inherent nature of a trust as a relationship in respect of property that a constructive

---

[1] There are of course circumstances where constructive trusts are imposed to give effect to the express or implied intention of the parties. The express intention of the parties is given effect to, for example, where a constructive trust is imposed to enforce an oral undertaking or agreement by a transferee of land who has subsequently sought to rely on the absence of the written formalities required by the Law of Property Act 1925. And the implied intention of the parties is given effect to, for example, where a constructive trust is imposed when a person has improved property on the understanding that he would thereby obtain a beneficial interest therein. (Both these types of constructive trusts are discussed in Chap. 2.). However, given that such constructive trusts only need to be imposed because the constructive trustee has gone back on what was originally envisaged, such cases in fact re-emphasise that constructive trusts arise independently of the intention of the parties.

trust can only be imposed if there is some identifiable property upon which to impose it. This does not of course mean that the property in question has to be identifiable in the hands of the constructive trustee at the time when the matter is brought before the courts; this requirement will equally be satisfied if that property has been identifiable in the hands of the constructive trustee at some earlier stage. But the existence of some identifiable property ought to be a prerequisite of the imposition of a constructive trust. There is indeed authority for this proposition. In *Re Barney*[2] Kekewich J. stated particularly clearly that:

> " . . . it is essential to the character of a trustee that he should have trust property actually vested in him or so far under his control that he has nothing to do but require that, perhaps by one process, perhaps by another, it should be vested in him."

This requirement is undoubtedly satisfied in the vast majority of the cases in which constructive trusts are imposed. However, there are some decided cases in which the courts have imposed constructive trusts where there has been no obviously identifiable property subject to the constructive trust. In all of these cases, the person upon whom the constructive trust was imposed had knowingly participated in a breach of trust as a result of which property subject to the trust had been transferred to third parties from whom it could not be recovered.[3] Some of these decisions are reconcileable with the principle enunciated in *Re Barney* because the property in question passed through the hands of the person upon whom the constructive trust was subsequently imposed—it is thus possible to argue that the constructive trust in question arose at the moment when the property was actually in the hands of the constructive

---

[2] [1892] 2 Ch. 265, 273.
[3] Such a case was *Lee* v. *Sankey* (1873) L.R. 15 Eq. 204, where trustees employed solicitors to receive the proceeds of sale of part of the trust property. The solicitors paid part of the money to one of trustees who employed the money in various improvident speculations and died insolvent. The other trustee and the beneficiaries successfully claimed that the solicitors were personally liable as constructive trustees to account for the sums so paid away on the grounds that they should have obtained the receipt of both trustees before parting with the proceeds of sale in their hands. There is a conflict of authority on the controversial question of whether the same liability will be imposed on agents who deal with trust property in accordance with the instructions of their trustees when they ought to realise but do not actually know that a breach of trust is being committed. This question was however answered in the affirmative in *Selangor United Rubber Estates* v. *Cradock (No. 3)* [1968] 1 W.L.R. 1555 and in *Karak Rubber Co.* v. *Burden (No. 2)* [1972] 1 W.L.R. 602 so that these cases also illustrate the proposition in the text.

trustee.[4] However, quite apart from the fact that none of the judges seems to have regarded as important the question of what property was subject to the constructive trust, there are other decisions which are, on any view, totally irreconcileable with the principle laid down in *Re Barney*. This is because in these cases constructive trusts were imposed on persons who had never received or in any way controlled the property in question.[5] The existence of these authorities, all of which will be discussed fully in Chapter 4, has led some commentators to contend that there is in fact a second kind of constructive trust which can arise without any necessity for there to be any identifiable trust property. This suggested second type of constructive trust obviously does not confer any proprietary rights on the beneficiary thereunder but merely imposes on the constructive trustee a personal liability to account to the beneficiary for his actions.[6] For this reason the constructive trusteeship so imposed has been described as "a fiction which provides a useful remedy where no remedy is available in contract or in tort."[7] It has to be admitted that it is virtually impossible to justify some of the existing authorities without accepting the argument that there is indeed such a second kind of constructive trust. Nevertheless, it is not easy to see how an obligation which is not imposed in respect of any identifiable property can properly be classified as a trust. This is not an appropriate moment to consider whether or not it is possible to justify the result of these decisions.[8] It is however suggested that, in any event, these decisions should

---

[4] Of the authorities discussed in n. 3, *Lee* v. *Sankey* can certainly be explained in this way since the solicitors actually received the proceeds of sale. However, it is much more difficult, although just about possible, to explain *Selangor United Rubber Estates* v. *Cradock (No. 3)* and *Karak Rubber Co.* v. *Burden (No. 2)* in this way since in both cases the constructive trustees were banks who had merely transferred funds from one account to another.

[5] Such a case was *Eaves* v. *Hickson* (1861) 30 Beav. 136, where a father produced a forged marriage certificate to the trustees of a settlement and thus convinced them that his children were legitimate and so entitled to the trust property which was duly distributed to them. (He had married the mother of the children after their birth but at that time there was no doctrine of legitimation by subsequent marriage. He thus changed the date on his marriage certificate so that the marriage appeared to have taken place before the birth of the children.) Those otherwise entitled to the property subsequently sued for its recovery and it was held that the father was personally liable to account for such of the property as could not be recovered from the children.

[6] This argument is set out particularly clearly in Ford & Lee, *Principles of the Law of Trusts*: pp. 992–995. See also Hayton & Marshall, *Cases and Commentary on the Law of Trusts* (8th ed.), pp. 443–446.

[7] D. J. Hayton: (1985) 27 *Malaya Law Review* 313, 314.

[8] This question will be considered in Chap. 4.

not be regarded as examples of the imposition of a constructive trust. It seems more appropriate to regard such cases as examples of equity imposing a quite distinct remedy—a personal liability to account in the same manner as a trustee. This is of course more a matter of terminology and classification than of substance. However, it is suggested that it is more in accordance with the inherent nature of a trust to regard such cases as examples of a quite distinct equitable remedy. Nevertheless, it has to be admitted that the argument that there are in fact two distinct types of constructive trust enjoys considerable support both from judges and from commentators.

## The consequences of the imposition of a constructive trust

It has already been seen that, when property is declared to be the subject matter of a constructive trust, the imposition of that trust produces liabilities both of a proprietary and of a personal nature for the constructive trustee. Not only will the beneficiary necessarily be entitled to proprietary rights in the subject matter of the constructive trust; the constructive trustee will also by virtue of his position as a trustee, be personally liable to account to the beneficiary for his actions as such. What is the relationship between these two distinct liabilities?

Where the property upon which the constructive trust is imposed is still identifiable in the hands of the constructive trustee, both these remedies will be available to the beneficiary who will be able to choose either to exercise his proprietary rights in the subject matter of the constructive trust, or to rely on the personal liability of the constructive trustee to account, or, in rare circumstances, to exercise both of these remedies. The position of a beneficiary who chooses to rely on his proprietary rights will obviously depend upon the precise nature of the constructive trust that has been imposed. In the vast majority of the cases in which a constructive trust is imposed on property in the hands of the constructive trustee, the beneficiary is held to have an absolute interest in the subject matter of the constructive trust, in which case he is obviously entitled to call for the transfer of the property to him together with any income or other fruits that the property has produced since the constructive trust arose. Such a situation will arise, for example, where a constructive trust is imposed to give effect to an oral undertaking by the transferee of land to reconvey that property to the transferor where the transferee has subsequently sought to rely on the absence of the writing which under section 53(1)(*b*) of the Law of Property Act 1925 is required to render such a trust enforceable.[9] In this case the transferor is entitled to call for the retransfer to him of the land in question together with all the income and other fruits which that property has produced since the property was transferred to the constructive trustee.[10] Alternatively, the beneficiary may be held to have less than an absolute interest in the subject matter of the trust, in which case he will have the rights appropriate to whatever beneficial interest he has. Such a situation will arise, for example, where a constructive trust is imposed to give effect to an oral agreement that the transferor of land is to retain a life interest therein where the transferee has subsequently sought to rely on the absence of the writing which under section 40 of the Law of Property Act 1925 is required to render such an agreement enforceable. In this case, the transferor will be entitled to all the rights appropriate to such a life tenancy.[11]

If the beneficiary instead chooses to rely on the personal liability of the constructive trustee to account, he will in effect be claiming damages for breach of trust from the constructive trustee. In the event that the beneficiary chooses to employ this remedy in the two situations which were used as examples in the preceding paragraph, he will in each case by virtue of the personal liability of the constructive trustee to account recover the value of the interest in question and so will recover, respectively, the value of the land and the value of his life interest therein as at the date when the constructive trust arose. In both cases, once this sum has been paid over, the constructive trust will be discharged and the constructive trustee will thereafter be absolutely beneficially entitled to the property upon which the constructive trust was imposed.[12]

Where the constructive trustee is solvent, the election between the two remedies will not normally have any particularly significant effects on the measure of the recovery of the beneficiary. When the property has neither produced income or other fruits nor changed in value while it has been in the hands of the constructive trustee, both remedies will lead to exactly the same measure of recovery. Where, on the other hand, the property upon which the constructive trust has been imposed has produced income or other fruits or has risen in value while it has been in the hands of the constructive trustee, it will obviously be preferable for the ben-

---

[9] Such a constructive trust is imposed on the grounds that a statute cannot be used as an instrument of fraud. The relevant authorities will be discussed in Chap. 2.

[10] *Re Duke of Marlborough* [1894] 2 Ch. 133.

[11] *Bannister* v. *Bannister* [1948] W.N. 261.

[12] There does not appear to be any decided case in support of this proposition but it seems sound as a matter of principle.

eficiary to choose to rely on his proprietary rights since this will enable him to recover the income, the other fruits or the increase in value in question. And where the property upon which the constructive trust has been imposed has fallen in value while it has been in the hands of the constructive trustee, it will obviously be preferable for the beneficiary to choose to rely on the personal liability of the constructive trustee since this will enable him to recover the amount that the property was worth when it reached the hands of the constructive trustee and so ignore the subsequent fall in its value. This will certainly be the best remedy for the beneficiary where the fall in the value of the property cannot be held to have been brought about by the conduct of the constructive trustee. But if, on the other hand, it can be shown that the constructive trustee was responsible for the fall in value of the property, there seems no reason why the beneficiary may not alternatively seek to rely on both the remedies available to him; if this is indeed possible, he will be able both to call for the transfer to him of the property and, by relying on the personal liability of the constructive trustee to account, to obtain damages for the fall in value of the property. This will not of course increase the measure of recovery but will enable the beneficiary to recover the property itself. There seems no reason whatsoever why such a process should not be possible in an appropriate case.

Where, however, the constructive trustee is insolvent, the election between the two remedies will be immensely significant. If the beneficiary chooses to rely on his proprietary rights, he will take priority over the general creditors of the insolvent constructive trustee, whereas if he instead chooses to rely on the personal liability of the constructive trustee to account, he will rank with rather than ahead of the general creditors. Consequently the only situation in which the beneficiary is likely to choose to rely on the personal liability of the constructive trustee to account will be where the property which is the subject matter of the constructive trust has fallen in value to a percentage of its original value smaller than the percentage that is likely to be paid out by the trustee in bankruptcy to the general creditors.[13] Except in this extremely unlikely situation, the beneficiary will in such circumstances inevitably

---

[13] In the event that it can be shown that the constructive trustee was responsible for the fall in value of the property, it will always be in the beneficiary's interest to take advantage of the possibility mentioned in the previous paragraph of the text to both recover the property and claim damages for the fall in its value (assuming of course that such a double claim is possible). This is because such a double claim will give him both the property and the same percentage of the claim for damages as is paid out to the general creditors.

choose to rely on his proprietary rights so as to obtain this priority. This will in turn diminish the mass of general assets available for distribution among the general creditors of the insolvent trustee so that each general creditor will therefore obtain a smaller proportion of the sum owed to him. Thus the imposition of a constructive trust upon a person who is, or subsequently becomes, bankrupt will almost inevitably prejudice the interests of his general creditors, who will *ex hypothesi* not be before the court to object to the imposition of the constructive trust in question. In such circumstances, the only possibility of avoiding the consequent prejudice to the interests of the general creditors will be for the trustee in bankruptcy of the constructive trustee to go to the court under sections 174 and 175 of the Insolvency Act 1985[14] and seek an order setting aside the constructive trust on the grounds that its imposition has conferred an unlawful preference on the beneficiary at the expense of the general creditors.

Thus far the consequences of the imposition of a constructive trust have been considered on the assumption that the constructive trust in question is imposed on property which is still identifiable in the hands of the constructive trustee. Where this is not the case, the property may nevertheless be identifiable in the hands of a third party. In such circumstances, it may be possible to recover the property by following it into the hands of that third party. Any third party in whose hands the property is identifiable other than a

---

[14] These sections enable the trustee in bankruptcy to apply to the court for an order restoring the *status quo* where a bankrupt has at a relevant time entered into a transaction at an undervalue or given a preference (the relevant time is determined by the nature of the transaction, the identity of the other party and the solvency of the bankrupt at the time of the transaction). An illustration of the kind of circumstances in which these sections are likely to be utilised is provided by *Re Densham (A Bankrupt)* [1975] 1 W.L.R. 1519, which concerned the predecessor of these sections, section 42 of the Bankruptcy Act 1914, which rendered void against the trustee in bankruptcy any settlement of property other than for value within fixed time limits before the bankruptcy. In this case, the court was faced by opposing claims to the matrimonial home of a bankrupt from his wife, who had contributed one-ninth of the purchase price on the strength of an agreement that she should have a half share therein, and from his trustee in bankruptcy who claimed that any such beneficial interest amounted to a settlement that was void against him. The wife obviously had a beneficial interest in the property in proportion to her contribution to the purchase price under a resulting trust and Goff J. held that the agreement entitled her to a half share in the property under a constructive trust. However, although the interest acquired under the resulting trust was clearly binding against the trustee in bankruptcy, he held that that part of the beneficial interest acquired under the constructive trust that exceeded her contribution to the purchase price had been acquired under a settlement that was caught by the section and so was void against the trustee in bankruptcy.

bona fide purchaser of a legal interest in the property for value
without notice of the adverse claim of the beneficiary under the
constructive trust will inevitably be liable to have the property
traced in equity into his hands. This is because the imposition of a
constructive trust gives rise to the relationship of trustee and beneficiary which, on any view, is sufficient to satisfy the prerequisites
of such an equitable tracing claim.[15] Where the trust property can
be followed in this way into the hands of a third party, the situation
will differ very little from that which has already been discussed.
The beneficiary will have a choice between, on the one hand, exercising his proprietary rights in the subject matter of the constructive trust by following that property into the hands of the third
party and, on the other hand, relying on the personal liability of
the constructive trustee to account. The election between the two
remedies will be dependent on exactly the same factors as have
already been discussed. Where both the third party and the constructive trustee are solvent, the only relevant factors will be the
presence or absence of income and other fruits and any changes in
the value of the property. Where the constructive trustee is insolvent, the beneficiary will almost inevitably choose to rely on his
proprietary rights and pursue his equitable tracing claim against
the third party.

It may, on the other hand, not be possible to recover the property upon which the constructive trust has been imposed. This will
be the case where the property either has disappeared as the result
of casual expenditure or dissipation by the constructive trustee or a
third party or has reached the hands of a third party against whom
it is not possible to maintain an equitable tracing claim because he
is a bona fide purchaser of a legal interest in the property for value
without notice of the adverse claim of the beneficiary under the
constructive trust. In this situation, the beneficiary will no longer
have any proprietary rights in the subject matter of the constructive trust. Consequently the only remedy available to him will be
to rely on the personal liability of the constructive trustee to
account. Where the constructive trustee is solvent, this will not
normally produce any particularly significant disadvantage, other
than the fact that the beneficiary will be unable either to recover
any income or other fruits that the property may have produced or
to take advantage of any increase in its value. Where, on the other
hand, the constructive trustee is insolvent, the absence of any pro-

---

[15] The rules of tracing trust property into its product are expounded and criticised
in R. Goff and G. Jones, *The Law of Restitution* (2nd ed. 1978), pp. 46–63. See
also (1975) *Current Legal Problems*, p. 64.

prietary rights will prevent the beneficiary from being able to claim priority over the general creditors of the constructive trustee since the liability of the constructive trustee to account will rank with, rather than ahead of, the claims of the general creditors. Such a situation will arise, for example, where a constructive trust is imposed upon a person who has received trust property in the knowledge that the transfer of the property to him constituted a breach of trust and that person has subsequently transferred the property to a third party into whose hands it cannot be traced in equity. In this case, the only remedy available to the beneficiary will be to rely on the personal liability of the constructive trustee to account and recover the value of the property with interest from the date of the transfer to the third party.[16] However, as has already been mentioned, such a claim will give the beneficiary no priority over the general creditors of the constructive trustee in the event of his bankruptcy.

Thus far the consequences of the imposition of a constructive trust have been considered on the assumption that the constructive trust is imposed on some property which either is or at some earlier stage has been in the hands of the constructive trustee. However, as was seen in the previous section of this chapter, it has been argued that it is possible for a constructive trust to be imposed without any necessity for there to be any identifiable property. It was suggested in the previous section that it is inappropriate to classify this remedy as a constructive trust. Whatever its correct classification, however, the consequences of the imposition of such a remedy are extremely clear. Such a remedy obviously does not confer any proprietary rights but merely imposes a personal liability to account in the same manner as a trustee. Thus the consequences of the imposition of this remedy are exactly the same as those considered above in the previous paragraph. The basic measure of recovery will be the value of the property lost and this will be the measure recovered when the person upon whom the remedy is imposed is solvent.[17] In the event of

---

[16] Such a remedy was sought and duly obtained in *Selangor United Rubber Estates* v. *Cradock (No. 3)* [1968] 1 W.L.R. 1555, where constructive trusts were imposed upon two successive transferees of the assets of the plaintiff company who had been aware that these assets were subsequently to be used, contrary to s.54 of the Companies Act 1948 (now repealed and replaced by ss.151–158 of the Companies Act 1985), to finance the purchase of the plaintiff company's own shares. Since the assets in question were necessarily not in their hands by the time of the action (they had by then already been utilised to purchase the shares), the transferees were held liable to repay the sums in question with interest.

[17] This seems to have been the case in all the decisions of this type discussed in the previous section of this chapter.

his bankruptcy, however, this remedy will not enjoy any priority over his general creditors since his personal liability to account will rank with, rather than ahead of, their claims. Thus the percentage of the value of the property recovered will be the same as that paid to every other general creditor.

### When and on what grounds will a constructive trust be imposed?

The most important single factor that will determine when, and on what grounds, a constructive trust will be imposed is the rôle which the courts consider that the constructive trust occupies in the legal system as a whole. Their perception of this rôle must inevitably take into account the various possible consequences of the imposition of a constructive trust that have just been considered. In this respect, the different common law jurisdictions adopt different attitudes.

American law has long adopted the attitude that the constructive trust is an instrument for remedying unjust enrichment. Thus a constructive trust may be imposed whenever the constructive trustee has been unjustly enriched at the expense of the constructive beneficiary. In other words, all that has to be shown is that the constructive trustee has received some benefit which, as against the constructive beneficiary, he cannot justly retain. Paragraph 160 of the American Restatement of Restitution provides:

> "Where a person holding title to property is subject to an equitable duty to convey it to another on the ground that he would be unjustly enriched if he were permitted to retain it, a constructive trust arises."

This provision unquestionably represents the attitude of American judges. As Cardozo J. has remarked:

> "A constructive trust is the formula through which the conscience of equity finds expression. When property has been acquired in such circumstances that the holder of the legal title may not in good conscience retain the beneficial interest, equity converts him into a trustee."[18]

Thus the attitude of American law is quite clear: the constructive trust is an instrument for remedying unjust enrichment.

---

[18] *Beatty* v. *Guggenheim Exploration Co.* (1919) 225 N.Y. 380, 386.

The attitude of English law is more uncertain. Few attempts have been made to lay down any general principle governing the imposition of constructive trusts. A fairly characteristic judicial pronouncement is this statement by Edmund Davies L.J. in 1969:

> "English law provides no clear and all-embracing definition of a constructive trust. Its boundaries have been left perhaps deliberately vague, so as not to restrict the court by technicalities in deciding what the justice of a particular case may demand."[19]

Despite this type of judicial reticence, the English attitude has been expressed in a number of ways. Professor R. H. Maudsley has stated in an oft-quoted passage, that "English law has always thought of the constructive trust as an institution"[20] as opposed to the American attitude that the constructive trust is "purely a remedial institution."[21] This terminology, however, causes some difficulty since it creates the impression that English law does not, in any sense, regard the constructive trust as a remedy. While it may indeed be accurate to state that English law does not regard the constructive trust as a remedy in the sense that it regards the injunction as a remedy, it can hardly be said that a litigant seeking the imposition of a constructive trust is not seeking a remedy. The English attitude to the constructive trust may, perhaps, rather be expressed in this way. English law has, generally speaking, only been prepared to impose a constructive trust where the conduct of the person upon whom the trust is to be imposed amounts to a legal wrong—where, in other words, a cause of action against the constructive trustee has arisen independently. This attitude seems to be inherent in the vast majority of the English authorities. At one stage it did indeed appear that English law might be moving towards an approach much more akin to that of the American decisions. In the years immediately before and after 1970, a number of decisions emanating from the Court of Appeal suggested that a constructive trust "is a trust imposed by law whenever justice and good conscience require it . . . it is an equitable remedy by which the court can enable an aggrieved party to obtain restitution."[22] However, the approach manifested in this series of cases has not been followed up and the more recent decisions have returned to the more traditional approach. It is therefore no

[19] *Carl-Zeiss Stiftung* v. *Herbert Smith (No.2)* [1969] 2 Ch. 276, 300.
[20] In (1959) 75 L.Q.R. 234, 237.
[21] These are words of Roscoe Pound in 33 Harvard L.Rev. (1920) 420 at p. 421.
[22] *Per* Lord Denning M.R. in *Hussey* v. *Palmer* [1972] 1 W.L.R. 1286, 1290.

longer possible to say[23] that English law may at present be in a transitional stage—the recent decisions indicate very clearly that English law, for at least the immediate future, will retain an attitude towards the constructive trust quite distinct from the attitude of American law.

What should be the attitude of English law towards the constructive trust? It has long been argued that the English courts should adopt the American approach and impose constructive trusts in order to prevent unjust enrichment. "What English law needs," wrote Professor D. W. M. Waters in 1964, "is a practical, down to earth remedy, as vivid as specific performance and injunction, and within which the courts are brought immediately face to face with the policy decisions or the equities that the courts must and do already respectively make or weigh."[24] Certainly, in principle, there is no reason why the categories of situations in which English courts will impose a constructive trust should be regarded as closed. However, the various consequences of the imposition of a constructive trust that have already been considered are strong arguments against the use of the constructive trust as a general equitable remedy to do justice in the instant case. The imposition of a constructive trust produces liabilities both of a proprietary and of a personal nature for the constructive trustee. Quite apart from the fact that such liabilities may be extremely burdensome for the constructive trustee, their proprietary nature affects the existing property rights both of the constructive trustee and, in the event of his bankruptcy, of his general creditors. As a matter of principle, such alterations of existing property rights should not be able to ensue merely from the desire of a court to do justice in the instant case. It has never been the practice of English courts to alter existing property rights merely in order to do justice *inter partes*.[25] The House of Lords has repeatedly stated that rights of property are not to be determined according to what is reasonable and fair or just in all the circumstances. This proposition was expressly asserted by four

---

[23] As was stated in the first edition of this work (on p. 3).

[24] *The Constructive Trust* (1964), p. 73.

[25] It has been suggested that the decision of the House of Lords in *Sinclair* v. *Brougham* [1914] A.C. 398 is an example of the alteration of priorities by the imposition of a constructive trust. Four members of the House of Lords did indeed hold that the depositors in an *ultra vires* banking business could trace the sums deposited into the hands of the Building Society who had run the bank on the grounds that the depositors were beneficiaries under a trust thereof. However, as was shown in *Current Legal Problems* (1975) 64, none of their lordships actually classified the trust in question as a constructive trust—in fact, the only member of the House to classify the trust (Viscount Haldane L.C., with whose speech Lord Atkinson concurred) stated that it was a resulting trust.

of the members of the House in *Pettitt* v. *Pettitt*[26] and was also crucial to the subsequent decision of the House in *Gissing* v. *Gissing*.[27] The fundamental nature of this principle was emphatically
stated by Bagnall J. in *Cowcher* v. *Cowcher*[28] where he said:

> "In any individual case the application of [established prin-
> ciples of property law] may produce a result which appears
> unfair. So be it: in my view that is not an injustice. I am con-
> vinced that in determining rights, particularly property rights,
> the only justice that can be attained by mortals, who are fal-
> lible and are not omniscient, is justice according to law; the
> justice that flows from the application of sure and settled prin-
> ciples to proved or admitted facts, So in the field of property
> law the length of the Chancellor's foot has been measured or
> is capable of measurement. This does not mean that equity is
> past child-bearing; simply that its progeny must be legit-
> imate—by precedent out of principle. It is as well that this
> should be so; otherwise no lawyer could safely advise on his
> client's title and every quarrel would lead to a law suit."

This principle is crucial for the maintenance of that certainty
which should be the hallmark of every system of laws. The imposition of a constructive trust in order to bring a dispute to a conclusion which appears to be just and equitable is inevitably contrary
to such a principle. The consequences of the imposition of a constructive trust thus constitute powerful arguments against the use
of the constructive trust as a means of doing justice *inter partes*.

These important considerations weigh heavily against the use of
the constructive trust as a general equitable remedy to do justice in
the instant case. Yet, as has already been seen, such a practice is
extremely common in the United States of America. Why do these
considerations bear no weight there? The answer to this question
appears to be that American law is much more ready to interfere
with existing third party rights than is the law of England. For
example, in America a claimant is permitted to trace his property
in equity whenever he can show that that property has been
wrongfully disposed of with knowledge of the wrongful nature of
the disposition.[29] The existence of a trust is not, as in English law,
a prerequisite of such a claim. A litigant to whom such a claim is

---

[26] [1970] A.C. 777, *per* Lord Reid at p. 793, *per* Lord Morris of Borth-y-Gest at pp.
801, 803 and 805, *per* Lord Hodson at p. 809, and *per* Lord Diplock at p. 825.
The principle is also implicit in the speech of Lord Upjohn.
[27] [1971] A.C. 886.
[28] [1972] 1 W.L.R. 425, 430.
[29] *The American Restatement of the Law of Restitution* (1937), para. 202. See also
A. W. Scott, (1955) 71 L.Q.R. 39, 48.

available will inevitably obtain priority over the third party creditors of the other party. Since the American courts are so ready to alter existing third party rights, the fact that the imposition of a constructive trust brings about such an alteration is not a particularly significant consideration. In England, on the other hand, the courts are extremely reluctant either to interfere with existing property rights or to grant priority over the general creditors of a bankrupt. Therefore, the fact that the imposition of a constructive trust has both these effects should be a much more significant consideration in England than it is in America.

It is therefore clear that the constructive trust is a remedy which has far-reaching ramifications not only for the person upon whom it is imposed but also for third parties. In England at least, the indiscriminate invocation and imposition of constructive trusts is therefore highly undesirable. The constructive trust should not be invoked by the courts as some sort of instant remedy to prevent what the court regards as an unjust result in an individual case. Thus, in this sense at least, constructive trusts should not be imposed merely in order to prevent unjust enrichment. This does not necessarily mean that the principle of unjust enrichment should not be accepted into the law of England, merely that the constructive trust is not an appropriate instrument for dealing out justice *inter partes*. Although the categories of situations in which English courts will impose constructive trusts should not be regarded as closed, these categories should be extended only where the courts are prepared to lay down some new principle which will apply generally. Any such principle must be capable of being applied with sufficient certainty to enable litigants to be safely advised as to the probable outcome of legal proceedings. Further, no such principle should be established without the fullest consideration of the effects thus produced on the general law and upon the interests of third parties nor should any such principle ever be established by deciding an individual case on grounds applicable only to that particular case.

### What trusts may properly be classified as constructive trusts?

There is a statutory basis for the classification of trusts in English law. Section 53 of the Law of Property Act 1925 lays down certain formal requirements for the valid creation of trusts and exempts from these formalities implied, resulting and constructive trusts.[30] It might therefore be expected that there would be

---

[30] This section is fully discussed by Professor G. Battersby in [1979] *The Conveyancer* 17.

general acceptance of a fourfold classification into express trusts, implied trusts, resulting trusts and constructive trusts. This, however, is not the case. The following basic definitions of express trusts, resulting trusts and constructive trusts are indeed generally accepted. Thus an express trust is said to arise where the settlor expressly creates a relationship of trustee and beneficiary; a resulting trust is said to arise where the settlor carries out some other transaction from which the court infers a relationship of trustee and beneficiary; and, as has already been seen, a constructive trust is said to arise where the court imposes upon certain persons a relationship of trustee and beneficiary. In other words, an express trust arises out of the intentional creation of the relationship, a resulting trust arises out of some other intentional act of the settlor and a constructive trust arises totally independently of the intention of anyone. On the other hand, however, there is no generally accepted definition whatsoever of implied trusts. It has sometimes been suggested that implied trusts are a quite distinct category of trust arising, like resulting trusts, where the settlor carries out some intentional act other than the creation of a relationship of trustee and beneficiary from which the court infers such a relationship—according to this view, therefore, trusts that arise in this way are divided into distinct categories of implied trusts and resulting trusts.[31] However, it is perhaps more common not to regard implied trusts as a distinct category of trusts and instead to utilise the term "implied trust" to denote one or more of the other categories of trusts. Thus the term "implied trust" has been said to be synonymous with the term "resulting trust"[32]; it has been said to embrace both resulting trusts and constructive trusts[33]; or to denote specific types of resulting and constructive trusts[34]; or, again, it has been used to denote express trusts in which the intention of the settlor has been inferred rather than been expressed

---

[31] This approach is adopted in P. H. Pettit: *Equity and the Law of Trusts*, (5th ed.), *passim*.

[32] "Implied trust" is used in this sense in *Snell's Principles of Equity* (28th ed.), pp. 176–191. This approach was also suggested in the first edition of this work at p. 9.

[33] "Implied trust" was used in this sense in *Cowcher* v. *Cowcher* [1972] 1 W.L.R. 425—this is regarded by D. J. Hayton as the normal meaning of the term today (see *Underhill's Law of Trusts and Trustees* (13th ed.), p. 22 and Hayton and Marshall: *Cases and Commentary on the Law of Trusts* (8th ed.), p. 52.)

[34] See *Soar* v. *Ashwell* [1893] 2 Q.B. 390 and the remarks of Sir Christopher Slade in *The Informal Creation of Interests in Land* (The Childe & Co. Oxford Lecture 1984), p. 4.

directly.[35] Given the confusion necessarily engendered by the use of the same term in so many different senses, it is hard to disagree with the recent comment that "[i]deally, since the concept of "implied trust" has no useful function it should cease to be used, but the compendious expression "implied resulting or constructive trusts" has its attractions to judges and parliamentary counsel who act on the principle *ex abundante cautela.*"[36] It is at least clear that no important consequence follows from giving the term "implied trust" one meaning rather than another. It is however suggested that, unless and until the ideal solution mentioned above is carried into effect, the simplest, and for that reason the best, view to adopt is to regard the terms "implied trust" and "resulting trust" as synonymous—at least that way it is only necessary to distinguish between three types of trusts, express trusts, implied or resulting trusts, and constructive trusts.

Despite the straightforward definitions of express trusts, resulting trusts and constructive trusts, the courts have always found considerable difficulty in deciding how to classify individual trusts. As Kay L.J. remarked in *Soar* v. *Ashwell*[37]; "The authorities do not seem to have drawn with any precision the line of distinction between express and constructive trusts." This, admittedly, is partly due to the historical accident that, until the enactment of the Limitation Act 1939, express trustees were unable to rely on the Statutes of Limitation as against the beneficiaries whereas the limitation period ran in favour of potential constructive trustees. This encouraged the courts to classify as express trusts certain trusts which were clearly nothing of the sort (*Soar* v. *Ashwell* itself was a case of this kind and contains a very full review of the situations in which the courts were prepared to do this). However desirable this may have been for the beneficiaries concerned, it has not exactly simplified the task of deciding whether an individual trust is express or constructive. There has also been, historically, some confusion between implied trusts, resulting trusts and constructive trusts and this confusion has not been helped by the recent tendency of certain judges to equate resulting and constructive trusts. Thus in *Hussey* v. *Palmer*[38] Lord Denning M.R. felt able to say:

---

[35] This view was adopted in *Lewin on Trusts* until its 15th edition (although not in the present (16th) edition) and also appears to be favoured by P. H. Pettit: *op. cit.* However, in accordance with the general view (now also adopted in *Lewin*), it is suggested that such trusts are in fact express trusts.

[36] D.J. Hayton in Hayton and Marshall, *op. cit.* p. 52.

[37] [1893] 2 Q.B. 390, 401.

[38] [1972] 1 W.L.R. 1286, 1289.

"Although the plaintiff alleged that there was a resulting trust, I should have thought that the trust in this case, if there was one, was more in the nature of a constructive trust; but this is more a matter of words than anything else. The two run together."

Despite these difficulties, however, the classification of many types of trusts has long been settled. Thus it is quite clear that an express trust arises whenever a settlor either declares that he is holding property on trust for another or transfers property to another to hold on trust for a third party or for himself.[39] It is also clear that an implied or resulting trust arises in two well-established situations: firstly, such a trust is presumed to arise (and such trusts are for this reason often described as "presumed resulting trusts"[40]) whenever a settlor purchases property in or transfers property into the name of a third party or the joint names of a third party and himself[41]: and, secondly, such a trust will arise automatically (and such trusts are for this reason often described as "automatic resulting trusts"[42]) whenever a settlor fails to dispose completely of the beneficial interest in property which he is settling. Further, it is also clear that a constructive trust arises in three well-established situations: first, where a person has obtained an advantage by acting fraudulently or unconscionably or (perhaps) inequitably; secondly, where a fiduciary has obtained an advantage as a result of a breach of his duty of loyalty; and, thirdly, where there has been a disposition of trust property in breach of trust. All these classifications are well established, long settled and generally agreed. However, there are certain other types of trust whose classification is less obvious. Such trusts include secret trusts, mutual wills, and the trusts that arise as a result of the creation of a contract of sale which is specifically enforceable, as a result of the exercise by a mortgagee of his powers under the mortgage, and in order to give effect in equity to a transfer of property which is at law incomplete. These types of trust are extremely difficult to classify and have been classified in many different ways by differ-

---

[39] *Milroy* v. *Lord* (1862) 4 De G.F. & J. 264.
[40] This classification was adopted by Megarry J. in *Re Vandervell's Trusts (No. 2)* [1974] Ch. 269, 294 (the classification was not affected by the subsequent reversal of the decision by the Court of Appeal).
[41] The presumption that such an implied or resulting trust arises may of course be rebutted either by contrary evidence or, in the case of a purchase in or transfer into the name of a child or ward by a father or guardian, by the presumption of advancement.
[42] See n. 40 above.

ent commentators. However, all have at various times been described by judges and commentators as constructive trusts.[43]

It thus appears that there are three types of situations which are
generally recognised as giving rise to constructive trusts and five
further types of trusts which are sometimes described as constructive trusts. These are the trusts which may be said to be classified
as constructive trusts. It therefore follows that the task of this work
must be to examine all the trusts which may be said to be classified
as constructive trusts, to consider to what extent these trusts satisfy
the principles which have been discussed in this introductory
chapter and to determine whether such trusts may properly be
classified as constructive trusts.

---

[43] It will be suggested in due course that secret trusts are in fact express trusts but
that all the other trusts mentioned are indeed constructive trusts.

Chapter 2

## CONSTRUCTIVE TRUSTS IMPOSED AS A RESULT OF FRAUDULENT, UNCONSCIONABLE OR INEQUITABLE CONDUCT

From its very earliest days, equity has always been prepared to grant relief against fraudulent and unconscionable conduct. Two of the most striking examples of this type of relief are the doctrine of undue influence and the principle that no criminal may benefit from his crime. In these situations, the courts impose constructive trusts upon the person who has exerted the undue influence and upon the criminal in respect of any property which has been obtained as a result of the undue influence or crime. Fraudulent or unconscionable conduct will also lead to the imposition of a constructive trust in other situations—such a constructive trust will be imposed, for example, to enforce an oral undertaking or agreement by a transferee of land who has subsequently sought to rely on the absence of the written formalities required by the Law of Property Act 1925. Cases of these types are, fortunately, extremely rare and until relatively recently it was generally thought that the intervention of equity was limited to the quite exceptional situations already outlined. However, in the years immediately before and after 1970, a number of decisions emanating from the Court of Appeal imposed constructive trusts of this type not only as a result of fraudulent or unconscionable conduct but also as a result of conduct which the individual judges were prepared to classify merely as inequitable. This approach was, of course, much closer to the American attitude to the constructive trust (already referred to in Chap. 1) and was thought to be symptomatic of a general change of attitude towards the constructive trust. However, the approach manifested in this series of cases has not been followed up in the more recent decisions of the Court of Appeal in which there has been a return to the more traditional approach. While it is therefore no longer possible to say that English law may at present be in a transitional stage in its attitude towards the constructive trust, none of the cases in which constructive trusts were imposed as a result of merely inequitable conduct has been formally overruled. Where these earlier decisions have been reconsidered and not followed, there are consequently conflicts of authority. Where on the other hand these earlier decisions have not yet been reconsidered, they clearly remain the law although it is generally thought that they would not now be followed if an opportunity for reconsideration arose. These uncertainties are only likely to be resolved when the House of Lords has an opportunity to consider this area of the law. However, there is of course no doubt whatever that fraudulent or unconscionable conduct will continue to lead to the imposition of a constructive trust.

### The doctrine of undue influence

Since the eighteenth century, it has been a rule of equity that a person who obtains a manifest and unfair disadvantage as a result of undue influence will be unable to retain the benefit of the transaction in question.[1] This equitable doctrine of undue influence, which applies only to *inter vivos* transactions,[2] was recently restated by the House of Lords in *National Westminster Bank* v. *Morgan.*[3] Lord Scarman, with whose speech the other members of the House agreed, emphasised that the principle upon which equity intervenes is not that "it is right and expedient to save persons from the consequences of their own folly" but "that it is right and expedient to save them from being victimised by other people."[4] He therefore held that the doctrine of undue influence will only apply where two distinct elements can be established: first, the transaction must have been procured by undue influence and, secondly, the transaction must have been wrongful in that an unfair advantage has been taken of the person seeking to avoid it. These two requirements must be considered in turn.

A transaction will be held to have been procured by undue influence in two distinct situations.[5] First, this will be held to be the case where the parties to a transaction are in such a relationship as to raise doubt whether one of the parties was able to exercise an independent will. Where a transaction takes place

---

[1] This doctrine is generally thought to have been evolved by Lord Hardwicke L.C. in *Morris* v. *Burroughs* (1737) 1 Atk. 398. A full discussion of the rules relating to the recovery of benefits conferred under undue influence is contained in Goff and Jones: *The Law of Restitution* (2nd ed.), pp. 192–198.

[2] The analogous probate doctrine is much more rigid.

[3] [1985] 2 W.L.R. 588.

[4] These are the words of Lindley L.J. in *Allcard* v. *Skinner* (1887) 36 Ch.D. 145, 182, which were cited with approval by Lord Scarman in *National Westminster Bank* v. *Morgan* at p. 598.

[5] This classification was adopted by Cotton L.J. in *Allcard* v. *Skinner* (1887) 36 Ch.D. 145, 171.

between, *inter alia,* a child and his parent, a client and his solicitor, a patient and his doctor, a beneficiary and his trustee, or, particularly, a religious devotee and his spiritual adviser,[6] the court will presume that undue influence has been exerted to bring about the transaction. This presumption can only be rebutted if the person who is presumed to have exerted the undue influence is able to prove affirmatively that no undue influence in fact occurred. This may most easily be done by showing that the other party received independent legal advice.[7] Secondly, a transaction will be held to have been procured by undue influence even though the parties to a transaction do not fall within a relationship of the type mentioned above where the person seeking to avoid the transaction can affirmatively prove that he entered into it as a result of the undue influence of the other party.[8]

Even when a transaction has been held to have been procured by undue influence, however, the person who has exerted the undue influence will nevertheless be able to retain the benefit of the transaction unless it can be shown that the transaction was wrongful in that it constituted "a disadvantage sufficiently serious to require evidence to rebut the presumption that in the circumstances of the relationship between the parties it was procured by the exercise of undue influence."[9] Where the transaction in question is a gift in favour of the person who exerted the undue influence, this requirement will be satisfied "if the gift is so large as not to be reasonably accounted for on the ground of friendship, relationship, charity, or other ordinary motives on which ordinary men act."[10] Where, on the other hand, the transaction in question is bilateral in nature, this requirement will be satisfied by any inadequacy of consideration in favour of the person who has exerted the undue influence. Thus in *Poosathurai* v. *Kannappa Chettiar,*[11] the Privy Council accepted that a sale at an undervalue would satisfy this requirement. On the other hand, in *National*

---

[6] Lindley L.J. stated in *Allcard* v. *Skinner* at p. 183 that "the influence of one mind over another is very subtle, and of all influences religious influence is the most dangerous and the most powerful."

[7] This was stated by Lord Hailsham L.C. in *Inche Noriah* v. *Shaik Allie Bin Omar* [1929] A.C. 127, 135.

[8] This burden of proof was successfully discharged in *Smith* v. *Kay* (1859) 7 H.L.C. 750.

[9] *National Westminster Bank* v. *Morgan* [1985] 2 W.L.R. 588 *per* Lord Scarman at p. 597.

[10] Lindley L.J. in *Allcard* v. *Skinner* (1887) 36 Ch.D. 145, 185.

[11] (1919) L.R. 47 I.A. 1, 3–4.

*Westminster Bank* v. *Morgan*[12] the House of Lords held that this requirement was not satisfied where a bank made a short term loan at a commercial rate of interest to enable the borrower to prevent a building society from going into possession of her home.

Where these two requirements are satisfied and the doctrine of undue influence therefore applies, it is normally sufficient for the courts simply to set aside the transaction. If property has actually been transferred to the person who exerted the undue influence, he will be bound to return it while if, as is often the case in bilateral transactions, the person who exerted the undue influence has obtained some mortgage or charge by way of security for the liabilities of the chargor or of a third party, that security will be unenforceable. In such circumstances, the courts do not need to classify the nature of the interest retained by the person upon whom the undue influence is exerted in any property which he has transferred away. Such classification is however necessary as soon as any third party becomes involved. It is clear that the right to have a transaction set aside on the grounds of undue influence is capable of being assigned both *inter vivos*[13] and upon death[14] and so may be enforced by the successors of the person upon whom the undue influence was exerted. It also seems clear that, in the event of the death or insolvency of the person who exerted the undue influence, the interest of the person whom he influenced is regarded as analogous to an interest arising under a trust; thus in effect the person who exerted the undue influence holds any property transferred to him as a result of that undue influence on constructive trust. His personal representatives or trustee in bankruptcy will therefore obviously be bound by this constructive trust so that the person who transferred the property will be able to trace it in equity into their hands and, if necessary, claim priority over the general creditors of the transferee. Thus far it seems entirely appropriate to contend that a person who obtains property from another through undue influence is a constructive trustee of that property for the person from whom he has obtained it. But where, on the other hand, the person exerting the undue influence transfers property which he has received on to a third party or causes property to be transferred directly to a third party in the first place, the interest of the transferor seems to be regarded as a mere equity rather than a full equitable interest. Such a mere equity clearly binds a volunteer[15] and any third party who has

---

[12] [1985] 2 W.L.R. 588 *per* Lord Scarman at p. 596.
[13] *Dickinson* v. *Burrell* (1866) L.R. 1 Eq. 337.
[14] *Stump* v. *Gaby* (1852) 2 De G.M. & G. 623.
[15] *Goddard* v. *Carlisle* (1821) 9 Price 169.

notice of the undue influence, even if he has purchased the property for value.[16] Further it seems to follow from the authorities that the transferor will be able to trace the property in equity into the hands of persons who are so bound by his interest.[17] However, a mere equity will not bind any bona fide purchaser for value of a legal or equitable interest in the property who has no notice of the undue influence. To the extent that a bona fide purchaser of an equitable interest without notice is thus able to take free of the interest of the transferor, his interest has clearly to be regarded as less than the full equitable interest obtained by the beneficiary under a constructive trust, which is enforceable against the whole world except a bona fide purchaser for value of a legal estate without notice. To this very limited and relatively insignificant extent, therefore, it has to be admitted that it is not appropriate to describe the interest of a person who transfers property as the result of undue influence as an interest arising under a constructive trust.

### The principle that no criminal may benefit from his crime

Equity has been concerned for many centuries to discountenance the acquisition of benefits from criminal acts.[18] However, until the Forfeiture Act 1870 abolished the rule that the property of a convicted felon was forfeit to the Crown, there was no way in which such a person could benefit from his crime and, consequently, no necessity for any formal rule. Thus it was not until 1891 that any general principle was laid down. In *Cleaver* v. *Mutual Reserve Fund Life Association*,[19] Fry L.J. stated the principle in simple terms:

> "It appears to me that no system of jurisprudence can with reason include among the rights which it enforces rights directly resulting to the person asserting them from the crime of that person. If no action can arise from fraud, it seems impossible to suppose that it can arise from felony or misdemeanour. This principle of public policy, like all such principles, must be applied to all cases to which it can be applied without reference to the particular character of the right asserted or the form of its assertion."[20]

[16] *Lancashire Looms* v. *Black* [1934] 1 K.B. 380.
[17] See *Lancashire Looms* v. *Black* [1934] 1 K.B. 380 *per* Lawrence L.J. at pp. 416–417.
[18] See *Bridgman* v. *Green* (1755) 2 Ves.Sen. 627, *per* Lord Hardwicke L.C. at p. 628.
[19] [1892] 1 Q.B. 147, 156.
[20] The operation of this principle has been exhaustively reviewed by T.G. Youdan: (1973) 89 L.Q.R. 235 and by T.K. Earnshaw & P.J. Pace: (1974) 37 M.L.R. 481.

There are two obvious areas where the principle so enunciated might be expected to operate: where property has been acquired by means of theft or some related offence and where property has been acquired as a result of an unlawful killing. There is in fact little scope for the operation of the principle in the former area. A thief has no title to the property which he steals and so is normally[21] unable to pass any title in such property to any third party to whom he transfers it. It is expressly provided that the title to stolen property is not affected by the conviction of the thief[22] so that the identity of the owner of stolen property is a question only for civil law, not for criminal law. Thus the only relevance of a conviction for theft is the fact that the court before whom a person is convicted may order that the property concerned be restored to its owner.[23] It is thus clear that only rarely[24] will the principle enunciated by Fry L.J. operate where property has been acquired by theft or some related offence.

On the other hand, there is very considerable scope for the operation of this principle where property has been acquired as a result of an unlawful killing. This is well illustrated by *In the Estate of Crippen.*[25] Crippen murdered his wife, who died intestate. He was indicted for her murder, convicted and hanged. The question then arose as to whether the beneficiary under his will (his mistress, Miss Le Neve) was entitled to Mrs. Crippen's estate. Sir Samuel Evans P. held that Crippen could not take under his wife's intestacy; her estate therefore passed to her intestate successors as if Crippen had not survived her. That this principle applies both to

---

[21] Title will only pass if there has been a sale in market overt or if the purchaser is protected by the provisions of the Sale of Goods Act 1979 or the Consumer Credit Act 1974.

[22] Theft Act 1968, s.31(2). (This provision changed the pre-existing law).

[23] Theft Act 1968, s.28. Where such an order is made and the person convicted has sold the goods to or has borrowed money on the security of them from a person acting in good faith, the criminal court may also order that there shall be paid to the purchaser or lender out of any money of the person convicted which was taken out of his possession when he was apprehended a sum not exceeding the purchase price or outstanding loan.

[24] In *Reading* v. *Att.-Gen.* [1951] A.C. 507, an ex-R.A.M.C. Sergeant brought a petition of right for the return of some £19,000 which had been paid to him by smugglers for riding in his uniform through Cairo in lorries in which smuggled goods were being transported and thus enabling the lorries to pass the civil police without search. This claim could undoubtedly have been denied on the basis of the principle enunciated by Fry L.J. (the claimant had been imprisoned for a breach of martial law and so had clearly committed a criminal offence) but the House of Lords did not consider this possibility, instead denying the claim on other grounds that will be considered in Chap. 3.

[25] [1911] P. 108.

testate and to intestate succession is illustrated by *Re Sigsworth*,[26] in which a murderer was absolutely entitled under the will of his victim, his mother, and was also, with his brother, her intestate successor. Following the suicide of the murderer, Clauson J. held that his estate could take neither under the will nor under the consequent intestacy. Thus the mother's entire estate passed to her other intestate successor, her other son.

The operation of the principle does not depend on a conviction having been secured in criminal proceedings nor are the results of any criminal proceedings decisive. Thus in *Re Sigsworth*[26] the fact that the murderer committed suicide before he could be brought to trial did not prevent the application of the principle, while in *Gray* v. *Barr*[27] the principle was applied even though the defendant had been acquitted of both murder and manslaughter.[28] There is, however, some controversy as to precisely what kinds of unlawful killing will bring the principle into operation. The authorities discussed in the previous paragraph establish the somewhat obvious proposition that a murderer may not enjoy any property which he may acquire under the will or intestacy of his victim, whether or not the acquisition of the property was the motive for the murder. It is equally clear that a killer who is found not guilty of murder by reason of insanity is entitled to take the property of his victim, since such a verdict constitutes an acquittal.[29] However, more controversy surrounds crimes such as manslaughter and causing death by reckless driving (this offence is synonymous with involuntary manslaughter except in name and maximum sentence).[30] It is clear that, as Salmon L.J. remarked in *Gray* v. *Barr*,[31] "manslaughter is a crime which varies infinitely in its seriousness." It has consequently been argued that the principle should not automatically be applied to such cases; since the reason for the acquittal of an insane killer is that he lacked the intention to kill, it is said that the principle should not apply either to a person convicted of unintentional manslaughter (involuntary man-

---

[26] [1935] 1 Ch. 89.

[27] [1971] 2 Q.B. 554.

[28] In the civil proceedings issues of fact only have to be decided on a balance of probabilities whereas a criminal conviction requires the jury to be satisfied beyond reasonable doubt. For this reason neither an acquittal nor a conviction is decisive in the civil proceedings. However, there is a statutory presumption that a person committed an offence of which he is convicted (Civil Evidence Act 1968, s.11, considered in *Stupple* v. *Royal Insurance Co.* [1970] 3 All E.R. 230.)

[29] Criminal Procedure (Insanity) Act 1964, s.1.

[30] *R.* v. *Seymour (Edward)* [1983] 3 W.L.R. 349.

[31] [1971] 2 Q.B. 554, 581.

slaughter or voluntary manslaughter on the ground of diminished responsibility) or to a person convicted of causing death by reckless driving.[32] However, this argument has not as yet been accepted by the courts. Although it has been stated that there may be some types of unlawful killing to which the principle does not apply,[33] English courts have so far taken the view that it is not appropriate to draw any distinction between voluntary and involuntary manslaughter and have applied the principle to both.[34] It seems to follow from this approach that the principle would similarly be applied to causing death by reckless driving (there seems to be no reported case in which this question has had to be considered, something which is rather surprising in view of the number of convictions there must have been in respect of accidents in which the spouse of the driver is killed). It thus remains uncertain what kind of unlawful killing would be held to be outside the operation of the principle.

It has already been seen that when the principle does operate the criminal will not be able to take any benefit under the will or intestacy of his victim. He is thus treated as being incapable of inheriting and the property devolves on this assumption. Thus in *Re Callaway*[35] a testatrix left her entire estate to her daughter, who murdered her and subsequently committed suicide. Her intestate successors were her daughter and her son. The daughter was obviously unable take under either the will or the intestacy and so, as in *Re Sigsworth*,[36] the entire estate passed to the son.[37] Similarly in *Re Peacock*[38] a testator disposed of his residue by way of a class gift to his wife, his son and his stepson. His wife murdered him

---

[32] See Youdan, *op. cit.*, at pp. 237–248, Earnshaw and Pace, *op. cit.*, at pp. 492–496.

[33] In *Gray* v. *Barr* [1971] 2 Q.B. 554, 581, Salmon L.J. said: "I am not deciding that a man who has committed manslaughter would, in any circumstances, be prevented . . . from inheriting under a will or upon the intestacy of anyone whom he has killed."

[34] *In the Estate of Hall* [1914] P. 1; *Re Giles* [1972] Ch. 544; *R.* v. *Chief National Insurance Commissioner, ex p. Connor* [1981] 2 W.L.R. 413; *Re Royse* [1984] 3 W.L.R. 784; *Re K. (deceased)* [1985] 2 W.L.R. 262.

[35] [1956] Ch. 559.

[36] [1935] 1 Ch. 89.

[37] Vaisey J. but for binding authority would have preferred to have held that the daughter's share had vested in her to the exclusion of the son and, because of her inability to take, passed to the Crown as bona vacantia. However such a conclusion appears to involve a return to the principle of forfeiture abolished in 1870 and it is therefore suggested that the result actually reached in the case is preferable.

[38] [1957] Ch. 310.

and subsequently committed suicide. The wife was obviously unable to take and so the estate was divided between the other two members of the class, the son and the stepson.[39] A much more difficult situation would have arisen, however, if in either *Re Sigsworth* or *Re Callaway* the murderer had left issue. Under the intestacy rules, the issue of a deceased child stand in the place of their parent. Is the incapacity of the murderer regarded as having the same consequences as if he had predeceased his victim or are his issue regarded as disqualified on the grounds that they are only able to claim through him? The authorities generally state that the will or intestacy provisions are applied on the basis that the murderer is struck out. While this has been sufficient to dispose of the cases that have come before the courts, it has never been made clear whether the effect of being struck out is or is not equivalent to predeceasing the victim. However, commentators have generally taken the view that the rights of third parties should indeed be established on the basis that the criminal predeceased his victim.[40] This question obviously awaits clarification by the courts. Similar problems arise where the criminal and his victim hold joint or successive interests. In the recent case of *Re K. (deceased),*[41] an English court had for the first time to consider the effect of one of two joint tenants unlawfully killing the other. The difficulty of such a situation is that, according to basic principles, the surviving joint tenant becomes, by virtue of the *jus accrescendi,* solely entitled both at law and in equity to the property which was the subject matter of the joint tenancy. To deprive the survivor of the whole of the property would be to deprive him of an interest in property which he already had and thus, in effect, would be a return to the principle of forfeiture. On the other hand, to permit the survivor to take advantage of the *jus accrescendi* would be to permit him to benefit from his crime. This situation had previously arisen in Canada,[42] in Australia[43] and in New Zealand[44] where it had been held that the survivor acquired the entire

---

[39] Upjohn J. but for binding authority would have preferred to have held that the wife's share had vested in her to the exclusion of the other two members of the class and, because of her inability to take, consequently passed on her intestacy. However such a conclusion would have enabled the wife's intestate successor to benefit from her crime; it is therefore suggested that the result actually reached in the case is preferable.

[40] See A.W. Scott, *Trusts*, para. 187; R. Goff and G. Jones, *Law of Restitution* (2nd ed.), p. 187.

[41] [1985] 2 W.L.R. 262.

[42] In *Schobelt* v. *Barber* (1967) 60 D.L.R. (2d.) 519.

[43] In *Rasmanis* v. *Jurewitsch* [1968] 2 N.S.W.R. 166.

[44] In *Re Pechar* [1969] N.Z.L.R. 574.

legal title to the property by virtue of the *jus accrescendi* but held that legal title as constructive trustee for himself and the representatives of his victim in equal shares. In *Re K. (deceased)*[45] Vinelott J.[46] referred to these authorities and reached the same conclusion, holding that under English law the same result can be reached more simply by treating the beneficial interest as vesting in the deceased and the survivor as tenants in common. (This does not, however, alter the fact that there is a constructive trust—the statutory trust for sale must necessarily determine on the death of the victim so that any tenancy in common can only arise under a constructive trust). This solution is obviously sound since it takes nothing away from the survivor other than the possibility that he might have survived beyond the natural death of his victim and so taken the entire property by survivorship—a deprivation of which the killer can hardly complain. An analogous problem arises where a person entitled to property in remainder unlawfully kills the holder of the prior life interest. This problem does not seem to have arisen in any common law jurisdiction[47] but it has been suggested[48] that the victim should be deemed to have lived as long as mortality tables predict. For that period, the benefit of the interest he would have held should pass to his representatives under a constructive trust and the remaining interests under the settlement should devolve as if he had died at the end of that period. This solution should be adopted if the problem ever arises. Finally, it should be noted that in the last two situations that have been discussed, the effect of the operation of the principle is the imposition of a constructive trust. It is not normally necessary for such a constructive trust to be imposed on property to which the criminal is entitled under the will or intestacy of his victim—this is simply because such property is normally intercepted before it reaches the hands of the criminal or his representatives. But if the property did reach their hands, as would be the case, for example, if the criminal was not apprehended for some considerable time, it cannot be doubted that the courts would impose a constructive trust upon the property for the benefit of those really entitled thereto. It is thus clear that one of the consequences of the operation of the principle

---

[45] [1985] 2 W.L.R. 262.

[46] The decision of Vinelott J. was subsequently affirmed by the Court of Appeal [1986] Ch. 180 but the point at present under discussion did not have to be considered in the Court of Appeal.

[47] Although this situation was postulated by Vaisey J. in *Re Calloway* [1956] Ch. 559.

[48] By Youdan, *op. cit.* at pp. 250–251.

enunciated by Fry L.J. in *Cleaver* v. *Mutual Reserve* is the imposition of a constructive trust.[49]

Where the principle does operate in one of the ways mentioned above as a result of an unlawful killing, it is however now possible for the court to grant relief against forfeiture under the provisions of the Forfeiture Act 1982.[50] Under this statute, where a court has determined that the principle has operated to bring about a forfeiture, that court is entitled, save in the case of a person who has been convicted of murder,[51] to make an order modifying the effect of the principle. No such order can be made unless the court "is satisfied that, having regard to the conduct of the offender and of the deceased and to such other circumstances as appear to the court to be material, the justice of the case requires the effect of the rule to be so modified in that case."[52] Such an order was made in *Re K.* (*deceased*)[53] where a wife had been convicted of the manslaughter of her husband who had over a number of years been subject to fits of uncontrollable rage which led him to make violent attacks on her; during one such attack, with the intention of frightening him and deterring him from following her out of the room, she picked up a loaded shot gun which went off and killed him. Vinelott J. held that this unlawful killing deprived her not only of all the benefits to which she was entitled under his will but also of his joint interest in their matrimonial home which would otherwise have vested in her by virtue of the *jus accrescendi*. However, he held that this was an appropriate case for the exercise of the discretion conferred upon him by the Forfeiture Act 1982 and made an order wholly relieving the wife from forfeiture. This decision was subsequently affirmed by the Court of Appeal.[54] The very

---

[49] The principle can also operate to deprive an unlawful killer of a pension to which he or she would otherwise have been entitled on the death in question (see *Reg.* v. *Chief National Insurance Commissioner, ex p. Connor* [1981] 2 W.L.R. 413) and can also have an effect on the right of the killer to claim under insurance policies (see *Cleaver* v. *Mutual Reserve* and *Gray* v. *Barr*). However such questions obviously have nothing to do with constructive trusts.

[50] Noted by P.H. Kenny: (1983) 46 M.L.R. 66.

[51] Forfeiture Act 1982, s.5 excludes such persons.

[52] Forfeiture Act 1982, s.2(2). No order may be made in respect of any interest in property acquired before the coming into force of the legislation (see n. 54 below).

[53] [1985] 1 W.L.R. 262.

[54] [1986] Ch. 180. Only two questions were raised on appeal. First, it was contended that, as a matter of statutory interpretation, because the death in question had occurred before the Act had come into force, no order thereunder could be made so as to deprive those otherwise entitled of interests which they had acquired at the moment of the death. Secondly, it was contended that the judge had exercised his discretion wrongly. Both contentions were rejected by the Court of Appeal.

extreme facts of this case ensured that his lordship had no great difficulty in deciding whether or not to exercise his statutory discretion. It obviously remains to be seen how the courts will apply the legislation in less clear-cut situations such as, for example, the case of a person convicted of causing the death of his spouse by reckless driving. While it is obviously desirable that the effects of the operation of the principle should be able to be modified in the light of the facts of each individual case, it is questionable whether it is entirely appropriate for judges to be obliged to make moral judgments of the type envisaged by the legislation. Only future decisions will show whether or not such doubts are justified.

**Other fraudulent or unconscionable conduct**

In addition to the two situations already discussed, the courts have always been prepared to impose a constructive trust upon a person who has acquired property by other types of fraudulent or unconscionable conduct. Thus a constructive trust will be imposed to enforce an oral undertaking or agreement by a transferee of land who has subsequently sought to rely on the absence of the written formalities required by the Law of Property Act 1925.[55] Such cases are manifestations of the principle that equity will not permit the provisions of a statute to be used as an instrument of fraud. As Lindley L.J. said in *Rochefoucauld* v. *Boustead*[56]:

> "It is a fraud on the part of a person to whom land is conveyed as a trustee and who knows it is so conveyed to deny the trust and to claim the land for himself. Consequently, notwithstanding the statute, it is competent for a person claiming land conveyed to another to prove by parol evidence that it was so conveyed upon trust for the claimant, and that the grantee, knowing the facts, is denying the trust and relying upon the form of conveyance and the statute to keep the land himself."[57]

Of course it is not always fraudulent to rely on the absence of the statutory formalities. Thus equity will neither prevent a party to a wholly executory oral contract for the sale of land from resist-

---

[55] The authorities are discussed and analysed by T.G. Youdan in [1984] C.L.J. 306.
[56] [1897] 1 Ch. 196, 206.
[57] His lordship went on to classify the trust established as an express trust. However, this view seems to have been taken largely because of the Statute of Limitations for the reasons discussed in Chapter 1. Now that such considerations do not apply, it seems more appropriate to classify the trust in *Rochefoucauld* v. *Boustead* as a constructive trust.

ing an action thereon by raising the absence of the writing required
by section 40 of the Law of Property Act 1925 nor prevent a settlor
who has made an oral declaration of trust respecting land from
resisting an action by the beneficiaries by raising the absence of the
writing required by section 53(1)(*b*) of the Law of Property Act
1925. What brings about the intervention of equity is the acquisition of property on the strength of an oral undertaking or agreement followed by an attempt to renege on the undertaking or
agreement because of the lack of the necessary statutory formalities.

*Bannister* v. *Bannister*[58] is a straightforward illustration of the
operation of this principle. The defendant owned two adjoining
cottages which she was negotiating to sell to the plaintiff, her
brother-in-law. They agreed orally that she could continue to live
in one of the two cottages rent-free for as long as she wished. However, the conveyance following the sale contained no mention of
the right of the defendant to so reside. Subsequently, the plaintiff
gave the defendant notice to quit and brought an action claiming
possession of the cottage. The defendant counterclaimed for a
declaration that the plaintiff held the cottage on trust for her for
her lifetime. The plaintiff sought to rely on the absence of the writing which the Law of Property Act 1925 requires for the creation
of the interest claimed by the defendant. However, the Court of
Appeal had no hesitation in rejecting the plaintiff's attempts to
claim possession by this means. The judgment of the court, which
was delivered by Scott L.J., was based fairly and squarely on the
fraudulent conduct of the plaintiff.

> "The fraud, which brings the principle on which a constructive
> trust is raised into play, arises as soon as the absolute character
> of the conveyance is set up for the purpose of defeating the
> beneficial interest, and that is the fraud to cover which the
> Statute of Frauds, or the corresponding provisions of the Law
> of Property Act, 1925, cannot be called in aid in cases in which
> no written evidence of the real bargain is available."

The Court of Appeal, therefore, imposed a constructive trust
upon the plaintiff and declared that the plaintiff held the cottage
on trust to permit the defendant to occupy it during her lifetime.
This decision clearly establishes that a constructive trust will be
imposed to prevent a person unconscionably relying on the

[58] [1948] W.N. 261.

absence of written evidence to defeat the interest of another[59]—a proposition which is entirely consistent with the earlier authorities.[60]

In cases such as *Bannister* v. *Bannister* where the person who made or procured the transfer of the property in question is himself entitled to the benefit of the oral undertaking or agreement, it is obvious that, where the principle enunciated in *Rochefoucauld* v. *Boustead* applies, that person will be entitled to enforce the undertaking or agreement in favour of himself. When, however, the person entitled to the benefit of the oral undertaking or agreement is a third party, the ability of that third party to enforce the undertaking or agreement in favour of himself is rather more questionable. If two parties agree orally that property will be held by

[59] What has created some difficulty, however, is the statement by the Court of Appeal that the imposition of this trust had the effect of making the defendant a tenant for life under the Settled Land Act 1925. Such a tenant is entitled, under the provisions of that Act, to have the legal estate conveyed to him by vesting deed and to sell it. How can the existence of such rights be consistent with the position that the parties in *Bannister* v. *Bannister* had originally intended to create? It seems absurd to interpret a sale from the defendant to the plaintiff as creating a settlement and thus entitling the defendant to call for the reconveyance of the cottage to herself. Doubts have been subsequently expressed as to whether the imposition of such a trust does create a settlement under the Settled Land Act 1925 (see the judgment of Lord Denning M.R. in *Binions* v. *Evans* [1972] Ch. 359 and the comments thereon in *Current Legal Problems* (1973) 17, 24–25). If such a settlement is indeed created, this result, despite its consequences, may not be completely undesireable in view of the unconscionable conduct of the plaintiff in *Bannister* v. *Bannister*. Nevertheless, it is one more reason why such constructive trusts should not be imposed lightly.

[60] *Bannister* v. *Bannister* has been applied in *Neale* v. *Willis* (1968) 19 P. & C.R. 839, *Binions* v. *Evans* [1972] Ch. 359 and *Lyus* v. *Prowsa Developments* [1982] 2 All E.R. 953. Unconscionable conduct may well also have been the grounds upon which a constructive trust was imposed in *Peffer* v. *Rigg* [1977] 1 W.L.R. 285. The plaintiff and the first defendant purchased registered land which was transferred into the name of the latter to be held by him on trust for the purchasers in equal shares. The first defendant subsequently purported to transfer the land as beneficial owner to the second defendant, his wife, as part of a divorce settlement. Graham J. held that the second defendant, by virtue of her notice of the trust, had taken the land subject to the beneficial interest of the plaintiff even though the latter had failed to protect that interest on the Land Register. (This conclusion has been much criticised as contrary to both the policy and the provisions of the Land Registration Act 1925—see D.J. Hayton [1977] C.L.J. 227—and, although not formally overruled, cannot really survive the subsequent decision of the House of Lords in *Williams & Glyn's Bank* v. *Boland* [1981] A.C. 487). His lordship then went on to hold, in a very few words, that in any event the land was subject to a constructive trust in favour of the plaintiff on the grounds that the second defendant had had notice of the trust. This conclusion, which his lordship based merely on "general equitable principles," can be supported on the basis that the second defendant was acting unconscionably in seeking to take the land free of a trust of which she had notice.

the transferee on trust for a third party, it is not immediately obvious that that third party has any right to enforce an agreement or undertaking to which he was not a party or that the undertaking should necessarily be enforced in favour of him rather than in favour of the transferor. It has been argued[61] that, as a matter of principle, the third party should be so entitled to enforce the oral undertaking or agreement in favour of himself; were he not able to do so, the property would undoubtedly finish up in the hands of the transferor since the transferee would be unable to resist a claim by him for its return; consequently the inability of the third party to enforce in his own favour would mean that the initial failure of the transferee to honour his word would have produced a benefit for the transferor at the expense of the third party. This argument has never actually been raised in any of the cases that have come before the courts. However, no doubt has ever been cast on the ability of the third party to enforce the undertaking or agreement in question in favour of himself. Thus in *Neale* v. *Willis*[62] a husband borrowed £50 from his mother-in-law towards the expenses of the acquisition of his matrimonial home on the understanding that the property acquired would be conveyed into the joint names of the husband and wife. The husband in fact had the property conveyed into his sole name and, following a divorce, the wife now claimed that he held the property on trust for both of them jointly. The Court of Appeal upheld this claim, applying *Bannister* v. *Bannister* and thus holding that the husband held the house on constructive trust to carry out the bargain which he had made with his mother-in-law. Similarly, in *Binions* v. *Evans*[63] the Tredegar Estate had entered into an agreement with the defendant, Mrs. Evans, who was the widow of one of their employees, under which she was permitted to live in a cottage rent-free for the rest of her life in return for keeping the property in good order. Subsequently, the Estate sold the cottage to the plaintiffs expressly subject to Mrs. Evans' interest, on account of which they paid a lower price. Nevertheless, six months later, they gave Mrs. Evans notice to quit and subsequently claimed possession. The majority of the Court of Appeal (Megaw and Stephenson L.JJ.)[64] applied *Bannister* v. *Bannister* and held that the plaintiffs held the property

---

[61] By T.G. Youdan, [1984] C.L.J. 306, 335–336.
[62] (1968) 19 P. & C.R. 839.
[63] [1972] Ch. 359.
[64] The third member of the court, Lord Denning M.R., reached the same conclusion by a different route; his judgment will be discussed in the next section of this chapter.

on constructive trust to give effect to Mrs. Evans' interest. Thus, although the issue has never been specifically raised, it is clear that the courts are prepared to allow a third party to enforce in favour of himself oral agreements or undertakings which fall within the principle enunciated in *Rochefoucauld* v. *Boustead.*

All the authorities discussed so far in which the principle in *Rochefoucauld* v. *Boustead* has been applied have concerned the imposition of constructive trusts to prevent a transferee of land from relying on the absence of the written formalities required by the Law of Property Act 1925. However, the principle has now also been applied to prevent a purchaser from relying on the failure of an incumbrancer to protect his interest under the provisions of the Land Registration Act 1925. This was in *Lyus* v. *Prowsa Developments.*[65] The plaintiffs entered into a contract to purchase a plot of land together with a house which was to be built thereon. The vendor subsequently became insolvent and his mortgagee duly sold and conveyed the plot to the defendant. Although the mortgagee was not in fact bound by the contract with the plaintiff, the plot was nevertheless sold subject to and with the benefit of the contract with the plaintiffs. However, the subsequent conveyance contained no mention of the contract and the plaintiffs had neglected to protect their contract in the way required by the Land Registration Act 1925. The defendant therefore claimed to have taken the plot free of their contract by virtue of section 20 of the Land Registration Act 1925.[66] As a general rule, when interests are required to be protected by registration, a purchaser who takes advantage of his strict statutory rights by relying on the absence of the necessary registration is not regarded as using the statutory provision in question as an instrument of fraud. This was made abundantly clear by the House of Lords in *Midland Bank Trust Co.* v. *Green.*[67] However, in *Lyus* v. *Prowsa Developments* Dillon J. held that, since the provision that the plot was sold subject to and with the benefit of the contract with the plaintiffs had been inserted with the express object of conferring new rights on the latter, the case fell within the principle enunciated in *Rochefoucauld* v. *Boustead.* Consequently the defendant could not use the pro-

---

[65] [1982] 2 All E.R. 953.
[66] Under this provision a bona fide purchaser for value of registered land is bound only by overriding interests and by entries on the register and takes free from all other interests whatsoever.
[67] [1981] A.C. 513. This was a decision on the Land Charges Act 1972 but similar decisions have been reached in relation to the Land Registration Act 1925 and the Companies Act 1985.

visions of the Land Registration Act 1925 to escape from its contractual obligations. His lordship therefore held that the defendant
held the plot on constructive trust to complete the house thereon
and convey the plot to the plaintiffs for the price agreed in the
original contract. At first sight, this decision appears to cast doubt
upon the ability of any purchaser to rely on his statutory right to
take free of incumbrances of which he is aware but which have not
been protected in the appropriate way. However, this is not in fact
the case. Dillon J. applied the principle in *Rochefoucauld* v. *Boustead* only because of his conclusion, reached as a matter of construction, that the provision that the plot was sold subject to and
with the benefit of the contract had been inserted with the express
object of conferring new rights on the plaintiffs. This finding
enabled his lordship to distinguish this provision from the normal
contractual provisions that land is being sold subject to incumbrances
such as restrictive covenants on the grounds that such provisions
are not intended to impose on the purchaser any new liability to
observe those covenants greater than that already imposed on the
vendor. Thus a purchaser who is aware of the existence of restrictive covenants which have not been protected in the appropriate
way will clearly be able to rely on his statutory right to take the
land free of those incumbrances. Only where such a purchaser has
expressly contracted with his vendor to confer new rights on those
entitled to the benefit of the restrictive covenants will he be caught
by the principle in *Rochefoucauld* v. *Boustead*. The decision in
*Lyus* v. *Prowsa Developments* is, therefore, confined to the situation where the purchaser has expressly agreed to take the property in question subject to a particular right in favour of a third
party. Such a situation is indistinguishable from the facts of cases
such as *Neale* v. *Willis* and it is therefore suggested that, in the
light of the decision reached by Dillon J. as a matter of construction, *Lyus* v. *Prowsa Developments* was correctly decided.

The imposition of constructive trusts in the cases that have been
discussed in this section can be supported simply because in each
case there was a finding that the person upon whom the constructive trust was imposed had attempted to rely on a statutory provision to escape from an obligation into which he had freely
entered. However, because of the considerable consequences of
the imposition of a constructive trust, such trusts should not be
imposed in the absence of such a finding and it must be emphasised
that the cases that have been discussed provide no support for the
proposition for which they have sometimes subsequently been
cited as authority, namely that the courts will impose a constructive trust whenever the result would, otherwise, be inequitable.

**Inequitable conduct**

Until relatively recently, the courts limited the imposition of constructive trusts of the type being discussed in this chapter to the extreme situations that have already been considered. However, in the years immediately before and after 1970, a number of decisions emanating from the Court of Appeal imposed constructive trusts of this type not only as a result of fraudulent or unconscionable conduct but also as a result of conduct which the individual judges were prepared to classify merely as inequitable. The underlying and indeed often expressed objective of the judges in question was to prevent results which would, otherwise, have been inequitable. If application of the basic principles of property law led to a result which, in the view of the court in question, was contrary to good conscience, that court acted upon the conscience of the party who would otherwise have obtained this unjust benefit and imposed a constructive trust upon him to bring the result into line with the requirements of justice.[68] This approach was, of course, much closer to the American attitude to the constructive trust (already referred to in Chap. 1) and was thought to be symptomatic of a general change of attitude towards the constructive trust. However, the approach manifested in this series of cases has not been followed up in the more recent decisions of the Court of Appeal in which there has been a return to the more traditional approach. It is therefore no longer possible to say that English law may at present be in a transitional stage in its attitude to the constructive trust. However, none of the cases in which constructive trusts were imposed as a result of merely inequitable conduct has been formally overruled. All these earlier decisions therefore remain authoritative at present, although where these earlier decisions have been reconsidered and not followed there are obviously now conflicts of authority. This necessarily means that this area of the law is at present in a somewhat uncertain state and these uncertainties are only likely to be resolved when the House of Lords has an opportunity to consider the matter.

The new principle enunciated by the Court of Appeal in this series of decisions immediately before and after 1970 seems to have originated in the area of matrimonial property disputes. Until the enactment of section 5 of the Matrimonial Proceedings and Property Act 1970 (now section 25 of the Matrimonial Causes Act 1973), the powers of the courts in relation to matrimonial property

---

[68] The principal decisions that manifested this approach were analysed in (1973) *Current Legal Problems*, p. 17.

on the termination of marriage were extremely limited. Apart from a power to vary ante-nuptial or post-nuptial settlements (defined by the courts as transactions making continuing provision for one or both spouses as such), the courts could only use their power under section 17 of the Married Women's Property Act 1882 to declare the existing property rights of the spouses. This power, according to the members of the House of Lords in *Pettitt* v. *Pettitt*[69] and *Gissing* v. *Gissing*,[70] had to be exercised in the light of the intentions of the parties at the time of acquisition of the property and not, as Lord Denning M.R. had held in a number of earlier cases, in the light of the intentions of the parties at the time of the action. Inherent in both *Pettitt* v. *Pettitt* and *Gissing* v. *Gissing* was the fundamental proposition that rights of property are to be determined according to the basic rules of property law, not according to what is reasonable and fair or just in all the circumstances. However, in the course of his speech in *Gissing* v. *Gissing*, Lord Diplock stated the following proposition[71]:

> "A resulting, implied or constructive trust—and it is unnecessary for present purposes to distinguish between these three classes of trust—is created by a transaction between the trustee and the *cestui que trust* in connection with the acquisition by the trustee of a legal estate in land, whenever the trustee has so conducted himself that it would be inequitable to deny to the *cestui que trust* a beneficial interest in the land acquired."

This statement, when thus isolated from its context, does indeed appear to suggest that the courts may impose a constructive trust to do justice *inter partes* whenever the result would, otherwise, be inequitable and it was indeed duly cited as authority for that proposition in several subsequent cases in the Court of Appeal. However those judges who cited this statement as authority for that proposition ignored the fact that Lord Diplock placed an immediate limitation on his statement in the following sentence, in which he said:

> "And he will be held so to have conducted himself if by his words or conduct he has induced the *cestui que trust* to act to his own detriment in the reasonable belief that by so acting he was acquiring a beneficial interest in the land."

[69] [1970] A.C. 777.
[70] [1971] A.C. 886.
[71] [1971] A.C. 886, 905.

The first cases in which the remarks of Lord Diplock were given this unjustifiably broad interpretation concerned the devolution of matrimonial property on the breakdown of marriage. The law contained in these cases no longer applies where the marriage in question has been terminated since the courts have now acquired an absolute discretion to vary matrimonial property rights at the termination of marriage under what is now section 25 of the Matrimonial Causes Act 1973 and thus have no need to resort to the imposition of a constructive trust. But the old rules continue to apply to disputes that arise during marriage concerning the property rights of the spouses and these cases have therefore been applied to disputes of this kind. Further the principle enunciated in these cases that a constructive trust will be imposed whenever the result would, otherwise, be inequitable has subsequently been extended outside the area of matrimonial property to analogous situations involving unmarried couples and to other types of joint enterprise. However, although these decisions remain authoritative at present, in each of the three areas mentioned above these decisions have been subsequently reconsidered and not followed. Thus in each of these three areas there is at present a conflict of authority.

Where a dispute arises during marriage concerning the property rights of the spouses, there is at present a conflict of authority between *Heseltine* v. *Heseltine*[72] and *Midland Bank* v. *Dobson,*[73] both decisions of the Court of Appeal. In *Heseltine* v. *Heseltine* the dispute was actually between the spouses, who had separated but had not divorced. The wife had very considerable means of her own. She had contributed four-fifths of the purchase price of the matrimonial home, which had been conveyed into the name of her husband. She had, at various times, transferred to the husband out of her own capital sums totalling £40,000, relying entirely on his advice that this would save estate duty if she predeceased him. She had also transferred to him a further £20,000 for the sole purpose of enabling him to raise the securities necessary to become a "name" at Lloyd's. During the marriage, the parties had purchased out of the wife's funds four houses, all of which had been conveyed into the name of the husband. What were the beneficial interests in these assets? According to the decisions of the House of Lords in *Pettitt* v. *Pettitt* and *Gissing* v. *Gissing,* this question should have been decided by the application of basic principles of property law; thus the court should have applied the principle that

---

[72] [1971] 1 W.L.R. 342.
[73] [1986] 1 F.L.R. 171.

where property is purchased in or transferred into the name of another there is a presumption that the property is held on a resulting trust for the purchaser or transferor. Application of this principle would have produced the following result: the matrimonial home (and the proceeds of its sale) would have been held on resulting trust for the parties in proportion to their contributions; the £40,000 and the £20,000 would have been held by the husband absolutely (the presumption of resulting trust is rebutted where the transferor intended the transferee to take beneficially) and the four houses would have been held on resulting trust for the wife. However, the Court of Appeal took a totally different attitude. Lord Denning M.R., citing as authority the first part of the passage from the speech of Lord Diplock in *Gissing* v. *Gissing* set out above in the text, imposed a constructive trust on the grounds that this was required by the circumstances. He therefore held that the proceeds of sale of the matrimonial home should be divided as to three-quarters to the wife and as to one-quarter to the husband (more or less the same result as that obtained by applying *Pettitt* v. *Pettitt* and *Gissing* v. *Gissing*) and that all the other property should be held on trust for the wife. Thus, in effect, the beneficial interests in the £40,000 and the £20,000 were transferred from the husband to the wife in order to reach a just result.

It is difficult to justify this result either as a matter of precedent or as a matter of principle. As a matter of precedent, the failure to follow the rules laid down by the House of Lords in *Pettitt* v. *Pettitt* and *Gissing* v. *Gissing* could only have been justified if the wife could have brought her case within the doctrine of undue influence; this was not attempted. As a matter of principle, it is not easy to justify the wife thus being given an advantage over the general creditors of her husband and being permitted (as the court expressly held) to trace the £40,000 into its product.

In *Midland Bank* v. *Dobson,* on the other hand, the dispute was between the wife and the husband's mortgagees. In this case, the spouses' matrimonial home had been purchased in 1953 and had been conveyed into the sole name of the husband. The purchase price was provided as to two-thirds by the husband's mother and as to the remainder by a mortgage which was in due course repaid in full by the husband. The wife had had no significant earnings until 1965 and had never made any direct contribution to the repayment of the mortgage or indeed to any other outgoings except household expenses. The husband subsequently mortgaged the property to the bank; he defaulted on the repayments and the bank now sought possession. The wife claimed a beneficial interest in the property on the basis that from 1953 onwards a common intention had existed between the spouses that the wife should have a joint beneficial interest therein. The Court of Appeal accepted the existence of such a common intention but held that this was not, without more, sufficient to give the wife a beneficial interest. Fox L.J. cited the whole of the passage from the speech of Lord Diplock in *Gissing* v. *Gissing* set out above in the text and held that the principle enunciated therein could only operate to give rise to a beneficial interest in favour of a person who had been induced to act to his detriment in pursuance of the agreement in question. Since there was no evidence that the wife was induced to act to her detriment on the basis of a common intention of ownership of the house, she could have no beneficial interest therein; consequently the bank's claim succeeded. As a matter of precedent, this decision is obviously entirely consistent with the rules laid down by the House of Lords in *Pettitt* v. *Pettitt* and *Gissing* v. *Gissing*. It is suggested that this decision is also, as a matter of principle, preferable to the decision in *Heseltine* v. *Heseltine* simply because its certainty and precision enables litigants to be safely advised as to their position, something which is totally impossible if the courts are free to alter existing property rights by the imposition of constructive trusts wherever the circumstances so require. This does not, of course, alter the fact that both *Heseltine* v. *Heseltine* and *Midland Bank* v. *Dobson* remain authoritative at present so that the judges are entirely free to choose which of the two to follow. However, given that all the most recent decisions of the Court of Appeal have adopted an approach similar to that adopted in *Midland Bank* v. *Dobson*, it is most unlikely that *Heseltine* v. *Heseltine* will now be followed.

The analogous area concerning the property rights of unmarried couples has had to be considered by the courts on a considerable number of occasions during the last twenty years. Initially the courts adopted exactly the same attitude to disputes of this kind as had been adopted in *Heseltine* v. *Heseltine*. In *Cooke* v. *Head*[74] the plaintiff was the mistress of the defendant. They decided to acquire some land on which to build a bungalow. The defendant paid all the outgoings save for a small amount, but the plaintiff helped him greatly in the actual task of building the bungalow, which the parties never in fact occupied because they split up before it was completed. The plaintiff brought an action claiming a share in the proceeds of sale. Plowman J. applied *Pettitt* v. *Pettitt* and *Gissing* v. *Gissing* and, since the plaintiff had contributed one-twelfth of the outgoings, awarded her a one-twelfth interest in the

---

[74] [1972] 1 W.L.R. 518.

proceeds. However, the Court of Appeal adopted a different approach. Lord Denning M.R. said that whenever two parties by their joint efforts acquire property to be used for their joint benefit, the courts may impose or impute a constructive or resulting trust. Applying this principle, he held that the plaintiff was entitled to a one-third interest in the proceeds. Once again, it is hard to support the imposition of a constructive trust. Apart from the fact that this approach renders the operation of the law uncertain and unpredictable, why should the plaintiff obtain an advantage over the general creditors of the defendant? However, the subsequent case of *Eves* v. *Eves*[75] showed very clearly that not all the members of the Court of Appeal were prepared to adopt the approach of Lord Denning M.R. The parties, who were living together as man and wife, purchased a delapidated house as a home for themselves and their children. All the purchase price was found by the defendant, the man, but the plaintiff did a very considerable amount of work on the house. The Court of Appeal held that she was entitled to a one-quarter share therein under a constructive trust. Lord Denning M.R. based this conclusion on the principle that he had enunciated in *Cooke* v. *Head*. But the other two members of the court, Browne L.J. and Brightman J., held that it could be inferred from the circumstances that there had been an arrangement between the parties whereby the plaintiff was to acquire a beneficial interest in the house in return for her labour in contributing to its repair and improvement. Hence her work in pursuance of this inferred arrangement gave her, under *Pettitt* v. *Pettitt* and *Gissing* v. *Gissing,* a beneficial interest in the house. On the assumption that such an arrangement could indeed be inferred, this was clearly an impeccable application of *Pettitt* v. *Pettitt* and *Gissing* v. *Gissing* and it is this approach that has been adopted in the subsequent decisions, most clearly in the two most recent decisions, *Burns* v. *Burns*[76] and *Grant* v. *Edwards.*[77] In *Burns* v. *Burns* the parties had lived together since 1961. In 1963 the man, the defendant, purchased a house paying the down payment, the costs and all the subsequent mortgage repayments out of his own funds. The woman had no significant earnings until 1975; she was never asked to make any direct contribution to household expenses, although she did purchase a number of items for the house, some of which she took with her when she left in 1980. She now claimed a beneficial interest in the house. Save that the par-

---

[75] [1975] 1 W.L.R. 1338.
[76] [1984] 1 All E.R. 244.
[77] [1986] 2 All E.R. 426.

ties were not married, the facts of this case were virtually identical with the facts of *Midland Bank* v. *Dobson*[78] and produced an identical result. The Court of Appeal applied *Pettitt* v. *Pettitt* and *Gissing* v. *Gissing* and held that the woman had no beneficial interest in the house.[79] The members of the court referred to a number of the earlier decisions in which constructive trusts were imposed to prevent results which would, otherwise, have been inequitable and stated quite clearly that such an approach was contrary to *Pettitt* v. *Pettitt* and *Gissing* v. *Gissing*. This emerges even more clearly from *Grant* v. *Edwards*. The parties had decided, following the birth of their son, to live together on a permanent basis. Consequently in 1969 a house was purchased in the name of the man and his brother; the man told the woman that her name was not going onto the title because that would cause some prejudice to her in the then pending matrimonial proceedings between her and her husband although this was clearly merely an excuse for not doing so. The purchase price was provided by a cash payment by the man and by two mortgages. The mortgage repayments were actually made by the man but the woman made regular weekly payments to him and when she was subsequently able to work made very substantial contributions to the housekeeping. Subsequently in 1975 the house was damaged by fire and the parties moved into council accommodation. The house was repaired with the insurance money, the balance of which was paid into an account opened in the joint names of the parties. The house was then let and the mortgage repayments were subsequently paid out of the rents. The woman now claimed a beneficial interest in the house. The Court of Appeal held that the facts, particularly the excuse made for not putting the woman's name on the title, clearly showed a common intention that the woman was to have a beneficial interest in the property. She had clearly acted to her detriment on the basis of this common intention by making substantial financial contributions. She was therefore entitled to a beneficial interest in the property which, given that the surplus of the insurance money had been paid into a joint account, was obviously a one half share. The members of the Court of Appeal based this result on *Pettitt* v. *Pettitt* and *Gissing* v. *Gissing* as applied in *Burns* v. *Burns* and by the majority in *Eves* v. *Eves*. Their lordships clearly rejected the view that constructive trusts could be imposed to prevent results which

---

[78] [1986] 1 F.L.R. 171 (discussed in the previous paragraph).
[79] The plaintiff applied for leave to appeal but this was denied by the Appeal Committee of the House of Lords. It is to be regretted that the House of Lords did not take advantage of this opportunity to review this area of the law.

would, otherwise, be inequitable, Nourse L.J. expressly stating that the ground upon which Lord Denning M.R. had decided *Eves* v. *Eves* "was at variance with the principles stated in *Gissing* v. *Gissing.*"[80] These two recent decisions suggest that little more will be heard either of *Cooke* v. *Head* or of the minority view of Lord Denning M.R. in *Eves* v. *Eves*. *Cooke* v. *Head* has not of course been formally overruled and therefore could still technically be followed but this is obviously highly unlikely following the clear contrary statements in *Burns* v. *Burns* and *Grant* v. *Edwards*.

The situation with respect to other types of joint enterprise is broadly similar. In *Hussey* v. *Palmer*[81] the plaintiff was invited by her son-in-law and daughter to live with them and, because their house was rather small, she paid for an extension to be built. Differences arose and she left after some fifteen months. She now claimed repayment of the sum spent on the extension under a resulting trust. The Court of Appeal, by a majority, held that she was entitled to the money under a constructive trust imposed on the just and equitable ground. Lord Denning M.R. stated expressly that this remedy was "to be applied in cases where the defendant cannot conscientiously keep the property for himself alone, but ought to allow another to have the property or a share in it."[82] While there is of course no doubt that the plaintiff was entitled to the return of her money, the imposition of a constructive trust does not seem to have been a particularly appropriate remedy to grant since this obviously gave her a right not just to the sum expended but to an interest in the house proportionate to the relative expenditure of the parties. For this reason, the view of the dissentient, Cairns L.J., that the transaction was one of loan, not of resulting trust, is much to be preferred. This view was also taken by Browne-Wilkinson J. in the later case of *Re Sharpe* (*a bankrupt*)[83] where the bankrupt purchased a property with the help of a sum lent to him by his aunt as part of an arrangement whereby the aunt was to live with the debtor and his wife in the property and they were to look after her. She claimed, *inter alia,* a beneficial interest in the property, relying on *Hussey* v. *Palmer*. Browne-Wilkinson J. held that where "moneys are advanced by loan there can be no question of the lender being entitled to an interest in the property."[84] His lordship attempted to distinguish *Hussey* v. *Palmer* on the grounds that in that case the parties had not really

[80] [1986] 2 All E.R. 426, 432.
[81] [1972] 1 W.L.R. 1286.
[82] [1972] 1 W.L.R. 1286, 1289.
[83] [1980] 1 All E.R. 198.
[84] [1982] 1 All E.R. 198, 201.

intended a loan but his approach was completely different to that adopted by the majority in that case and cannot really be reconciled with it. (His lordship then went on to impose a constructive trust on another ground which will be considered in the next section of this chapter). The decision in *Hussey* v. *Palmer* obviously remains authoritative despite the very different approach adopted by Browne-Wilkinson J. in *Re Sharpe* (*a bankrupt*). However, this latter approach is identical to that adopted in the more recent decisions of the Court of Appeal that have been discussed in the two previous paragraphs and it is therefore unlikely that much more will be heard of *Hussey* v. *Palmer*.

In the three areas which have just been discussed the decisions imposing a constructive trust on the grounds that the result would, otherwise, have been inequitable have, therefore, not been followed in the more recent cases that have come before the courts. While there thus remain conflicts of authority in all three of these areas, it is obviously highly unlikely that the earlier decisions will now be followed. By comparison, the next group of cases in which constructive trusts have been imposed on the just and equitable ground have yet to be reconsidered at all and thus clearly remain the law at present. This group of cases go considerably further and purport to alter fundamental rules of English property law.

This group of cases has emerged as a result of the judgment of Lord Denning M.R. in *Binions* v. *Evans*.[85] In this case, the Tredegar Estate had entered into an agreement with the defendant, Mrs. Evans, who was the widow of one of their employees, under which she was permitted to live in a cottage rent-free for the rest of her life in return for keeping the property in good order. Subsequently, the Estate sold the cottage to the plaintiffs expressly subject to Mrs. Evans' interest, on account of which they paid a lower price. Nevertheless, six months later, they gave Mrs. Evans notice to quit and subsequently claimed possession. As was seen earlier in this chapter, the majority of the Court of Appeal (Megaw and Stephenson L.JJ.) classified this conduct as unconscionable and imposed a constructive trust in accordance with *Bannister* v. *Bannister*[86] and *Rochefoucauld* v. *Boustead*.[87] No criticism can possibly be made of this decision. However Lord Denning M.R. reached the same conclusion by a different route. He held that Mrs. Evans was a contractual licensee. The status of such a contractual licence is uncertain. Until 1952, it was clear that

[85] [1972] Ch. 359.
[86] [1948] W.N. 261 (discussed on p. 31).
[87] [1897] 1 Ch. 196 (discussed on p. 30).

a contractual licence bound no purchaser, even a purchaser with full notice of the licence. However, in 1952 in *Errington* v. *Errington and Woods*[88] the Court of Appeal enunciated the wholly novel and highly controversial principle that a contractual licence binds all the world other than a bona fide purchaser for value without notice.[89] Lord Denning M.R., since he was a party to the decision in *Errington* v. *Errington,* naturally enough followed that authority and held that the plaintiffs were bound by Mrs. Evans' contractual licence. On that basis, his lordship could then have imposed an injunction restraining the plaintiffs from evicting Mrs. Evans—this would surely have been sufficient protection against any act of the plaintiffs or their successors. However, his lordship did not consider the possibility of an injunction. Instead he imposed a constructive trust upon the plaintiffs on the grounds that it would be inequitable to do otherwise. It is difficult to justify this conclusion either as a matter of precedent or as a matter of principle. Lord Denning M.R. cited three authorities— *Bannister* v. *Bannister,* the first part of the passage from the speech of Lord Diplock in *Gissing* v. *Gissing* set out in the text at the beginning of this section, and the statement by Cardozo J. in *Beatty* v. *Guggenheim Exploration Co.* which was referred to in Chapter 1. Of these authorities, *Bannister* v. *Bannister* is no authority for the imposition of a constructive trust in the absence of fraudulent or unconscionable conduct and it has already been shown that to cite only this part of Lord Diplock's statement is to take it out of context and that the American and the English attitudes towards the constructive trust are very different. As a matter of principle, it is clear that the implications of the imposition of such a constructive trust are contrary to some of the most fundamental principles of English land law. If the mere statement in the contract of sale of an interest in the land creates an interest enforceable by a constructive trust, to what effect are the rules relating to the annexation and assignment of restrictive covenants? Under such a constructive trust, an otherwise unenforceable posi-

---

[88] [1952] 1 K.B. 290.

[89] This proposition has been criticised extensively, principally because it cannot be reconciled with *King* v. *David Allen & Sons, Billposting* [1916] 2 A.C. 54, where the House of Lords held that a contractual licence does not bind any third party purchaser, even if he has notice thereof. The matter was expressly left open for future discussion in *National Provincial Bank* v. *Hastings Car Mart* [1968] A.C. 1175, 1239, 1251 and a contrary view was preferred at first instance in *Re Solomon (a bankrupt)* [1967] Ch. 573, 583. Nevertheless, *Errington* v. *Errington,* with the support it has received from the authorities discussed in the text, clearly remains authoritative at present.

tive covenant might well be enforceable. Further, by means of such a constructive trust a purchaser of registered land might well find himself bound, contrary to section 20 of the Land Registration Act 1925, by interests which are neither overriding interests nor minor interests protected on the register.[90] Fundamental rules of English land law should not thus be overridden by a side wind. Consequently the imposition of a constructive trust on the just and equitable ground in *Binions* v. *Evans* cannot be supported either upon precedent or upon principle. The imposition of a constructive tive trust in that case can only be justified on the approach taken by Megaw and Stephenson L.JJ. However, the imposition of a constructive trust to protect a contractual licence on the just and equitable ground has since been approved and followed by all the members of the Court of Appeal in *DHN Food Distributors* v. *London Borough of Tower Hamlets*.[91] In this case, the issue before the court was whether the plaintiffs, a company in possession under an irrevocable contractual licence of land compulsorily acquired by the defendants, could recover compensation for disturbance. The Court of Appeal found in favour of the plaintiffs on three separate grounds but the imposition of a constructive trust to protect the contractual licence on the just and equitable ground formed a clear part of the ratio of all three members of the court. A similar result occurred in *Re Sharpe (a bankrupt)*,[92] where the bankrupt purchased a property with the help of a sum lent to him by his aunt as part of an arrangement whereby the aunt was to live with the debtor and his wife in the property and they were to look after her. Browne-Wilkinson J., as has already been seen, rejected the aunt's claim to a beneficial interest in the property. Instead he classified her interest as a contractual licence and applied *DHN Food Distributors* v. *London Borough of Tower Hamlets* by imposing a constructive trust to protect this contractual licence on the just and equitable ground.[93] The judgment of Lord Denning M.R. in *Binions* v. *Evans* was also cited as authority for

---

[90] It might be thought that this actually occurred in *Lyus* v. *Prowsa Developments* [1982] 2 E.R. 953, which was discussed on p. 34. However, in this case the constructive trust in question was imposed in accordance with the principle in *Rochefoucauld* v. *Boustead* so that this case is not an example of section 20 of the Land Registration Act 1925 being overridden by the imposition of a constructive trust imposed on the just and equitable ground.

[91] [1976] 1 W.L.R. 852.

[92] [1980] 1 All E.R. 198.

[93] Her interest was thus enforceable against the trustee in bankruptcy. He had in fact already sold the property to a third party but this third party was not before the court so his lordship did not have to decide whether or not he was also bound.

the proposition that a contractual licence can be protec,
imposition of a constructive trust on the just and equitabi
in *Lyus* v. *Prowsa Developments.*[94] However, as has alrea
seen, in this case the constructive trust in question was ii ͵ᴜsed
under the principle in *Rochefoucauld* v. *Boustead* so that this
decision is not an example of the imposition of a constructive trust
on the just and equitable ground. Nevertheless the judgment of
Lord Denning M.R. in *Binions* v. *Evans* and its application in
*DHN Food Distributors* v. *London Borough of Tower Hamlets*
and in *Re Sharpe* (*a bankrupt*) provide considerable authority for
the proposition that a contractual licence can be protected by the
imposition of a constructive trust on the just and equitable ground.
No doubt has yet been cast on this proposition in any subsequent
decision so that these authorities clearly represent the law at present. It has already been suggested that this proposition cannot be
supported either as a matter of precedent or as a matter of principle. It is obviously possible that the rejection of the imposition of
constructive trusts on the just and equitable ground in the recent
decisions of the Court of Appeal that were discussed earlier in this
section and/or the continuing uncertainty about the status of a contractual licence may cause these authorities to be reconsidered if
an opportunity arises. Until that time, however, these decisions
clearly remain authoritative.

## Conclusion

The traditional and admittedly extreme situations in which constructive trusts of this type have been imposed are clearly justifiable even though some of the ramifications of these situations have
not yet been fully clarified. On the other hand, the proposition
that a constructive trust may be imposed whenever the result of a
case would, otherwise, be inequitable cannot be supported either
as a matter of precedent or as a matter of principle and it is much
to be hoped that such authority as there is in support of this proposition will be overruled by the House of Lords when a suitable
opportunity arises.

[94] [1982] 2 All E.R. 953 (discussed on p. 34).

## Chapter 3

## CONSTRUCTIVE TRUSTS IMPOSED AS A RESULT OF A BREACH OF FIDUCIARY DUTY

One of the best known situations in which constructive trusts are imposed is where a fiduciary has obtained a benefit as a result of a breach of the duty of loyalty which he owes to his principal. The many different aspects of the law governing fiduciary relationships are considered in very great depth in Finn, *Fiduciary Obligations*, while the particular aspects of this area of law considered in this chapter are fully discussed and analysed in Goff and Jones, *The Law of Restitution* and in an article by Professor Gareth Jones.[1] This chapter owes a considerable debt to all these works.

No comprehensive definition of the expression "fiduciary" has ever been attempted. This is perhaps because the classification of a particular relationship as fiduciary in nature does not automatically bring into play a series of fixed rules and principles—indeed, it has been suggested, most persuasively, that the use of the expression "fiduciary" "has generally been descriptive, providing a veil behind which individual rules and principles have been developed."[2] It is difficult to disagree with Dr. Finn when he states that, for the purposes of the rules which form the subject matter of this chapter, a fiduciary "is, simply, someone who undertakes to act for or on behalf of another in some particular matter or matters. That undertaking may be of a general character. It may be specified and limited. It is immaterial whether the undertaking is or is not in the form of a contract. It is immaterial that the undertaking is gratuitous. And the undertaking may be officiously assumed without request."[3] The majority of the decided cases have concerned four relationships: trustee and beneficiary, agent and principal, director and company, and partner and co-partner. Such relationships are inevitably classified as fiduciary. However, solicitors, accountants, guardians, promoters and receivers have also been held, in certain circumstances, to be fiduciaries and in one case, the House of Lords even held that a member of the

---

[1] (1968) 84 L.Q.R. 472.

[2] Finn, *op. cit.* p. 1, adopting the view propounded by L. S. Sealy in [1963] C.L.J. 119. Dr. Finn decribes this conclusion as 'incontestable.'

[3] Finn: *op. cit.* p. 201.

armed forces of the Crown was a fiduciary in respect of the use of his uniform and the opportunities and facilities attached to it.[4] On the other hand, the courts will not normally classify as fiduciary a commercial relationship entered into at arm's length and on an equal footing.[5] Thus what determines whether or not any particular relationship is fiduciary is a simple question of fact—whether or not one of the parties to the relationship has undertaken to act for or on behalf of the other.

Given the lack of any comprehensive definition of what constitutes a fiduciary relationship, it is hardly surprising that English law does not adopt a particularly consistent attitude towards fiduciaries. It is only to be expected that the law will differ from fiduciary relationship to fiduciary relationship. This is the case even as between the four main fiduciary relationships—a director is in a more favourable position with regard to property transactions with his company than is a trustee with regard to property transactions with his trust. But, more unexpectedly, the law governing a fiduciary relationship also differs depending on the nature of the benefit obtained by the fiduciary. Some of the distinctions are quite absurd—an agent who receives a commission will be liable to account for that commission as a constructive trustee, while an agent who receives a bribe to induce him to deal with the property of his principal in a particular way will not be obliged to account for that bribe as a constructive trustee but will be obliged merely to pay over its value to his principal. Thus a constructive trust is imposed on remuneration which has been honestly earned but not on an illicit unearned payment. Despite inconsistencies of this kind, however, the attitude of English law towards fiduciaries is, generally speaking, a harsh one. As James L.J. remarked in *Parker* v. *McKenna*[6] the rule that a fiduciary may not profit from his position without the knowledge and consent of his principal "is an inexorable rule, and must be applied inexorably by this court, which is not entitled, in my judgment, to receive evidence, or suggestion or argument as to whether the principal did or did not suffer any injury in fact by reason of the dealing of the [fidu-

---

[4] *Reading* v. *Att.-Gen.* [1951] A.C. 507, discussed *infra*.

[5] *Jirna* v. *Mister Donut of Canada* (1973) 40 D.L.R. (3d) 303; *United States Surgical Corp.* v. *Hospital Products International* [1984] A.L.J.R. 587. However, such a relationship will nevertheless be classified as fiduciary if one of the parties did indeed undertake to act for or on behalf of the other (*Walden Properties* v. *Beaver Properties* [1973] 2 N.S.W.L.R. 815, *Reid-Newfoundland Co.* v. *Anglo-American Telegraph Co.* [1912] A.C. 555.)

[6] (1874) L.R. 10 Ch. 96.

ciary]." There are innumerable examples of courts adopting this kind of attitude and penalising fiduciaries (particularly trustees) totally irrespective of whether there was any serious conflict of interest between their duty to their principal and their personal interests. However, as Lord Herschell remarked in *Bray* v. *Ford*[7] this rule "might be departed from in many cases, without any breach of morality, without any wrong being inflicted, and without any consciousness of wrongdoing." Indeed, there have been some indications that the English courts might be prepared to relax the strict penal rule in favour of a more flexible rule that fiduciaries should only be penalised where there has been a serious conflict between their duty and interest. However, this approach is not without its problems. Is the conflict of interest and duty to be measured prospectively or retrospectively? Prospective measurement would involve inquiring whether, at the commencement of the course of conduct which led to the advantage in question, there was a real sensible possibility of conflict between interest and duty. Retrospective measurement, on the other hand, would involve inquiring, at the end of that course of conduct, whether any serious conflict between interest and duty had in fact occurred. No clear answer to this question has been given in the decisions in which this approach has been adopted but it is suggested that the retrospective approach is preferable. In other words, the question of whether there is a serious conflict of interest and duty should be decided by inquiring, at the end of the course of conduct which has produced the advantage in question whether any serious conflict between interest and duty in fact occurred. Whatever the answer to this problem, however, it is at least clear that at present English law does not adopt a consistent attitude towards the fiduciary. Inconsistencies appear no matter how the decided cases are classified—a number of different classifications have been suggested by the various commentators. The classification adopted in this chapter is that which was drawn up and developed by Dr. Finn.[8] He divides the authorities into three main groups: first, cases where a fiduciary has as a result of his position obtained unauthorised remuneration; secondly, cases where a fiduciary has entered into a transaction in a double capacity in that he has purported to represent the interests both of his principal and of himself; and, thirdly, cases where a fiduciary has as a result of his position obtained a benefit to the exclusion of his principal.

[7] [1896] A.C. 44, 51.
[8] *Op. cit.* pp. 204–205.

### Unauthorised remuneration obtained by a fiduciary as a result of his position

The first and most obvious question that has to be considered is the extent, if at all, to which a fiduciary is entitled to claim from his principal remuneration for his services. As might be anticipated, very different rules apply to the different fiduciary relationships. It is a long-established rule of English law that a trustee is under a duty to act without remuneration[10]; this is the case even where the trustee in question devotes a considerable amount of time and trouble to managing the trust business. This rule does not of course prevent a trustee from reimbursing himself for his expenses; this right has been placed upon a statutory basis by section 30(2) of the Trustee Act 1925.[9] However, every case in which a trustee may obtain remuneration constitutes an exception to the general rule. The remuneration of professional executors and trustees is therefore normally governed by express provisions of the will or trust deed in question. However the presence of such a clause in a will achieves nothing if the estate in question is either insufficient to pay all the pecuniary legacies or is exhausted by specific gifts or is insolvent because in such situations there will be no assets available out of which the remuneration can be paid. This rather startling proposition emerges from the decision of the Court of Appeal in *Re White*[10] and of course means that a professional executor who has administered the estate under the impression that he is to receive his normal fees may find himself deprived of them because the estate is destroyed by some unexpected claim that has priority over his. The existence of this trap for professional trustees was criticised by the Law Reform Committee in their 1982 Report on the Powers and Duties of Trustees[11]; they proposed that sums due under charging clauses should be treated as administration expenses provided that the charges are properly incurred and have been authorised by the testator. However, unless and until this proposal is given statutory effect, every professional trustee who acts as an executor runs an inherent risk of finishing up without any remuneration whatever. In the absence of a charging clause, a trustee will only be able to obtain remuneration if he is able to bring himself within one of the other exceptions. It is, theoretically, possible for a trustee to contract with the beneficiaries for his remuneration. However, such a contract will only be

---

[9] All provisions of the Trustee Act 1925 are in the absence of contrary intention implied into all trust instruments.
[10] [1898] 2 Ch. 217.
[11] Law Reform Committee, 23rd Report (1982) Cmnd. 8733, para. 3.45.

feasible if all the beneficiaries are *sui juris* and would certainly be scrutinised very closely by the courts. Further, in the case of an existing trustee, there is also the possibility that such a contract might be held to be unenforceable for lack of consideration (unless of course the contract were by deed) on the grounds that the trustee was merely contracting to perform his existing legal duties— this admittedly would not apply to an incoming trustee who could obviously point to his acceptance of appointment as constituting the necessary consideration. If such a contract is not feasible, the only other possibility is to go to court and ask for a charging order to be made, either under the provisions of the Trustee Act 1925 or under the inherent jurisdiction of the court. Section 42 of the Trustee Act 1925 does indeed enable the court to authorise corporate trustees to charge such remuneration for their services as the court thinks fit but this power can only be used when the court is actually appointing a corporate trustee. The only other relevant provision of the Trustee Act 1925 is section 57 which enables the court to authorise any dealing with the trust property which it thinks fit. However, it is abundantly clear from the decided cases that the jurisdiction under this section is extremely limited and will only be rarely applied. So far as the inherent jurisdiction is concerned, it is now clear, following the decision of the Court of Appeal in *Re Duke of Norfolk's Settlement Trusts*,[12] that the courts can, upon the appointment of a trustee, direct that he be remunerated and that such an order can be made whether the application is made before or after he has accepted appointment. Thus this jurisdiction can be used both to obtain remuneration for work already done and to enable future work to be charged. The Court of Appeal also held expressly that this jurisdiction also extends to increasing the remuneration authorised by the deed or will in question. However, the mere existence of this jurisdiction does not mean that it will automatically be exercised. The courts have always emphasised that the office of trustee is, as such, gratuitous. Thus remuneration or increased remuneration in respect of future work will only be ordered if the court considers that, having regard to the nature of the trust, the experience and skill of a particular trustee is of great importance for the interests of the beneficiaries, while such orders will only be made in respect of work already done if the work in question has been wholly outside what could have been anticipated at the time of appointment. Thus it is clear that, save in the case of corporate trustees appointed by the court, the possibilities of a trustee obtaining remuneration in the absence

[12] [1981] 3 W.L.R. 455.

of a charging clause are very limited. Finally, it should be noted that a trustee may retain any remuneration to which he is automatically entitled under the law of another jurisdiction in which he is administering trust property[13] and that special rules govern the payment of remuneration to solicitor-trustees acting in their professional capacity. Prima facie, a solicitor-trustee may not pay either himself or another member of his firm for work done for the trust.[14] However, where a solicitor-trustee can properly employ an outside solicitor, he may employ and pay another member of his firm provided that it has been expressly agreed that the solicitor-trustee will not take any share in the profits.[15] Similarly, under the rule in *Cradock* v. *Piper*,[16] where a solicitor-trustee is merely one of several trustees, he or his firm may receive the usual fees for work done in the course of legal proceedings on behalf of the trust.

These are the rules which govern the payment of remuneration to a trustee as such. However, it is not uncommon for a trustee, by virtue of his position, to hold an office of profit, such as a directorship in a company in which the trust has a shareholding. In this situation, the basic rule is the same. Since the trustee is supposed to act without remuneration, he will be liable to account to the trust for any remuneration he receives as a result of holding that office. Thus, in *Re Macadam*[17] under the articles of association of a company, the trustees of a will had power for so long as the trust held shares in that company to appoint two persons to directorships. The trustees appointed themselves and were held liable to account to the trust for the directors' fees they received from the company. Once again, however, there are a number of exceptions to this rule. First, the trust instrument may expressly authorise the trustees to retain such remuneration and may well be held to do so impliedly if, as in *Re Llewellin's Will Trusts*,[18] a testator or settlor expressly authorises his trustees to use the trust shares to secure their own appointment as directors. Secondly, although there does not seem to be any decided case in which this has actually happened, the beneficiaries can presumably authorise a trustee to retain such remuneration; however such an authorisation has exactly the same potential problems for the trustee as the contract between him and the beneficiaries for the payment of remuneration which was discussed in the previous paragraph. Thirdly, a

[13] *Re Northcote's Will Trusts* [1949] 1 All E.R. 442.
[14] *Christophers* v. *White* (1847) 10 Beav. 523.
[15] *Clack* v. *Carlon* (1861) 30 L.J.Ch. 639.
[16] (1850) 1 Mac. & G. 664.
[17] [1946] Ch. 73.
[18] [1949] Ch. 225.

trustee who, as in *Re Dover Coalfield Extension*[19] becomes a director before becoming a trustee is entitled to retain any remuneration obtained. Fourthly, a trustee who secures his appointment as
director by the use of shares held in his personal capacity will be
able to retain any remuneration received provided that, as Harman J. stated in *Re Gee*[20], he would still have been appointed even
if he had used the trust shares to vote against himself. Finally, the
court has an inherent jurisdiction to allow the trustees to retain the
whole or some part of the remuneration if satisfied that they were
the best persons to be directors. Following the decisions in *Re
Keeler's Settlement*[21] and in *Re Duke of Norfolk's Settlement
Trusts*,[22] it is now clear that this jurisdiction is exercisable on the
same basis as the jurisdiction to order the payment of remuneration which was discussed in the previous paragraph. Thus the jurisdiction will not automatically be exercised. Retention of future
fees will only be ordered if the court considers that, having regard
to the nature of the trust, it is of great importance for the interests
of the beneficiaries that the office in question should be held by a
trustee and that the effort and skill required is over and above that
normally required of a director representing the interests of a substantial shareholder, while retention of past fees will similarly only
be ordered if the effort and skill required was over and above that
ordinarily required of a director representing the interests of a substantial shareholder. With such criteria the possibilities of this jurisdiction being exercised are clearly very limited.

The position of fiduciaries other than trustees is, however, more
favourable simply because they are not, generally speaking,
expected to act without remuneration. Consequently, they may
not only be remunerated for their services as fiduciaries but may
also retain the benefits of any other office to which they are
appointed by virtue of their fiduciary position, provided, of
course, that the appointment has been disclosed to their principal.
A director of a company who is appointed by the board to a directorship of a subsidiary may undoubtedly retain both sets of directors' fees and a partner who is appointed by the partners to a
directorship in a company in which the partnership holds shares
may similarly retain his director's fees.

[19] [1908] 1 Ch. 65.
[20] [1948] Ch. 284.
[21] [1981] 2 W.L.R. 499. This case was decided after the first instance decision but
before the Court of Appeal decision in *Re Duke of Norfolk's Settlement Trusts*
and therefore must now be read in the light of the latter decision.
[22] [1981] 3 W.L.R. 455.

Where a fiduciary is liable to account for remuneration received as such, he will in principle clearly be liable as a constructive trustee in respect of the remuneration so obtained. However, only where the remuneration in question is still identifiable at the date of action (as will be the case where the remuneration takes the form of shares) will there be any purpose in imposing such a trust. Where the remuneration has already passed into the general funds of the fiduciary (as will obviously be more usual), then the fiduciary will be liable merely to account to his principal for the value of the remuneration as, in effect, damages for breach of fiduciary duty.[23] In this situation, there will obviously be no need for the imposition of a constructive trust since any fiduciary liable to account for remuneration of this kind will inevitably be an express fiduciary.

In addition to his liability to account for any unauthorised remuneration received as a result of holding an office of profit, a fiduciary will also be liable to account for any other payments that he may receive as a result of his position. Such payments are generally known as secret profits. It is clearly established that no fiduciary who receives a secret profit may retain that profit as against his principal unless such retention is either authorised in advance or subsequently ratified by the principal with full knowledge of all relevant facts. In the case of all secret profits other than bribes, it is quite clear that the fiduciary will be a constructive trustee of the profit in question. A straightforward illustration of this rule is *Williams* v. *Barton*.[24] A trustee used a firm of which he was a member to value trust securities. His action was completely bona fide but he was nevertheless held liable to account as a constructive trustee to the trust for the commission he had made out of the introduction of the trust business. However, rather different rules seem to apply in the case of bribes. In *Lister & Co.* v. *Stubbs*'[25] the plaintiff employed the defendant as a purchasing agent. The latter regularly gave orders to a third party in return for a commission. In an action to recover these bribes the plaintiff sought an order restraining the defendant from dealing with certain investments purchased with the money received on the basis that, since the defendant was a constructive trustee of the bribes, the plaintiff would be entitled to follow the money into its product, the investments. But the Court of Appeal declined to grant this order, hold-

---

[23] As was seen in Chap. 1, such a claim gives the principal no priority over the general creditors of the fiduciary in the event of his bankruptcy.

[24] [1927] 2 Ch. 9.

[25] (1890) 45 Ch. D. 1.

ing that the only obligation of the defendant was to pay over the
sums received to the plaintiff—the relationship between them
being that of debtor-creditor rather than trustee-beneficiary. This
conclusion seems quite extraordinary. The defendant in *Williams*
v. *Barton* is held to be a constructive trustee of a commission
which he has earned in good faith yet the defendant in *Lister &
Co*. v. *Stubbs* is held not to be a constructive trustee of an illicitly-
obtained bribe. It used to be thought that the principal in a bribe
case had the consolation that he could recover the amount of the
bribe twice over—once from the fiduciary and once from the third
party who bribed him provided that the third party realised the
nature of the payment made (see *Salford Corporation* v. *Lever*).[26]
However, in *Mahesan* v. *Malaysia Government Officers Co-operative Housing Society*[27] the Privy Council held that these two possible claims are alternative, not cumulative. In any event, this
inconsistency in the imposition of constructive trusts cannot be justified. It is therefore suggested that, despite the eminence of the
members of the Court of Appeal who decided *Lister & Co*. v.
*Stubbs*, a constructive trust should have been imposed in that case.
Nevertheless the decision remains English law.[28] Therefore, while
all secret profits other than bribes received by a fiduciary as a
result of his fiduciary position will be subject to a constructive trust
in favour of his principal (assuming, as always, that the profits can
be sufficiently identified), a fiduciary who receives a bribe will
merely be obliged to pay over its value to his principal.

   When considering secret profits of this type, the courts take a
particularly wide view of what constitutes a fiduciary relationship.
In *Reading* v. *Attorney-General*,[29] the House of Lords had to consider the case of an ex-R.A.M.C. Sergeant who had obtained large
sums from smugglers for riding in his uniform through Cairo in
lorries in which smuggled goods were being transported—his presence enabled the lorries to pass the civil police without search.
When he was apprehended, some £19,000 found in his hands was
confiscated. He now brought a petition of right for the return of
this money. This action predictably failed but the basis of the
Crown's right to confiscate the money caused some little difficulty.

[26] [1891] 1 Q.B. 168.
[27] [1978] 2 All E.R. 405.
[28] The decision has been followed on several occasions, although in Australia the
   opinion has been expressed that the decision is anomalous and should be confined to its own facts (*Consul Development* v. *D.P.C. Estates* [1974] 1
   N.S.W.L.R. 443 (New South Wales Court of Appeal—the point was left open
   on the further appeal to the Australian High Court (1975) 132 C.L.R. 373)).
[29] [1951] A.C. 507.

At first instance[30] Denning J. held that there was no fiduciary relationship between the suppliant and the Crown but that no such
relationship was necessary. In the Court of Appeal[31] Asquith L.J.
took a different view and held that, assuming a fiduciary relationship to be necessary, such a relationship arose from the use by the
suppliant of his uniform and the opportunities attached to it.
Asquith L.J. admitted that this was using the concept of fiduciary
relationship "in a very loose . . . sense" but this did not stop the
House of Lords from confirming his view. Admittedly this was an
extreme case but it is regrettable that the concept of fiduciary relationship should thus have been deprived of certainty. A more
satisfactory basis for the decision might well have been the principle (discussed in Chap. 2) that no criminal may benefit from his
crime. The suppliant had undoubtedly committed a criminal
offence (he had been imprisoned for a breach of martial law) so
there seems no reason why this principle could not have been
invoked to justify the retention of the money by the Crown as
against him. Nevertheless, it is interesting to reflect whether,
ignoring the fact of sovereign immunity from suit, the Egyptian
authorities (who were obviously the real losers) could have
recovered from the Crown the sums which had been confiscated.

The Supreme Court of New Jersey approved the decision in
*Reading* v. *Attorney-General* in the equally extreme case of *Jersey
City* v. *Hague*.[32] The defendant mayor of New Jersey had used his
position to extort some 3 per cent. of the salary of each employee
of the city in consideration of continued employment. Over a
period of 30 years the sums extorted amounted to at least $15 mil-
lion. The City now sought to impose a constructive trust for this
amount on the assets of the defendant for its own benefit or,
alternatively, for the benefit of its defrauded employees. Clearly
the City had suffered no loss—the extortion had in no way
increased the salaries paid. All the loss had fallen upon the
employees. Therefore, three members of the court held that the
City was not the proper plaintiff, since it had no claim on its own
behalf and lacked the capacity to act as a trustee for its employees.
However, the other four members of the Supreme Court held that
the defendant stood in a fiduciary relationship to the people of Jersey City. Hence the City could seek to impeach the defendant's
breach of fiduciary duty and so was a proper plaintiff—it mattered
not that two mutually inconsistent claims had been made. Once

[30] [1948] 2 K.B. 268.
[31] [1949] 2 K.B. 232.
[32] (1955) 115 At. (2d) 8.

again this result, albeit by a bare majority, was predictable but it would be interesting to know what proportion, if any, of the sums recovered was distributed to the defrauded employees.

It is apparent that the rules established by this first group of cases are neither satisfactory nor consistent in that constructive trusts are automatically imposed on commissions which have been earned in good faith while totally illicit payments such as bribes are not held on constructive trust. The law would be very much more satisfactory if *Lister* v. *Stubbs* were overruled. However, it has to be admitted that there seems little likelihood of a decision handed down so long ago by so distinguished a Court of Appeal not being followed.[33]

### Transactions into which a fiduciary has entered in a double capacity

This second group of cases concerns transactions in which a fiduciary has purported to represent the interests both of his principal and himself. Such situations produce an obvious conflict between the personal interest of the fiduciary in the transaction and his duty towards his principal. Consequently, no matter how fair the transaction, the principal has the right to have the transaction set aside unless he was fully aware of the facts.

One of the most obvious situations of this type is where the fiduciary purchases property from his principal. Most of the reported cases have concerned purchases of property by a trustee from his trust. The basic rule governing such purchases was laid down by Lord Eldon L.C. in *Ex p. Lacey*.[34] Since in such a purchase the trustee is both vendor and purchaser, it is impossible to determine from the evidence whether or not he has obtained an advantage from the purchase; hence, the court has no option but to set aside the sale at the instance of the beneficiaries. This rule is sometimes known as the self-dealing rule.[35] On the other hand, where a trustee purchases the beneficial interest of one of the beneficiaries under the trust, then the mischief which the rule in *Ex p. Lacey* was intended to solve does not arise since the trustee is not both

---

[33] The decision was very recently cited with approval in *Att.-Gen. Ref. (No. 1 of 1985)* [1986] 2 All E.R. 219, where the Court of Appeal, Criminal Division, held that the decision in *Lister* v. *Stubbs* must have been borne in mind by the draftsmen of section 5 of the Theft Act 1968 and that, for that reason, an employee who in breach of contract sold his own goods on his employer's premises was neither a constructive trustee of the profit nor had committed an offence under the Act.

[34] (1802) 6 Vesey 625.

[35] See the judgment of Megarry V.C. in *Tito* v. *Waddell (No. 2)* [1977] Ch. 106, 240.

vendor and purchaser. Hence the courts have always been prepared to uphold such purchases provided that the trustee is able to convince the court that he obtained no advantage by virtue of his position.[36] This rule is sometimes known as the fair-dealing rule.[37]

The many cases in which the rule in *Ex p. Lacey* has been applied have illustrated that it is quite irrelevant that the trustee was honest, the sale open and the price fair. In *Wright* v. *Morgan*[38] a testator devised property to two trustees on trust for sale for one of them. The will stated that the trustees were required to offer the trustee-beneficiary the land at a price to be fixed by independent valuers. The trustee-beneficiary assigned his beneficial interest to the other trustee, who bought the property at the price fixed by the independent valuers in accordance with the terms of the will. The Privy Council held that this sale had to be set aside. Lord Dunedin said that the testator had authorised only a sale to the trustee-beneficiary and so the sale to the other trustee had to be set aside. What was the possible conflict of interest? Lord Dunedin said that the conflict of interest arose not from what the purchaser had done but from what he might have done. But what could the purchaser possibly have done, given that the sale had to be at the price fixed by the independent valuers? In reality, Lord Dunedin can only have been applying a penal rule on the grounds that any relaxation of Lord Eldon's principle might lead to wholesale defrauding of beneficiaries.

However, both the rule and the rationale of *Ex p. Lacey* were doubted by two of the members of the Court of Appeal in *Holder* v. *Holder*.[39] One of the executors of a will renounced his executorship after carrying out certain acts which, it was conceded, amounted to intermeddling. He was the tenant of certain farms which the other executors offered for sale by auction subject to his tenancy. At the auction he purchased the farms at a good price, probably higher than would have been paid by anyone other than a sitting tenant and well above the reserve price (which had been fixed by an independent valuer). One of the beneficiaries sub-

---

[36] *Chalmer* v. *Bradley* (1819) 1 J. & W. 51. In *Coles* v. *Trecothick* (1804) 9 Vesey 234 it was stated that the trustee must be able to show that he did not abuse his position as trustee, that he concealed no material facts, that the price paid was fair and that the beneficiary did not rely solely on his advice. This burden of proof will be almost incapable of discharge where the beneficiary in question is an infant (see *Sanderson* v. *Walker* (1807) 13 Vesey 601); in such circumstances the only course the trustee can adopt is to obtain the approval of the court in advance by bringing an action for a declaration.

[37] See n. 35, above.

[38] [1926] A.C. 788.

[39] [1968] Ch. 353.

sequently sought to have the sale set aside. The Court of Appeal
refused to do so. Harman L.J. held that the rule in *Ex p. Lacey*
was based on the principle that no man may be both vendor and
purchaser. Here the purchaser had renounced his executorship
long before the sale. All the beneficiaries were aware of this and so
could not have been looking to him to protect their interests. Thus
the mischief that the rule was intended to prevent did not arise and
there was no reason to set aside the sale. Such an attitude, while
quite different from that of Lord Dunedin in *Wright* v. *Morgan*,
does not in any way affect the principle in *Ex p. Lacey*. But both
the other members of the court declined to accept the principle of
that decision. Danckwerts L.J. said that Chancery judges were
daily engaged in ascertaining the knowledge and intentions of parties to proceedings; the court could unquestionably sanction such a
sale and so the rule in *Ex p. Lacey* could be no more than a rule of
practice. So, he held, this type of issue was a matter for the discretion of the judge. Sachs L.J. took very much the same view. All
three members of the court then went on to hold that, in any
event, the beneficiary had acquiesced in the purchase and could
not now seek to set it aside. The approach taken in this case by
Danckwerts and Sachs L.JJ. suggested that the courts might be
about to move away from the automatic application of the self-
dealing rule and instead apply the fair-dealing rule to purchases of
property by a trustee from his trust. This would mean that such
purchases would be set aside only where the trustee was unable to
convince the court that he obtained no advantage by virtue of his
position. The adoption of this sort of flexible approach would
undoubtedly be preferable to the automatic application of the rule
in *Ex p. Lacey* at the instance of the beneficiaries. However,
*Holder* v. *Holder* has not in fact been interpreted in this way. In *Re
Thompson's Settlement*[40] Vinelott J. instead took the view that the
decision in *Holder* v. *Holder* had been reached for the reasons
enunciated by Harman L.J. and consequently held that the self-
dealing rule had not been applied in that case simply because the
same person had not in fact been both vendor and purchaser. In
*Re Thompson's Settlement*, a trust owned two farms which were
leased to and run by a company of which the settlor was managing
director and the two trustees directors. It was agreed at a meeting
of this company that the lease of one of the farms should be
assigned to a new company of which one of the trustees was
managing director and, with his family, majority shareholder and
that the lease of the other farm should be assigned to a partnership

---

[40] [1985] 2 All E.R. 720. The facts have been somewhat simplied.

formed by the other trustee and his family. The original company was then wound up. The trustees, as freeholders, never gave the necessary consent to the assignments and no formal assignments were in fact ever executed. It was argued that *Holder* v. *Holder* had limited the self-dealing rule to direct purchases by trustees from their trusts and that the fair-dealing rule now applies to all other transactions. Vinelott J. held that the self-dealing rule "is applied stringently in cases where a trustee concurs in a transaction which cannot be carried into effect without his concurrence and who also has an interest in or holds a fiduciary duty to another in relation to the same transaction"[41] and held that there were no valid leases of the farms in favour of either the new company or the partnership. Thus it appears that the self-dealing rule retains its full force for the moment.

While the self-dealing rule thus clearly applies to purchases of property by a trustee from his trust, purchases of property by other fiduciaries from their principals are governed by the fair-dealing rule and thus will be upheld if the fiduciary did not abuse his position in any way, revealed his interest in the property and any information which he possessed concerning it, and paid a fair price.[42] In applying the appropriate rule, the courts ignore technicalities and concentrate on realities. Thus the self-dealing rule will apply where a trustee retires from his office in order to purchase trust property[43] and where the purchaser is not the trustee himself but a company controlled by him or a partnership of which he is a member.[44] On the other hand, the rule will not apply merely because the purchaser is a retired trustee if he has not obtained any advantage by virtue of his former trusteeship[45] nor where the purchaser is a public company of which the trustee happens to be a minority shareholder.[46]

Where a purchase is impeachable under the principles discussed above, the purchase is nevertheless not void. It is merely voidable at the instance of the principal who must avoid the transaction within a reasonable time. If the sale is so avoided, the result is as follows. If the fiduciary still has the property, the principal has a choice. He may opt to have the property (together with any income received meanwhile) retransferred to him in exchange for the purchase money, interest thereon and the value of any

---

[41] *Ibid.* p. 730.
[42] *Edwards* v. *Meyrick* (1842) 2 Hare 60.
[43] *Carter* v. *Palmer* (1842) 8 Cl. & F. 657.
[44] *Re Thompson's Settlement* [1985] 2 All E.R. 720.
[45] *Re Dole's & British Land Co.'s Contract* (1902) 71 L.J.Ch. 130.
[46] *Farrar* v. *Farrars* (1888) 40 Ch. D. 395.

improvements.[47] Alternatively, he may direct the fiduciary to offer the property for resale at no less than the purchase price plus the cost of repairs and improvements and then recover from him the profit on the original purchase price. If, on the other hand, the fiduciary has already resold the property, he will be obliged to account as a constructive trustee for the profit made on the resale (assuming that this is sufficiently ascertainable) plus interest thereon.[48]

Similar considerations arise where a fiduciary sells his own property to his principal. In this situation, it is clear that, unless the fiduciary has fully disclosed the nature of his interest in the transaction, the sale will be set aside at the instance of the principal, no matter how honest the fiduciary or fair the price.[49] Such a sale may be set aside even where the fiduciary purchased the property in question before he entered into the fiduciary relationship. However, where the principal seeks not to set aside the sale but to recover the profit made by the fiduciary out of the transaction, the time when the fiduciary purchased the property will be crucial. In *Re Cape Breton Co.*,[50] a director acquiesced in the sale to his company of certain mining claims in which he had a beneficial interest. After discovering the facts, the company elected not to set aside the sale but to claim the profit made by the director. This action failed because the director had acquired the property more than two years before the company in question had been formed. On the other hand, in *Bentley* v. *Craven*,[51] the defendant was responsible for the purchase of sugar for a partnership of sugar refiners of which he was a member but also carried on an independent business as a sugar dealer. He purchased a quantity of sugar which he later resold to the partnership at a price which, although resulting in a profit to him, was the fair market price of the day. He was held liable to account for his profit to the partnership since he had been a fiduciary at the date of purchase and so should have purchased the sugar for the partnership rather than for himself. Thus, where the right to rescind the sale has passed (as will be the case whenever any of the usual bars to rescission, such as affirmation, lapse

---

[47] It is probable that this option will require the consent of all the beneficiaries because of the risk that the property may not be able to be resold at a higher price.

[48] The rate of interest awarded has traditionally been 4% but it seems, following the remarks of Brightman J. in *Bartlett* v. *Barclays Bank Trust Co.* [1980] Ch. 515, 547, that the rate will now be that of the court's short-term investment account (established under the Administration of Justice Act 1965, s.6(1)).

[49] *Gillett* v. *Peppercone* (1840) 3 Beav. 78.

[50] (1885) 29 Ch. D. 795.

[51] (1853) 18 Beav. 75.

of time or bona fide purchase, has occurred) the principal will have no remedy where the fiduciary acquired the property in question before he entered into the fiduciary relationship. It will be noticed that all the decisions discussed deal with fiduciary relationships other than that of trustee and beneficiary. In fact there seems to be no English authority dealing with a purchase by a trustee of his own property for his trust. However an American decision[52] and dicta in *Bentley* v. *Craven* suggests that the same rules will apply to such a transaction.

The examples that have been given of situations falling within this second group of cases[53] illustrate that in this area the law is at least consistent and clearly established. It has already been suggested that the adoption of the more flexible approach that seems to emerge from the judgments of Danckwerts and Sachs L.JJ. in *Holder* v. *Holder* would undoubtedly be preferable to the automatic application of penal rules such as the rule in *Ex p. Lacey*. However, at present there seems little likelihood of such an approach being adopted.

### Benefits obtained by a fiduciary as a result of his position to the exclusion of his principal

The most extreme example of a fiduciary obtaining as a result of his position a benefit to the exclusion of his principal and almost the only situation within this third group of cases which is wholly uncontroversial arises where a fiduciary engages in speculation with the property of his principal. In such a case, the principal will obviously be entitled to all the profits made by the fiduciary under a constructive trust.[54] A somewhat extreme example of the operation of this principle is the decision of the Privy Council in *Reid-Newfoundland Co.* v. *Anglo-American Telegraph Co.*[55] Under the terms of a contract, the respondent telegraph company erected a special telegraph wire for use in the operation of the railway run by the appellant. The contract expressly provided that no commercial messages should be passed over this wire except for the account of the respondent. The appellant having used the wire for such commercial messages, the respondent brought an action claiming an account of the profits so made. This action succeeded, the Privy Council holding that these profits were held by the appellant on

---

[52] *Cornet* v. *Cornet* (1916) 269 Mo. 298.
[53] Dr. Finn includes two further situations: trade dealing with a business managed as a fiduciary and loans by a fiduciary to his principal (*op. cit.* pp. 228–231).
[54] *Brown* v. *I.R.C.* [1965] A.C. 244.
[55] [1912] A.C. 555.

constructive trust for the respondent. The basis upon which this constructive trust was imposed does not emerge very clearly from the only opinion (which is concerned principally with the Statutes of Limitation) but it appears that the Privy Council regarded the appellant as the agent of the respondent in respect of its use of the latter's telegraph wire. Thus the appellant had made a profit out of the property of the respondent and was therefore bound to account for that profit under a constructive trust. In this type of case, where the principal has been owner of the property throughout, and in cases where the fiduciary is already holding the property in question on trust for the principal, the constructive trust will be imposed merely on the profit. But if the property has reached the hands of the fiduciary in some other way, both the property and the fiduciary's profit will be subject to a constructive trust. If the speculation results in a loss, a constructive trust may still be imposed, if necessary, upon any of the property remaining in the hands of the fiduciary but the loss will only be recoverable by an action for damages.

At the other extreme, there are certain circumstances in which a fiduciary will be unable to compete with the business of his principal. Distinct rules apply to the different fiduciary relationships. Whether a trustee may compete with a business carried on by the trust on behalf of the beneficiaries seems to depend on the nature of the business. In *Re Thomson*,[56] a testator directed his executors to continue his yacht broking business after his death and it was held that one of the executors was not able to start a similar competing business. However, the decision appears to have been based almost entirely on the highly specialised nature of yacht broking. Thus it may well be that this decision would not be applied where the business in question was less unusual even if there were some conflict of interest between the two enterprises. *A fortiori*, a trustee who at the time of his appointment already runs a business in competition with that of the trust cannot be under any duty to cease competing.

It might be expected that, if an unpaid trustee may thus be prevented from competing, the paid director and partner would necessarily be prohibited from so doing. Partners are indeed under a statutory duty not to compete with the partnership business[57] but the position of directors is both obscure and anomalous. At common law, a director is not under any obligation not to compete with his company—at least, this is the time-honoured rule laid

---

[56] [1930] 1 Ch. 203.
[57] By virtue of Partnership Act 1890, s.30.

down in *London and Mashonaland Exploration Co.* v. *New Mashonaland Exploration Co.*[58] and approved by Lord Blanesburgh in *Bell* v. *Lever Bros.*[59] However, the position may well be different as a result of a provision in the Articles of Association of any particular company or in the service contract of any individual director. Further, in the light of authority that an employee may not compete with the business of his employer,[60] it seems likely that an executive director will be under a similar duty not to compete with his company—this seems to have been recognised by Lord Denning in *Scottish Co-operative Wholesale Society* v. *Meyer.*[61] However, at present, although the situation where there is a clear conflict of duty is covered by Part XVII of the Companies Act 1985, merely to accept directorships in competing companies is not a breach of the director's duty of loyalty to the first company. It would be preferable, however, if directors, like partners, were restrained from such activities. Where a fiduciary has breached his duty of loyalty by competing with the business of his principal, it is quite clear that the principal may obtain an injunction restraining such competition. Further, although there seems to be no case in which this has actually been held, the fiduciary should be liable to account to his principal for any profits he has made out of this competition under a constructive trust.

The two situations that have just been considered are relatively straightforward. However the majority of authorities that constitute this third group of cases have concerned the much more controversial question of what opportunities a fiduciary is entitled to utilise for his own benefit. The starting point of any discussion of this issue is unquestionably *Keech* v. *Sandford,*[62] decided by Lord King L.C. as long ago as 1726. The case actually concerned the right of a trustee to renew for his own benefit a lease which the landlord had refused to renew in favour of the trust. The decision has had two quite distinct effects. First, it has produced a line of authority concerning the extent to which a fiduciary may renew for his own benefit a lease held by his principal (the actual issue that arose in *Keech* v. *Sandford*) and the associated question of whether a fiduciary may purchase the freehold reversion of property of which his principal is lessee. Secondly, and totally unconnected with any question of the renewal of leases or the purchase of reversions, the decision has had a profound effect on the

---

[58] [1891] 1 W.N. 165.
[59] [1932] A.C. 161, 195.
[60] *Hivac* v. *Park Royal Scientific Instruments* [1946] Ch. 169.
[61] [1959] A.C. 324, p. 366–367.
[62] (1726) Sel. Cas. Ch. 61.

general question of what opportunities a fiduciary is entitled to utilise for his own benefit. These two questions will be considered in turn.

In *Keech* v. *Sandford* a lease of a market was held on trust for an infant. The trustee sought, unsuccessfully, to renew the lease for the benefit of the trust. However the landlord, although not prepared to renew the lease to the trust, was prepared to grant a renewal to the trustee in his personal capacity and the trustee duly took the lease in his own right. Lord King L.C. held that any trustee who abuses his position by entering into a transaction with a third party must account for the benefit of the transaction as a constructive trustee. Consequently the trustee held the benefit of the lease on constructive trust for the infant. His lordship stated the rationale of the rule both simply and cynically: if a trustee on the refusal of a lessor to renew a lease to the trust were permitted to take a lease himself, few leases would ever be renewed in favour of trusts. The rule thus enunciated applies strictly speaking only to trustees but has repeatedly been applied to all types of fiduciaries.

The precise limits of the rule were discussed very fully in *Re Biss*.[63] A lessee died intestate, leaving a widow and three children, all of whom were obviously entitled under his intestacy. The widow became administratrix of the estate and sought a renewal of the lease on behalf of the estate. This the lessor refused to grant and instead granted a lease to one of the children in his personal capacity. The administratrix claimed that the child held the lease on constructive trust for the estate. The Court of Appeal held that the rule in *Keech* v. *Sandford* applies with all its stringency to persons clearly occupying a fiduciary position such as trustees and agents. There is an irrebuttable presumption that such persons cannot retain the benefit of transactions entered into in their personal capacity. (Thus, had the administratrix renewed the lease for her personal benefit, it would have been subject to a constructive trust.) On the other hand, persons owing a special, but non-fiduciary, duty are subject only to a rebuttable presumption. Thus if such a person can show that he did not abuse his position, he can retain the benefit of the transaction. The Court of Appeal considered mortgagees, tenants for life, joint tenants and (rather unexpectedly) partners to be in this category. The child was merely one of those who would be entitled upon intestacy if the estate turned out to be solvent and so was merely a possible beneficiary and tenant in common. Such a person, if indeed he was

---

[63] [1903] 2 Ch. 40.

under any duty at all, clearly fell into the second category and, since he had not abused his position, was able to retain the benefit of the lease.

Thus, fiduciaries (with the possible exception of partners) are clearly within the rule in *Keech* v. *Sandford*, whereas those occupying a special, but non-fiduciary, position will only be caught by the rule if they have in fact obtained an advantage by abusing their position. It is rather difficult to see why partners, who are quite clearly fiduciaries, should be in the latter rather than the former category. The basis of this classification seems to have been a statement to this effect by Turner L.J. in *Clegg* v. *Edmondson*[64] but there seems to be no decision in which a partner has been allowed to retain the benefit of a transaction on this ground. It is suggested that the position of all fiduciaries should be the same in this respect and that, so long as the rule in *Keech* v. *Sandford* governs the position of trustees, agents and directors, it should also govern that of partners. This may well now be the law following the decision in *Thompson's Trustee* v. *Heaton*[65] (which will be discussed later), where the rule in *Keech* v. *Sandford* was applied in its most strict form to a partner. However, *Re Biss* was not very fully discussed in that case and so the matter has not yet been finally settled.

The rule in *Keech* v. *Sandford* is clearly not limited to situations where a fiduciary obtains the renewal of a lease formerly held by his principal. It has been extended to cases where the fiduciary has acquired the freehold reversion in property of which his principal is lessee. Where the fiduciary has acquired the reversion by means of an abuse of his fiduciary position or has only obtained the opportunity to purchase because, as fiduciary, he is the nominal lessee, it is clearly in accordance with principle for a constructive trust to be imposed. This was held by Parker J. in *Griffith* v. *Owen*.[66] Similarly, where the lease in question is renewable by custom, the fiduciary will hold the reversion on constructive trust for his principal since, otherwise, he would be able to prejudice the interests of his principal by declining to renew the lease. This was held by the Court of Appeal in *Phillips* v. *Phillips*.[67] On the other hand, where the lease in question is not renewable by custom or by right, the acquisition of the reversion by the fiduciary can hardly be said to prejudice his principal. Hence in *Randall* v.

---

[64] (1857) 8 De G.M. & G. 787.
[65] [1974] 1 W.L.R. 605.
[66] [1907] 1 Ch. 195.
[67] (1885) 29 Ch. D. 673.

*Russell*[68] and *Bevan* v. *Webb*[69] it was held that, in such circumstances, a fiduciary who had not abused his position was entitled to retain the reversion for his own benefit. Thus far the law was both clear and in accordance with principle. Two more recent cases, however, have raised some doubt as to whether a fiduciary can ever purchase a reversion for his own benefit. In *Protheroe* v. *Protheroe*[70] a husband held a leasehold on trust for himself and his wife in equal shares. After they had separated, the husband acquired the freehold reversion. The Court of Appeal, without referring to any of the authorities just discussed, held that a trustee of leasehold property cannot acquire the freehold for himself and imposed a constructive trust. Now it may well be that the husband only obtained the opportunity to acquire the reversion because he was, as trustee, the nominal lessee. If this was the case, discussion and application of the earlier authorities would have made no difference. However, the broad principle thus enunciated has since been applied in *Thompson's Trustee* v. *Heaton*.[71] After the dissolution of a partnership, one of the partners remained in possession of land of which the partners had been and remained joint lessees. After that partner's death his executors acquired the freehold reversion and subsequently resold the land. The trustee in bankruptcy of the other partner now claimed to be entitled to one half of the profit so obtained, a claim which was upheld by Pennycuick V.C. He held that on the facts the leasehold interest remained an undistributed asset of the partnership and thus, by virtue of *Protheroe* v. *Protheroe*, neither partner could acquire the reversion for his sole benefit. There are two difficulties about his conclusion. First, in *Re Biss* the Court of Appeal stated that partners were only to be caught by the rule in *Keech* v. *Sandford* if it could be shown that an advantage had actually been obtained by virtue of their fiduciary position. This dictum has already been criticised but should it not at the very least have been discussed? Secondly, and more significantly, the application of the broad statement enunciated in *Protheroe* v. *Protheroe* prevented any discussion of the earlier authorities, application of which might well have led to a different result. Thus it may well be that *Protheroe* v. *Protheroe* has swept away all the earlier distinctions and has established that a fiduciary may never purchase for his own benefit a reversion in

[68] (1817) 3 Mer. 190.
[69] [1905] 1 Ch. 620.
[70] [1968] 1 W.L.R. 519.
[71] [1974] 1 W.L.R. 605.

property of which his principal is lessee. Such a rule seems unnecessarily harsh and it is therefore suggested that the approach of the earlier authorities was preferable.

Dr. Finn has commented that "One of the hazards of a judge-made system of law is that a mechanical application of the doctrine of precedent can produce a body of law devoid of any satisfactory, or reasonable, unifying principle. Such has been the fate of the case law that has built up upon the actual decision in *Keech* v. *Sandford* . . . [which] is now applied in an arbitrary and mechanical fashion irrespective of any actual conflict of duty and interest, or of any actual misuse of a position of trust."[72] It cannot be denied that the group of decisions that has just been discussed manifests the harsh and unyielding application of a penal rule whose ambit is even at the present time still being widened by the courts. It is obviously impossible to justify the existing law governing the rights of a fiduciary to renew for his own benefit a lease held by his principal or to purchase the freehold reversion of property of which his principal is lessee. However, as has already been mentioned, the decision in *Keech* v. *Sandford* has also had a profound effect on the general question of what opportunities a fiduciary is entitled to utilise for his own benefit. The effect of the application of the decision in *Keech* v. *Sandford* to this general question has been to produce equally harsh results; the only difference is that the application of that decision has been somewhat less mechanical in that the courts have on occasions attempted to consider whether or not there has been any actual conflict of interest and duty or misuse of a position of trust.

It is of course obvious that a fiduciary is entitled to utilise for his own benefit opportunities which have nothing whatever to do with the fiduciary relationship in question. The mere fact that a person is a trustee of an investment fund does not prevent him from purchasing shares in his personal capacity—were this not the case it would be impossible to find anyone prepared to accept a trusteeship. Equally obviously, if such a trustee obtains the opportunity to take up a rights issue by virtue of the fact that the trust is a shareholder in the company in question, then he is not entitled to take up that rights issue in his personal capacity and if he does so the shares in question will be subject to a constructive trust in favour of the fund. A fiduciary will only be in breach of his duty of loyalty to his principal if the transactions into which he enters in his personal capacity fall within the scope of his fiduciary obli-

---

[72] *Op. cit.* p. 261.

gations to his principal. As Oliver L.J. stated in *Swain* v. *The Law Society*[73]:

> "What one has to do is ascertain first of all whether there was
> a fiduciary relationship and, if there was, from what it arose
> and what, if there was any, was the trust property; and then to
> inquire whether that of which an account is claimed either
> arose, directly or indirectly, from the trust property itself or
> was acquired not only in the course of, but by reason of, the
> fiduciary relationship."

The question of whether a transaction falls within the scope of a
fiduciary obligation may be capable of being resolved by reference
to the terms of the agreement between the fiduciary and principal
in question. Thus in *Aas* v. *Benham*[74] a member of a ship-broking
partnership utilised information which he had received in his
capacity as partner to help form a ship-building company of which
he became a director. An action by his partners for an account of
the benefits received from the company failed on the grounds that
the business of the company was quite different from the business
of the partnership, the Court of Appeal holding that there was
nothing to prevent a partner utilising information obtained in his
fiduciary capacity provided that he was not competing with the
partnership business. A similar decision was reached by the
Supreme Court of Oklahoma in *British American Oil Producing
Co.* v. *Midway Oil Company*.[75] The two oil companies agreed
jointly to exploit the petroleum resources of a particular area
under the terms of a contract which contained detailed provisions
both as to the area in question and as to their mutual obligations.
As a result of work carried out in performance of this contract the
British American Oil Producing Company obtained information
which caused that company to take oil leases over an adjoining
area. The Supreme Court of Oklahoma rejected a claim by the
Midway Oil Company for a half-share in these leases on the
grounds that the agreement between the two companies had a
specifically defined nature and scope, holding that "no court has the
right to enlarge the duty of British American and create new rights

---

[73] [1982] 1 W.L.R. 17, 37. The case concerned the liability of The Law Society to
account for commissions received from an insurance company in respect of pre-
miums paid by solicitors under the Solicitors' Indemnity Scheme. The House of
Lords, reversing the Court of Appeal, held that The Law Society was not a fiduciary in that it was performing a public duty and so was not accountable but Lord
Brightman approved the approach adopted by Oliver L.J. ([1983] 1 A.C. 598,
619).

[74] [1891] 2 Ch. 244.

[75] (1938) 82 P. (2d) 1049.

in Midway by decreeing to Midway a share of profits made by British American from a private risk in a separate enterprise."[76]

However it is not often that the scope of a fiduciary obligation is defined so closely by the parties thereto. In such circumstances rather more difficulties can be encountered. Cases of clear misconduct by the fiduciary are of course quite straightforward. In *Cook* v. *Deeks*[77] three of the directors of a company, with the intention of excluding the fourth member, arranged for a contract which they had negotiated on behalf of the company to be made with them in their private capacities. The excluded director claimed that the company was entitled to the benefit of this contract. This claim was upheld by the Privy Council who held that the whole reputation of the three had been obtained with the company. They could have excluded the plaintiff quite legitimately by using their majority shareholding to wind up the company. Instead they had abused their position as directors to deprive the company of any chance of obtaining the contract. Thus the benefit of the contract belonged in equity to the company. This decision cannot be faulted since the directors had clearly abused their fiduciary position. However the English courts have adopted an identical attitude where the misconduct of the fiduciary in question has been much more questionable. The decided cases of this type have generally arisen when the principal in question has been unable or unwilling to utilise an opportunity and the fiduciary has subsequently utilised that opportunity for his own benefit.[78]

In *Regal (Hastings)* v. *Gulliver*,[79] the plaintiff company owned a cinema in Hastings and wished to acquire two other local cinemas with the intention of selling the whole enterprise as a package. A subsidiary, with a capital of 5,000 £1 shares, was formed to take a lease of these two cinemas. The original scheme was for only 2,000 of these shares to be paid up but the owner of the cinemas declined to grant a lease on this basis. Since the company could not afford

---

[76] *Ibid*. p. 1053 *per* Welch J.

[77] [1916] A.C. 554.

[78] Dr. Finn has argued that there are in fact two separate rules that arise as a result of the decision in *Keech* v. *Sandford*: "These rules, though interlocking, have distinct applications and applications which illustrate both the conflict and the profiting facets of the general rule. They are: (1) a fiduciary cannot, on his own account, derive any benefit which his undertaking authorises or requires him to pursue in his representative capacity; and (2) a fiduciary, even though acting in a matter outside the scope of his undertaking to his beneficiary, cannot retain a private profit made, if it has been made only through some actual misuse of his representative position." (*op. cit.* pp. 231 *et seq.*) Dr. Finn is the first to admit that these two distinct questions are often confused by the courts but his analysis provides considerable assistance when considering the authorities.

[79] [1942] 1 All E.R. 378; [1967] 2 A.C. 134n.

to put more than £2,000 into the subsidiary, four of the directors
and the company solicitor each subscribed for 500 shares and the
fifth director found some outsiders to take up the remaining 500.
The combined concern was then sold not as a whole but by way of
takeover and each holder of shares in the subsidiary obviously
made a profit. The purchasers then brought an action against all
five directors and the company solicitor claiming that this profit
had been made out of a breach of their fiduciary duty and therefore had to be accounted for to the company. (The action, in
effect, was an attempt to recover some of the purchase price
already paid for the companies.) The action against the director
who had not subscribed for any shares obviously failed, for he had
made no profit. So too did the action against the company solicitor, for he had subscribed for his shares with the consent of the
board of directors as then constituted. But the actions against the
other four directors succeeded in the House of Lords. Thus
the purchasers in the event paid less for the companies than they
had bargained to pay and the directors were deprived of any return
on the money they had invested. The decision of the House of
Lords was based fairly and squarely on *Keech* v. *Sandford*. Lord
Russell of Killowen (who gave the principal speech) stated that the
directors had unquestionably acquired their shares by virtue of
their fiduciary position. It made no difference that the company
could not itself have subscribed for the shares—the trust in *Keech*
v. *Sandford* could not itself have obtained a new lease and that had
made no difference. Thus the directors had to surrender their
profit.

This decision seems extremely harsh. Given that the company
could not afford to put more than £2,000 into the subsidiary, what
alternative did the directors have? Lord Russell of Killowen
clearly thought that the directors should have obtained the consent
of the shareholders in general meeting. He stated that the directors "could, had they wished, have protected themselves by a resolution (either antecedent or subsequent) of the Regal shareholders
in general meeting."[80] This statement appears at first sight to conflict with the decision in *Cook* v. *Deeks*[81] since in that case the
Privy Council held that the three majority shareholders were not
protected by such a resolution in general meeting. However in
*Prudential Assurance Co.* v. *Newman Industries (No. 2)*[82] Vinelott
J. stated that "there is no obvious limit to the power of the major-

[80] [1942] 1 All E.R. 378, 389, [1967] 2 A.C. 134, 150.
[81] [1916] 1 A.C. 554 (discussed on p. 71).
[82] [1980] 2 All E.R. 841, 862.

ity to authorise or ratify any act or transaction whatever its character provided that it is not ultra vires or unlawful and that the majority does not have an interest which conflicts with that of the company," explaining *Regal (Hastings)* v. *Gulliver* on the grounds that there was no evidence in that case that the directors did in fact control the majority. This suggests that any utilisation by a director of an opportunity for his own benefit may be ratified by the company in general meeting provided that the director in question does not control the majority of the votes. However a very much more generous attitude towards the question of ratification was demonstrated by the Privy Council in *Queensland Mines* v. *Hudson*.[83] Hudson was the managing director of Queensland Mines which had been formed to exploit certain mining operations. In 1961 Hudson, in his own name but in fact on behalf of the company and utilising its reputation and funds, sought and obtained two mining exploration licences from the Tasmanian Government. Immediately thereafter the source of the company's finance dried up. Hudson, faced by the immense personal obligations owed by him to the Tasmanian Government and a total lack of resources with which to meet them, resigned his managing directorship (although he remained a director for a further ten years) and devoted himself entirely to the task of raising sufficient funds to exploit the licences. In 1962 the board of Queensland Mines, fully informed of all relevant facts, decided to renounce all interest in the exploitation of the licences and assented to Hudson taking over the venture for his own benefit. By 1963 he had proved the existence of valuable mineral resources and subsequently he succeeded in interesting an American company to whom a mineral lease of the land in question was finally granted in 1966. Under his contract with the American company Hudson was entitled to the payment of royalties on the ore mined. Queensland Mines now claimed to be entitled to these payments. The Privy Council held that Hudson had obtained the opportunity to earn these royalties by virtue of his position as managing director of Queensland Mines. Hudson was therefore liable to account for his profit unless he could show that Queensland Mines had renounced its interest in the transaction and had assented to Hudson proceeding in his personal capacity.[84] However, the Privy Council held that the decision taken by the board in 1962 was sufficient to satisfy this

---

[83] (1977) 18 A.L.R. 1.
[84] The Board cited as authorities *Regal (Hastings)* v. *Gulliver* and the decision of the House of Lords in *Phipps* v. *Boardman* [1967] 2 A.C. 46 which will be discussed later.

requirement and that, consequently, Hudson was entitled to retain the royalties. This decision was undoubtedly influenced by the fact that Hudson had worked extremely hard and risked everything while Queensland Mines had risked nothing and was now attempting to deprive Hudson of the fruits of his success. Nevertheless it is hardly appropriate for a decision of the board, albeit unanimous, to be regarded as sufficient ratification of some action of a director and on this point the decision of the Privy Council is clearly inconsistent with the decision in *Regal (Hastings)* v. *Gulliver* where, since all the directors took part, directly or indirectly, in the transaction, they must necessarily have consented to it and the the transaction was nevertheless successfully impeached. The only ground upon which it may be possible to justify the decision of the Privy Council on the question of consent is that Queensland Mines had only two shareholders: a company controlled by Hudson had a 49% shareholding and was represented on the board by Hudson while the 51% shareholder was represented on the board by the other two directors; since all the shareholders of the company were thus represented on the board, it may just about be possible to regard the decision of the board as a decision of the shareholders which, since the shareholder represented by Hudson had a minority interest, would satisfy the test suggested by Vinelott J. in *Prudential Assurance Co.* v. *Newman Industries (No. 2)*. However this possible justification of the decision is scarcely satisfactory. It is therefore suggested that, when the consent of a company is necessary in respect of some action of a director, that consent should only be able to be given in the circumstances indicated by Vinelott J., namely by the company in general meeting provided that the director in question does not control the majority of the votes.

While the decisions in *Regal (Hastings)* v. *Gulliver* and *Queensland Mines* v. *Hudson* are thus mutually inconsistent on the question of consent, the two decisions are entirely consistent on the question of the liability of the directors in question to account. In both cases it was assumed that, in the absence of the appropriate consent, any director who obtained an opportunity by virtue of his fiduciary position was liable to account to the company for his profit. Thus it is clear that the English courts are not prepared to countenance a fiduciary exploiting an opportunity for his own benefit and are more concerned to penalise him for having taken up an opportunity of entering into a profitable transaction on his own behalf than to ascertain whether or not there has been a conflict between his duty of loyalty to his principal and his own self-interest. Other jurisdictions have felt able to adopt a more flexible

approach. In *Peso Silver Mines* v. *Cropper*[85] the Supreme Court of
Canada had to consider a situation very similar to that in *Regal*
(*Hastings*) v. *Gulliver*. The defendant was on the board of the
plaintiff company at a time when the company geologist invited
and advised that board to purchase certain mining claims, some of
which were contiguous to claims already owned by the company.
The board rejected this offer partly for financial reasons and partly
because some of the directors considered the claims to be an unin-
viting business risk. Subsequently, the geologist, with the defendant and two other directors of the plaintiff, formed a company to
purchase and exploit these claims. In due course, the plaintiff was
taken over and its new board claimed that the defendant held his
shares in the new company on a constructive trust for the plaintiff.
This claim failed. The British Columbia Court of Appeal rejected
*Regal* (*Hastings*) v. *Gulliver* and held, by a majority, that the strict
penal rules of equity had been carried far enough and were not
appropriate for a modern country in a modern era.[86] But the
Supreme Court took a much narrower view and distinguished
*Regal* (*Hastings*) v. *Gulliver* on the grounds that the defendant had
acted entirely in good faith in participating in the initial decision of
the board not to purchase the claims. He had not obtained any
advantage at all as a result of participating in this decision and
therefore was entitled to take up a subsequent offer in his private
capacity without being liable to account for his profit. This
approach seems preferable in every way to that adopted by the
House of Lords in *Regal* (*Hastings*) v. *Gulliver*. It is of course possible to criticise this decision as a matter of policy on the ground
that to permit a director to take up opportunities which his company is unable to utilise is to encourage him to refrain from exerting his strongest efforts on behalf of the company.[87] But for
present purposes the point that must be emphasised is that the sort
of penal attitude adopted by the House of Lords in *Regal* (*Hastings*) v. *Gulliver* prevents such matters of policy being raised at all.

The High Court of Australia adopted an attitude similar to that
of the Canadian Supreme Court in *Consul Development* v. *D.P.C.
Estates*.[88] The case concerned the activities of one Grey who had
been employed by a group of property companies, of which the
plaintiff was one, to find properties for purchase. He was under an
express duty of confidentiality in respect of all group business and

---

[85] (1966) 58 D.L.R. (2d) 1.
[86] (1966) 56 D.L.R. (2d) 117.
[87] See (1967) 30 M.L.R. 450 (D. D. Prentice). These sentiments were also
expressed by Swan J. in *Irving Trust Co.* v. *Deutsch* (1934) 73 Fed. (2d) 121, 124
[88] (1975) 49 A.L.J.R. 74.

had undertaken not to engage in real estate business other than for the group. However, he came to collaborate with one Clowes, who was both an employee of the group and managing director of the defendant company. Grey provided Clowes with information about properties which were then acquired by the defendant but told Clowes that the group was not interested in these properties for reasons which were quite plausible. The plaintiff now claimed that these properties were subject to a constructive trust. It was quite clear that Grey, who had been guilty of a deliberate breach of his duty of loyalty to the plaintiff, was liable to account for his own profit. But a majority of the High Court held that if the group had in fact declined to buy the properties Grey would have been entitled to buy the properties for himself. Clowes (and therefore the defendant) believed and were entitled to believe that the group had declined to buy the properties and so the defendant was entitled to enter into the transaction for its own benefit. Thus, the defendant neither held the properties on trust for the plaintiff nor was liable to account for its profit. This attitude is wholly consistent with that taken in *Peso Silver Mines* v. *Cropper* and, once again, is much to be preferred to that of the House of Lords in *Regal (Hastings)* v. *Gulliver*.

The contrast between the two approaches emerges extremely clearly in the controversial decision of the House of Lords in *Phipps* v. *Boardman*.[89] A testator established a trust for the benefit of his widow and children. Some 12 years after his death, the trust solicitor, one Boardman, became concerned about one of the principal investments of the fund—a 27 per cent. holding in a private company. After an unsuccessful attempt to bring about the election of one of the testator's sons to the board of the company, Boardman reached the conclusion that the only way of protecting the trust investment was to acquire a majority holding in the company. He suggested this to the managing trustee, who said that it was entirely out of the question for the trust to acquire such a holding. Boardman and the son then decided to purchase the outstanding shares themselves. They duly obtained control of the company and, by capitalising some of the assets, were able to make a distribution of capital to the shareholders without reducing the value of the shares. The trust benefitted by this distribution to the tune of £47,000 and Boardman and his colleague made a profit of about £75,000. However, in the course of negotiations leading up to the take-over, Boardman had purported to represent the trust and

[89] [1967] 2 A.C. 46.

thereby had incontrovertibly obtained information which would not have been made available to the general public. One of the other sons of the testator, who had not been particularly fully consulted, therefore claimed that this profit of £75,000 had been made by the utilisation of information which had reached Boardman while acting on behalf of the trust and so in a fiduciary capacity. This claim was upheld by the House of Lords, who held that the shares which had been acquired were subject to a constructive trust in favour of the trust. Thus, in effect, the trust obtained the whole of the profit made on the take-over, less an allowance which the House awarded under its inherent jurisdiction to Boardman by way of remuneration for the work he had done.

All the members of the House of Lords agreed that the defendants had placed themselves in a fiduciary relationship by acting as representatives of the trust for a number of years and that out of this fiduciary relationship they had obtained the opportunity to make a profit and the knowledge that a profit was there to be made. The majority adduced two inter-connected reasons for going on to hold that the defendants were therefore liable as constructive trustees to account for their profit to the trust. Lord Hodson and Lord Guest both clearly held that, since the only basis on which the defendants had obtained their information was the fact that they had been purporting to represent the trust, this information was trust property. Therefore, the defendants had, in effect, made a profit out of speculating with trust property and thus were clearly liable. Lord Cohen reached the same conclusion by a slightly different route. He held that information was not property in the strict sense of the word and that it did not necessarily follow that a fiduciary must account for any profit obtained by the use of information acquired in his fiduciary capacity. In this case, however, the information had been acquired while the defendants had been purporting to represent the trust. Thus, the defendants were liable to account for their profit under the principle in *Regal (Hastings)* v. *Gulliver*.

Further, all three felt that Boardman had placed himself in a position where his duty and interest might conflict (such a conflict would have arisen, for example, had the trustees sought his advice as to the merits of the trust acquiring a majority holding in the company). No matter how remote the possibility of such a conflict arising, a fiduciary who placed himself in this position was bound to account to his principal for any profit he had made. Since the defendants had accepted that their positions were the same, both were thus liable for their profit. In the opinion of the majority, it was quite immaterial that the defendants had acted honestly and openly in a manner highly beneficial to the trust in a situation where the trust itself could not have utilised the information they had received.

Both the dissentients (Viscount Dilhorne and Lord Upjohn) took the view that the remoteness of the possibility of any conflict of interest arising and the various factors just referred to which the majority had found irrelevant led inescapably to the conclusion that the defendants had not breached their duty of loyalty to the trust. Lord Upjohn said that a conflict of interest only arose where the reasonable man, looking at all the relevant circumstances, would think that there was a real sensible possibility of conflict and not where the only possibility of conflict arose from events not contemplated as real sensible probabilities by any reasonable person. Boardman knew when he decided to proceed on his own behalf that there was no possibility of the trustees seeking his advice as to the merits of a purchase by the trust—the managing trustee had already told him that this was quite out of the question. Further, Lord Upjohn doubted the classification of the information as trust property. He said that information was not in any normal sense property; equity would merely restrain its transmission to another in breach of confidence. This was not such a case.

The decision of the majority in *Phipps* v. *Boardman* is open to criticism on two distinct grounds: first, because of the classification of the information as trust property and, secondly, because of the decision that the fiduciaries were not entitled to exploit the opportunity for their own benefit. These two grounds will be considered in turn. It is of course apparent that if the information was indeed properly classifiable as trust property, then the defendants had of course made a profit out of speculating with trust property and were thus clearly liable as constructive trustees under the principle laid down in *Reid-Newfoundland Co.* v. *Anglo-American Telegraph Co*[90] which was discussed at the beginning of this section. However, Professor Gareth Jones[91] has produced forceful arguments in support of the minority view of Lord Upjohn that information is not in any normal sense trust property. Professor Jones argues that it is wholly inappropriate to classify the information received by the defendants as the property of the trust and draws support for this contention from *Aas* v. *Benham*[92] where, as has

---

[90] [1912] A.C. 555.
[91] (1968) 84 L.Q.R. 472.
[92] [1891] 2 Ch. 244 (discussed on p. 70).

already been seen, a member of a ship-broking partnership utilised information which he had received in his capacity as partner to help form a ship-building company of which he became a director. The Court of Appeal, in rejecting a claim by his partners for an account of the benefits received from the company, declined to classify the information as the property of the partnership. Further support for Professor Jones' contention may be found in a number of North American cases, in all of which, admittedly, the fiduciary relationship arose under a commercial contract. In *Pine Pass Oil & Gas* v. *Pacific Petroleum*,[93] the Supreme Court of British Columbia declined to classify as trust property information obtained by a trustee as such and held that the trustee was able to use the information for its own benefit when not acting in its fiduciary capacity. A similar decision was reached by the Supreme Court of Oklahoma in *British American Oil Producing Co.* v. *Midway Oil Co.*,[94] which has already been discussed. Professor Jones also draws attention to a further consequence of classifying information as trust property: if the information is trust property in the normal sense of that expression, it can presumably be followed into the hands of the whole world other than a bona fide purchaser thereof for value without notice. Given the essential nature of information, which can be divulged in its entirety to any number of persons, such a conclusion could lead to quite absurd results. This is not to say that a fiduciary should automatically be entitled to utilise for his own benefit information which has come to him in his fiduciary capacity. A fiduciary who by the utilisation of such information abuses his fiduciary position should clearly be liable as a constructive trustee. But this liability should arise not as a result of the automatic classification of the information as the property of his principal but rather as a result of the application of the principles which have already been discussed. A case in which it was entirely appropriate for a constructive trust to be imposed upon a fiduciary who had utilised for his own benefit information which had come to him in his fiduciary capacity was *Industrial Development Consultants* v. *Cooley*.[95] The defendant was managing director of the plaintiff company. In 1968 he had been attempting, on behalf of the plaintiff, to obtain a contract to design certain depots for the Eastern Gas Board. These attempts had failed because the Gas Board did not like the plaintiff's organization and were not

---

[93] (1968) 70 D.L.R. (2d) 196.
[94] (1938) 82 P. (2d) 1049 (discussed on p. 70).
[95] [1972] 1 W.L.R. 443.

prepared to deal with that company in any capacity. In 1969, a representative of the Gas Board sought a meeting with the defendant in his private capacity and intimated to him that if he could free himself from his ties with the plaintiff he had a very good chance of obtaining the contract for himself. The defendant therefore secured his release from his contract with the plaintiff by a totally false representation that he was on the verge of a nervous breakdown and accepted an offer from the Gas Board to do substantially the same work which he had unsuccessfully attempted to obtain for the plaintiff in 1968. The plaintiff now claimed that the defendant was a trustee of that contract for the benefit of the plaintiff and sought an account of the defendant's profits. This action succeeded. Roskill J. held that at the time when the defendant first realised that he had an opportunity of obtaining the contract for himself the only capacity in which he was carrying on business was as managing director of the plaintiff. He was under a fiduciary duty to pass on to the plaintiff information which reached him while carrying on business in that capacity.[96] Since he had failed to do so and had instead utilised the information for his own ends, he was a trustee of the contract for the plaintiff and must account for his profit. In reaching this conclusion, Roskill J. relied heavily upon *Boardman* v. *Phipps*. However, it is clear that even if the majority view in that case is rejected in favour of the view of Lord Upjohn (whose speech, interestingly enough, was the only one to be cited) the result would be the same. In the light of the conduct of the defendant, this was the clearest possible case for the imposition of a constructive trust. Similarly extreme conduct and a similar result occurred in the Canadian case of *Pre-Cam Exploration Co.* v. *McTavish*,[97] where the defendant was employed by the plaintiff to inspect certain mining claims. The inspection showed that the mineralized zone extended onto unclaimed land so the defendant, instead of informing the plaintiff, severed his employment and staked the claims himself. The Supreme Court of Canada held that he held these claims on constructive trust for the plaintiff. These decisions show that a fiduciary who abuses his fiduciary position by utilising information which has come to him in his fiduciary capacity should clearly be liable as a constructive trustee but not

---

[96] A director is not normally obliged to pass on to his company all the information which he receives in any capacity (see pp. 64–65). Consequently this fiduciary duty must have arisen because the defendant had undertaken some specific duty to the plaintiff in respect of this source of information by virtue of his prior negotiations with the Gas Board on behalf of the plaintiff. (See Finn, *op. cit.* pp. 240–241.)

[97] [1966] S.C.R. 551.

by virtue of the automatic classification of the information as the property of his principal.[98]

The decision of the majority in *Phipps* v. *Boardman* that the fiduciaries were not entitled to exploit the opportunity for their own benefit has also been the subject of considerable criticism. Professor Gareth Jones[99] has argued that courts of other jurisdictions have declined to impose constructive trusts upon fiduciaries who have profited from their fiduciary position unless it has been shown that a real conflict of interest has arisen. He cites as illustrations both the Canadian decision, *Peso Silver Mines* v. *Cropper*[1], which has already been discussed, and the decision of the Supreme Court of the United States of America in *Manufacturers Trust Co.* v. *Becker*.[2] In this latter decision, the directors of a company encouraged their associates to purchase debentures at a time when the market price of the debentures was a fraction of their face value. At the time, the company was a going concern but subsequently went into liquidation, at which point an objection was

---

[98] It is possible that, quite apart from any question of the imposition of a constructive trust, a fiduciary may be held liable under the equitable obligation of confidence. English law clearly recognises that "he who has received infomation in confidence shall not take unfair advantage of it. He must not make use of it to the prejudice of him who gave it without obtaining his consent" (*Seager* v. *Copydex* [1967] 1 W.L.R. 923, 931 *per* Lord Denning M.R.). In a number of cases where information obtained in confidence has been used without such consent, the courts have been content to consider the whole gamut of remedies open to them and award that remedy which is most appropriate to the situation. Thus in *Seager* v. *Copydex*, the plaintiff had been endeavouring, unsuccessfully, to interest the defendants in an invention of his, the nature of which he obviously had to disclose to them. Subsequently, the defendants unconsciously made use of this information to produce a virtually identical article. The Court of Appeal held that neither an account of profits nor an injunction was the appropriate remedy for such a case. Instead the court ordered damages to be assessed on the basis of reasonable compensation for the use of the confidential inforation given to the defendants. This book is not an appropriate place for a detailed discussion of the equitable obligation of confidence but there can be no doubt that the approach adopted in cases such as *Seager* v. *Copydex* gives to the law of breach of confidence a very desirable flexibility. This approach has been consistently adopted in cases involving a breach of confidence where there was no pre-existing fiduciary relationship between the parties and has been adopted in one case involving principal and agent (*North and South Trust* v. *Berkeley* [1971] 1 W.L.R. 471). It is arguable that the utilisation by a fiduciary of information which he has obtained as a result of his fiduciary position should be governed by the equitable obligation of confidence rather than by an automatic classification of the information as the property of his principal. (See Goff and Jones, *op. cit.* pp. 512–522 and Finn, *op. cit.* pp. 130–168).

[99] (1968) 84 L.Q.R. 472.

[1] (1966) 58 D.L.R. (2d) 1, discussed on p. 75.

[2] (1949) 338 U.S. 304.

taken to these purchases. Clearly, there was a possibility of a conflict of interest between the directors' duty to the company and their interest in benefitting their associates but the Supreme Court decided that the directors had acted in the best interests of the company and upheld the transactions. It was clear that the company had suffered no loss, the purchasers' profits having been made at the expense of the selling bond-holders, who had in no way been misled or deceived. (This approach is, of course, similar to that advocated by Lord Upjohn in *Phipps* v. *Boardman* and adopted by two members of the Court of Appeal in *Holder* v. *Holder*.[3]) Professor Jones therefore concludes that the constructive trust should not be used as a penal remedy against any fiduciary who has obtained a personal advantage from his fiduciary position. Such a trust should only be imposed where it is clear on an examination of all the facts that, by seeking to obtain this advantage, the fiduciary placed himself in a position where there was a serious possibility of conflict between his interest and his duty. To these highly persuasive arguments of Professor Jones should be added the comments of Dr. Finn.[4] Given that the conflict of interest found by the majority in *Phipps* v. *Boardman* arose out of the mere possibility that Boardman might in the future have been asked to advise the trustees, he observes that in this eventuality Boardman could, like any solicitor, have declined to advise the trustees or, if they insisted, he could have declared his interest. He therefore concludes that the effect of *Phipps* v. *Boardman* is that "if a person thinks he might be asked in the future to undertake duties for another which will clothe him with a fiduciary character, he cannot beforehand benefit himself in any matter in which he might be asked to advise." If this is indeed the law, it is difficult to see how any professional person can ever safely enter into a transaction on his own behalf in any area in which he habitually advises. For all these reasons, it is suggested that *Phipps* v. *Boardman* was wrongly decided. Nevertheless, there is not the slightest doubt that the approach adopted by the majority in that decision is at present English law.[5]

The authorities which have been considered illustrate clearly

---

[3] [1968] Ch. 353, discussed on pp. 59–60.

[4] *Op. cit.* pp. 244–246.

[5] *Phipps* v. *Boardman* was cited by the Privy Council in *Queensland Mines* v. *Hudson* (1977) 18 A.L.R. 1 (discussed on pp. 73–74) as authority for the proposition that a director who utilises for his own benefit an opportunity which he has obtained as a result of his fiduciary position must account for his profit to the company unless the company has consented to the director proceeding in his personal capacity.

that English law is not prepared to allow a fiduciary to utilise for his own benefit an opportunity which falls within the scope of his fiduciary obligations to his principal unless the principal gives his fully informed consent. The English courts seem more concerned to penalise a fiduciary for having taken up an opportunity of entering into a profitable transaction on his own behalf than to ascertain whether or not there has been a conflict between his duty of loyalty to his principal and his own self-interest. Other jurisdictions have, however, been prepared to adopt a more flexible approach and have permitted fiduciaries to enter into transactions on their own account where they are able to demonstrate that there was no real conflict of interest and duty. This approach is much to be preferred. It is time that English law reconsidered the stringent rule in *Keech* v. *Sandford* both in relation to the specific question of the renewal of leases and the purchase of reversions and in relation to the more general question of what opportunities a fiduciary is entitled to utilise for his own benefit. Nevertheless *Keech* v. *Sandford* and all the cases in which that decision has been applied stand and establish that a fiduciary may not, without the fully informed consent of his principal, take up on his own account an opportunity which has come to him in his fiduciary capacity. Such a rule is both harsh and unnecessary but is unquestionably English law.

## Conclusion

It is apparent that, with the outstanding and inexplicable exception of the rule established by the decision of the Court of Appeal in *Lister* v. *Stubbs*, the attitude of English law towards fiduciaries is consistently harsh. A fiduciary is liable to account to his principal for any unauthorised remuneration and for any other payments that he may receive as a result of his fiduciary position; any transaction into which he has entered in a double capacity is avoidable at the instance of his principal; and he may not without the fully informed consent of his principal take up on his own account an opportunity which he has obtained as a result of his fiduciary position. Admittedly in cases such as *Holder* v. *Holder, Re Cape Breton Co.* and *Re Thomson* and above all in the minority speech of Lord Upjohn in *Phipps* v. *Boardman* there have been indications that English courts are prepared to consider the facts of an individual case and decide whether or not there has been a significant conflict of duty and interest. However these hints only stress still more the underlying penal nature of the present English law. It is suggested that English law should adopt the more flexible attitude manifested in these decisions and in other jurisdictions. Of course, it could be argued that the adoption of such a flexible approach would make the operation of the law unpredictable and uncertain—a criticism which was earlier directed towards the recent decisions in which constructive trusts have been imposed in order to prevent the result of a case from being inequitable. However, it is eminently possible to predict how the more flexible attitude which has been advocated would be applied to the facts of any given case—it is possible to ascertain whether or not a price was the market price and whether or not any advantage was gained in exactly the same way as English courts at present determine whether or not fully informed consent has been given. On the other hand, it is quite impossible to predict what results a particular judge will find inequitable. Therefore, there does not seem to be any inconsistency between criticising the cases in which constructive trusts have been imposed to do justice *inter partes* and advocating the adoption of a more flexible attitude towards fiduciaries. If this approach were indeed to be adopted, a fiduciary would be liable as a constructive trustee for benefits obtained as a result of his fiduciary position only if it could be shown that he had actually abused that fiduciary position. Whether or not such an abuse had occurred would, as has already been suggested, be determined by an examination of the entire course of events which had led to the acquisition of the benefit in question. It is suggested that such a position would be greatly preferable to the existing law. Nevertheless, English law is still as far as it has ever been from such a position.

Chapter 4

# CONSTRUCTIVE TRUSTS IMPOSED AS A RESULT OF A DISPOSITION OF TRUST PROPERTY IN BREACH OF TRUST

When trust property has been disposed of in breach of trust, the courts will, in certain circumstances, impose a constructive trust on any person who has intermeddled in the administration of that trust, on any person who has assisted in bringing about the disposition of the property in breach of trust, and on the recipient of the trust property in question. The imposition of such a constructive trust will not of course necessarily be the only remedy available to the beneficiaries of the trust. It may be possible for them to follow the trust property into its product. Additionally, or alternatively, it may be possible for them to maintain an action for damages against the persons responsible for committing the breach of trust. However, there are many circumstances in which no such tracing claim will be available; this will be the case, for example, where the property in question has been dissipated and where the recipient is either a bona fide purchaser for value without notice of the trust or is able to rely on one of the established defences to such equitable tracing claims. Further, an action for damages against those responsible for committing the breach of trust will achieve little if those persons are insolvent. Consequently the imposition of a constructive trust of this type will often be the only effective remedy available to the beneficiaries. This is illustrated by the large number of cases in which the imposition of this type of constructive trust has been sought. [1]

## Intermeddlers in the administration of a trust

A person who intermeddles in the administration of a trust is often described as a trustee de son tort. This expression was defined by A. L. Smith L.J. in *Mara* v. *Browne*,[2] where he said:

"... if one, not being a trustee and not having authority from

---

[1] The recent authorities have produced considerable academic comment. Particular reference should be made to: C. Harpum: (1986) 102 L.Q.R. 114 & 267; D. J. Hayton, (1985) 27 *Malaya Law Review* 313; R. P. Austin: *Essays in Equity* (ed. Finn, 1985) p. 196.
[2] [1896] 1 Ch. 199, 209.

a trustee, takes upon himself to intermeddle with trust matters or to do acts characteristic of the office of trustee, he may thereby make himself what is called in law a trustee of his own wrong—*i.e.*, a trustee de son tort, or, as it is also termed, a constructive trustee."

A good illustration of the operation of this principle is *Blyth* v. *Fladgate*.[3] Trust funds were, by direction of the sole trustee, paid to a firm of solicitors and invested in Exchequer bills, which were deposited in the name of the firm. Subsequently, following the death of the sole trustee and before any new trustees had been appointed, the Exchequer bills were sold and the proceeds of sale invested in a mortgage, the security for which proved to be insufficient. Stirling J. held that the partners of the firm were liable to account to the trust for the sums so lost on the basis that, by selling the Exchequer bills and reinvesting the proceeds of sale at a time when there are no trustees, they had themselves been carrying out the functions of the trustees; consequently they had intermeddled in the administration of the trust and so were clearly constructive trustees of the proceeds of sale and, as such, responsible for any improper investment thereof. It is obviously entirely proper that the law should thus impose the office of trustee upon a person who purports to act as such without authority. Such a person should clearly be burdened with all the same responsibilities and liabilities as an express trustee.[4] Thus he will not only, as in *Blyth* v. *Fladgate*, be a constructive trustee of any property of the trust which he has received and, consequently, be responsible for any diminution or depreciation thereof. He will also be subject, like any other fiduciary, to all the rules that were discussed in Chapter 3. Thus if an intermeddler obtains a secret profit, he will be in exactly the same position as an express trustee in relation to that profit.

Similar principles apply to fiduciaries other than trustees. Thus a person who takes it upon himself to act as an agent will be subject to exactly the same liability to account to his principal as if he had been expressly appointed. This is illustrated by the decision of the House of Lords in *Lyell* v. *Kennedy*[5]. The owner of land near Manchester died without having made any will dealing with this land, which therefore passed to her heir at law. It took 22 years to resolve the identity of the heir and during this period the defendant, who had previously managed the property for its owner, con-

---

[3] [1891] 1 Ch. 337. The explanation of the decision given in the text is that adopted by Vinelott J. in *Re Bell's Indenture* [1980] 3 All E.R. 425 (discussed on p. 103).

[4] This was stated by Lord Esher M.R. in *Soar* v. *Ashwell* [1893] 2 Q.B. 390, 394.

[5] (1889) 14 App.Cas. 437.

tinued to collect the rents from the tenants without telling them of the death of their landlord. The House of Lords held that, since he had taken it upon himself to receive the rents of property which he knew to belong to another, he held these sums (which had been placed in a separate bank account) on constructive trust for the heir. Lord Selborne stated extremely clearly that the motives which induce a person to intermeddle in the administration of a trust or other fiduciary relationship are totally irrelevant to the imposition of the constructive trust. Whether the intermeddler intervenes with the intention of protecting the interests of the beneficiaries or with the intention of taking the benefit for himself, a constructive trust will be imposed on any property acquired by him in the course of his intervention.[6]

These authorities clearly establish that any person who takes it upon himself to act as a trustee or other fiduciary without having been appointed as such will be a constructive trustee of any property acquired by him in the course of his intervention and will in every respect be treated as if he had been expressly appointed to the office in question.

### Persons who have assisted in bringing about a disposition of trust property in breach of trust

The imposition of a constructive trust upon a person who has assisted in bringing about a disposition of trust property in breach of trust, although clearly established by the authorities, is as a matter of principle somewhat difficult to reconcile with the inherent nature of a trust. As has already been mentioned in the Introduction,[7] given that a trust is a relationship in respect of property, it might be expected to follow that a constructive trust can only be imposed if there is some identifiable property upon which to impose it. There is indeed authority for this proposition. In *Re Barney*[8] Kekewich J. stated particularly clearly that:

"... it is essential to the character of a trustee that he should have trust property actually vested in him or so far under his

---

[6] Thus in *English* v. *Dedham Vale Properties* [1978] 1 W.L.R. 93, a prospective purchaser, purporting without authority to act as agent for the prospective vendors, submitted an application for planning permission in respect of part of the subject matter of the proposed sale and was held liable to account to the vendors for the profits made thereby. This case will be fully discussed in Chapter 6 at pp. 165–166.

[7] On pp. 1–4.

[8] [1892] 2 Ch. 265, 273.

control that he has nothing to do but require that, perhaps by one process, perhaps by another, it should be vested in him."[9]

However, in the cases in which the courts have imposed constructive trusts upon persons who have assisted in bringing about a disposition of trust property in breach of trust, there is often no obviously identifiable property subject to the trust. Where the person upon whom the constructive trust is imposed has played an active part in the disposition of the trust property in breach of trust, as in the case of a bank or a solicitor who, following the instructions of the trustees, has actually made the disposition in question, it is possible to reconcile the imposition of a constructive trust with the principle enunciated in *Re Barney*. This is because the fact that the property in question passed through the hands of the person upon whom the constructive trust was imposed makes it possible to argue that the constructive trust in fact arose at the moment when the property was actually in the hands of the constructive trustee.[10] However, quite apart from the fact that none of the judges seems to have regarded as important the question of what property was subject to the constructive trust, there are other decisions which are, on any view, totally irreconcileable with the principle laid down in *Re Barney*. This is because in these cases constructive trusts were imposed on persons who had never received or in any way controlled the property in question. This occurs, for example, when a constructive trust is imposed upon a person on the grounds that he has induced the trustees to make the disposition in question.[11] As has already been mentioned in the Introduction, the existence of these authorities has led some commentators to contend that there are in fact two types of constructive trust. According to this view, while the vast majority of cases in which constructive trusts are imposed satisfy the principle enunciated in *Re Barney* and consequently confer proprietary rights on the beneficiaries in question, it is also possible for a constructive trust to be imposed without there being any identifiable trust property. This suggested second type of constructive trust obviously does not confer any proprietary rights on the beneficiary thereunder but merely imposes on the constructive trustee a personal

---

[9] The question under consideration in *Re Barney* was whether or not the defendants were liable as intermeddlers so that Kekewich J. was admittedly not directing his attention to the point under discussion. That does not, however, detract from the fundamental nature of the proposition set out in the text.

[10] This was the reconciliation adopted in the first edition of this work.

[11] Such a case was *Eaves* v. *Hickson* (1861) 30 Beav. 136, which is discussed on pp. 90–91.

liability to account to the beneficiary for his actions.[12] For this reason the constructive trusteeship so imposed has been described as "a fiction which provides a useful remedy where no remedy is available in contract or in tort."[13] It has to be admitted that it is virtually impossible to justify some of the existing authorities without accepting the argument that there is indeed such a second kind of constructive trust. Nevertheless, it is not easy to see how an obligation which is not imposed in respect of any identifiable property can properly be classified as a trust. As will be seen in the course of this section, there is no doubt that, in at least some of the cases in which constructive trusts of this type have been imposed, it was entirely appropriate for the person who had assisted in bringing about the disposition in question to have been held liable. It is, however, suggested that these decisions should not be regarded as examples of the imposition of a constructive trust. It seems more appropriate to regard such cases as examples of equity imposing a quite different remedy—a personal liability to account in the same manner as a trustee. Consequently, throughout this section, the remedy in question will be described as a personal liability to account rather than as the imposition of a constructive trust. This is admittedly more a matter of terminology and classification than of substance. However, it is suggested that it is more in accordance with the inherent nature of a trust to regard such cases as examples of a quite distinct equitable remedy. Nevertheless, it has to be admitted that the argument that there are in fact two distinct types of constructive trust and that, consequently, the remedy that will be discussed in this section is indeed the imposition of a constructive trust, enjoys considerable support both from judges and from commentators.

No matter how the liability imposed upon a person who has assisted in bringing about a disposition of trust property in breach of trust should properly be described, however, there is no doubt whatsoever as to where to commence consideration of the authorities. The classic statement of the law enunciated by Lord Selborne L.C. in *Barnes* v. *Addy*[14] has been used as the starting point in almost every subsequent decision. The Lord Chancellor said this:

". . . strangers are not to be made constructive trustees merely

---

[12] This argument is set out particularly clearly in Ford & Lee, *Principles of the Law of Trusts*, pp. 992–995. See also Hayton & Marshall, *Cases and Commentary on the Law of Trusts* (8th ed.), pp. 443–446.

[13] D. J. Hayton, (1985) 27 *Malaya Law Review* 313, 314.

[14] (1874) 9 Ch.App. 244, 251–252.

because they act as the agents of trustees in transactions within their legal powers, transactions, perhaps of which a Court of Equity may disapprove, unless those agents receive and become chargeable with some part of the trust property, or unless they assist with knowledge in a dishonest and fraudulent design on the part of the trustees. Those are the principles, as it seems to me, which we must bear in mind in dealing with the facts of this case. If those principles were disregarded, I know not how any one could, in transactions admitting of doubt as to the view which a Court of Equity might take of them, safely discharge the office of solicitor, of banker, or of agent of any sort to trustees. But, on the other hand, if persons dealing honestly as agents are at liberty to rely on the legal power of the trustees, and are not to have the character of trustees constructively imposed upon them, then the transactions of mankind can safely be carried through; and I apprehend those who create trusts do expressly intend, in the absence of fraud and dishonesty, to exonerate such agents of all classes from the responsibilities which are expressly incumbent, by reason of the fiduciary relation, upon the trustees."

In this passage Lord Selborne was clearly primarily concerned to protect the agents of a trust, such as solicitors or bankers, who as a result of following the instructions of the trustees, have assisted in bringing about a disposition of trust property in breach of trust. His lordship was not concerned to protect either persons who "receive and become chargeable with some part of the trust property" or persons who induce the trustees to make the disposition in question, or agents who engage in activities beyond the scope of their agency or exceed their authority. All such persons will clearly be liable to the beneficiaries. The liability of recipients of property disposed of in breach of trust, whether or not such recipients are agents of the trust, will be considered in the next section. The liability of persons who induce the trustees to make the disposition in question is clearly established as a result of the decision in *Eaves* v. *Hickson*.[15] A father produced a forged marriage certificate to the trustees of a settlement and thus convinced them that his children were legitimate and so entitled to the trust which was duly distributed to them. He had in fact married the mother of the children after their birth but at that time there was no doctrine of legitimation by subsequent marriage. He (or some

---

[15] (1861) 30 Beav. 136.

other person presumably acting in accordance with his instructions) therefore changed the date on the marriage certificate so that the marriage appeared to have taken place before the birth of the children. Those otherwise entitled to the property subsequently sued for its recovery and it was held that the father was personally liable to account for such of the property as could not be recovered from the children. The liability of agents who engage in activities beyond the scope of their agency or exceed their authority is also clearly established. An agent who, in the absence or incapacity of his principal, takes it upon himself to carry out acts which can only properly be carried out by that principal will be liable as an intermeddler under the authorities discussed in the previous section. An agent who exceeds his authority will be similarly liable. Thus in *Lee* v. *Sankey*[16] trustees employed a firm of solicitors to receive the proceeds of sale of part of the trust property. The solicitors paid part of this money to one of the trustees who employed the money in various improvident speculations and died insolvent. The other trustee and the beneficiaries successfully claimed that the solicitors were liable to account for the sums so paid away on the grounds that they should have obtained the receipt of both trustees before parting with the proceeds of sale in their hands. In *Barnes* v. *Addy*, however, the defendants were not liable under any of the above heads. They had instead assisted in bringing about a disposition of trust property in breach of trust. Lord Selborne therefore held that such persons will only be personally liable to account if they "assist with knowledge in a dishonest and fraudulent design on the part of the trustees." What conduct will give rise to this liability?

In *Baden* v. *Société General*,[17] Peter Gibson J. isolated four distinct elements: first, the existence of a trust; secondly, the existence of a dishonest and fraudulent design in the part of the trustee of the trust; thirdly, the assistance by the agent in that design; and, fourthly, the knowledge of the agent. However, his lordship emphasised that "it is important not to lose sight of the requirement that, taken together, those elements must leave the court satisfied that the alleged constructive trustee was a party or privy to dishonesty on the part of the trustee."[18] The first three elements so isolated cause no difficulties. Peter Gibson J. held that the existence of any fiduciary relationship between the trustee and the

---

[16] (1873) L.R. 15 Eq. 204.
[17] [1983] B.C.L.C. 325, 404. The full name of this case is *Baden, Delvaux and Lecuit* v. *Société General pour Favoriser le Développement du Commerce et de l'Industrie en France S.A.*
[18] *Ibid.*

property of another person would satisfy the first element, the existence of the trust. As to the second element, the existence of a dishonest and fraudulent design on the part of the trustee of the trust, his lordship followed and applied the statements of the members of the Court of Appeal in *Belmont Finance Corporation* v. *Williams Furniture*[19] to the effect that the adjectives "dishonest" and "fraudulent" have the same meaning and signify something more than mere misfeasance or a breach of trust. His lordship held, quoting *R* v. *Sinclair*,[20] that what was required was "the taking of a risk to the prejudice of another's rights, which risk is known to be one which there is no right to take."[21] His lordship then went on to hold that the third element, the assistance by the agent in the design of the trustee, was simply a question of fact. It is obviously unlikely that any of these first three elements will pose problems. On the other hand, the fourth element, the knowledge of the agent, has provoked considerable judicial disagreement.

The initial attitude of the courts as to the level of knowledge that has to be shown before a personal liability to account can be imposed upon an agent is well illustrated by the facts of *Barnes* v. *Addy* itself. The surviving trustee of a fund appointed as sole trustee of part of the fund the husband of the life tenant, who duly sold the trust property, misapplied the proceeds of sale and became bankrupt. The beneficiaries sought to impose a personal liability to account upon the solicitors of the two trustees, who had advised against the appointment but had prepared the requisite deeds. The Court of Appeal in Chancery dismissed this action. Lord Selborne L.C., having made the statement of principle which has already been quoted, said that the solicitors had had no knowledge or suspicion of any dishonest intention on the part of the trustees and so could not be personally liable to account. This approach has been followed in a number of other cases. In *Williams* v. *Williams*[22] a solicitor was instructed to sell lands and use the proceeds of sale to discharge the debts of the vendor. He inquired whether the lands were subject to any settlement and, from the information which he was given, reasonably came to the conclusion that the

---

[19] [1979] 1 All E.R. 118, *per* Buckley L.J. at p. 130, *per* Orr L.J. at p. 132, *per* Goff L.J. at pp. 134–135.

[20] [1968] 1 W.L.R. 1246.

[21] In *Selangor United Rubber Estates* v. *Cradock (No.3)* [1968] 1 W.L.R. 1555 at pp. 1582 and 1590, Ungoed-Thomas J. had held that these adjectives must be understood in accordance with equitable principles for equitable relief and consequently conduct which is morally reprehensible therefore suffices. However this view was rejected in *Belmont Finance Corporation* v. *Williams Furniture*.

[22] (1881) 17 Ch.D. 437.

lands were not so encumbered. In due course it transpired that there had been a settlement and the beneficiaries sought to make the solicitor personally liable to account for the proceeds of sale received by him. This action failed. Kay J. said that, although the solicitor had been somewhat negligent, he had had a bona fide conviction that there had been no settlement and so could not be personally liable to account. However his lordship emphasised[23] that the case would have been very different if the solicitor had "wilfully shut his eyes" to the existence of a settlement. Similarly, in *Williams-Ashman* v. *Price & Williams*[24] trust solicitors, following the instructions of the sole trustee, paid out part of the trust fund to persons who were not in fact beneficiaries and invested the residue of the fund in unauthorized securities. At all times the solicitors had had in their possession a copy of the trust deed but had not actually been aware that the trustee was acting in breach of trust. The beneficiaries sought to impose upon the solicitors a personal liability to account for the sums they had paid away. Bennett J. dismissed this claim on the grounds that the solicitors had been acting honestly in the course of their agency without actual knowledge of any breach of trust.

These decisions clearly established that an agent of a trust who has assisted in bringing about a disposition of trust property in breach of trust will not be personally liable to account to the beneficiaries unless he either has actual knowledge of the breach of trust in question or has wilfully closed his eyes to the possibility of such a breach. The law thus appeared to be settled. However, in *Selangor United Rubber Estates* v. *Cradock (No.3)*[25] Ungoed-Thomas J. took a different view and held that an agent who has assisted in bringing about a disposition of trust property in breach of trust will be personally liable to account to the beneficiaries if he either knew or ought to have known of the breach of trust.

This case resulted from an attempt by the first defendant, Cradock, to buy the plaintiff company with its own money.[26] The plaintiff company had formerly carried on business as a rubber company in Malaya but, following the nationalisation of the Malayan rubber estates, no longer had a business. It did, however,

---

[23] *Ibid*. p. 445.
[24] [1942] 1 Ch. 219.
[25] [1968] 1 W.L.R. 1555.
[26] At that time such conduct was unlawful under s.54 of the Companies Act 1948 which prohibited the provision of direct or indirect financial assistance by a company for the acquisition of its own shares. The section has now been repealed and has been replaced by ss. 151–158 of the Companies Act 1985.

have substantial assets, of which £232,500 were in a current banking account with the National Bank. Contanglo, a banking company who were acting as agents for an undisclosed principal (Cradock), made an offer for the shares in the company. This offer was accepted by 79 per cent. of the shareholders. Cradock now had to find £195,000 to pay for the shares. His own bank account at the District Bank was only barely in credit. However, he told his bank manager that he would arrange for the plaintiff's bank account to be transferred to that branch of the District Bank and asked him to prepare a banker's draft for £195,000 in favour of Contanglo (who actually had to pay for the shares). A representative of the bank was then to take that draft to the meeting at which the takeover was to be effected and exchange it for a draft for £232,500 in favour of Cradock (which would, of course, cover the payment of the £195,000). However, what actually happened at this meeting was rather different. The representative of the District Bank was induced to hand over the draft for £195,000 without receiving anything in return. The takeover was then completed and a new board of directors of the plaintiff company (consisting entirely of nominees of Cradock) was elected. The new board then resolved to transfer the company's bank account to the District Bank and duly transferred the balance of the account from the National Bank to the District Bank. They then resolved to lend £232,500 to a company called Woodstock at a commercial rate of interest and drew a cheque for this amount in favour of Woodstock on their new bank account with the District Bank. Woodstock, having already agreed to lend the money at a slightly higher rate of interest to Cradock, immediately endorsed the cheque in favour of Cradock. He then paid the cheque into his own account with the District Bank and thus covered the banker's draft which had paid for the shares. Thus the District Bank had covered the draft with which the shares had been purchased by a cheque drawn on the company's bank account and duly endorsed in favour of Cradock. Thus the Bank, without being aware of the fact, had enabled Cradock to purchase the plaintiff company with its own money. In due course the true facts emerged and an action was brought in the name of the company against Cradock, Contanglo, Woodstock, the nominee directors of the plaintiff company, and the District Bank. Clearly, the directors of the plaintiff company were liable for breach of trust in that they had paid away the property of the company for an improper purpose. Equally clearly, Cradock, Contanglo, and Woodstock were all liable as constructive trustees as recipients of property disposed of in breach of trust under the rules that will be discussed in the next section. Much more controversial, however, was the decision of Ungoed-Thomas J. to impose upon the District Bank a personal liability to account to the company. The District Bank had clearly acted in good faith without any actual knowledge of the breach of trust being perpetrated by the directors. The authorities that have already been discussed clearly establish that an agent of a trust who has assisted in bringing about a disposition of trust property in breach of trust will not be personally liable to account to the beneficiaries unless he either has actual knowledge of the breach of trust in question or has wilfully closed his eyes to the possibility of such a breach. How then could the District Bank have been held to be personally liable to account to the company? Ungoed-Thomas J. held that a reasonable banker would have realised that, by allowing the company's money to be paid into Cradock's account, he was enabling the latter to purchase the company with its own money. His lordship then held that an agent of a trust who has assisted in bringing about a disposition of trust property in breach of trust will be personally liable to account if he either knew or ought to have known of the breach of trust in question, distinguishing the earlier authorities on the grounds that they were concerned with persons who were intermeddling in the administration of the trusts in question. It is extremely difficult to accept this distinction since in *Williams-Ashman* v. *Price & Williams* (one of the cases which Ungoed-Thomas J. specifically so distinguished), Bennett J. had expressly held that the defendant solicitors were not intermeddlers. It is therefore suggested that, in imposing a personal liability to account upon an agent on the grounds that he ought to have known of the breach of trust, Ungoed-Thomas J. was departing from the principles established by the earlier authorities.

Subsequently, while an appeal in *Selangor United Rubber Estates* v. *Cradock (No. 3)* was pending,[27] that decision had to be considered by the Court of Appeal in *Carl-Zeiss Stiftung* v. *Herbert Smith (No.2)*.[28] This was a subsidiary action in a claim brought by an East German Company against a West Germany Company. Each claimed to be the original Zeiss Foundation and hence to be entitled to use the Zeiss trademark (the company had become divided due to the division of Germany after the Second World War). In the main action, the East German Company claimed that the property and the assets of the West German Company either belonged to or were held on trust for them. In the subsidiary action, the East German Company claimed that the solicitors act-

[27] This appeal was not in the end pursued.
[28] [1969] 2 Ch. 276.

ing for the West German Company in the main action held their legal fees on constructive trust for them. This claim was based on the fact that the solicitors had notice that the East German Company claimed to be entitled to all the assets of the West German Company including, obviously enough, any legal fees paid to the solicitors. The case thus principally concerned the question of whether the solicitors had received property which had been disposed of in breach of trust. At first instance, Pennycuick J. denied the claim on the grounds of public policy but indicated that, but for such considerations, the claim would have succeeded.[29] Both sides appealed to the Court of Appeal who declined to reach any decision on the public policy ground. All the members of the court held that notice of an adverse claim to the property of the West German Company did not amount to notice of a trust since difficult questions both of fact and law were involved in the claim. The action therefore failed on the grounds that the solicitors had had no effective notice of any adverse claim to the property they had received and therefore were, in effect, bona fide purchasers for value without notice.[30] However, for present purposes, what is important about this decision is the fact that two of the members of the court (Sachs and Edmund Davies L.JJ.) went on to state that, in any event, an agent of a trust who has assisted in bringing about a disposition of trust property in breach of trust cannot be personally liable to account unless he has actual knowledge of the breach of trust. Their lordships clearly preferred the view established by the older authorities to that taken in *Selangor United Rubber Estates* v. *Cradock (No.3)*. However, their lordships took pains to refrain from any criticism of the latter decision since they did not wish to prejudice the appeal which was then pending. Consequently, despite the statements of Sachs and Edmund Davies L.JJ. in *Carl-Zeiss Stiftung* v. *Herbert Smith (No.2)*, the conflict between the older authorities and *Selangor United Rubber Estates* v. *Cradock (No. 3)* remained unresolved.

Neither has this conflict been resolved in the subsequent authorities since each of the two conflicting views has been cited with approval on a number of occasions. *Selangor United Rubber Estates* v. *Cradock (No. 3)* was followed and applied in *Karak Rub-*

---

[29] [1968] 2 All E.R. 1233.

[30] This decision has been criticised (see D. M. Gordon, (1970) 44 A.L.J. 261) on the grounds that notice of an adverse claim, no matter how tenuous, has always hitherto been regarded as effective notice. In principle, there seems much to be said for this criticism but this aspect of the decision is not relevant to the liability of an agent of a trust who has assisted in bringing about a disposition of trust property in breach of trust.

*ber Company* v. *Burden (No.2).*[31] This case also resulted from a successful attempt to purchase a company with its own money, the means by which this was achieved (and for that matter the persons involved) being substantially the same as in *Selangor United Rubber Estates* v. *Cradock (No. 3)*. On this occasion the unlucky bank was Barclays and, not surprisingly in the light of the very considerable similarity between the two cases, Brightman J. followed *Selangor United Rubber Estates* v. *Cradock (No. 3)* and held that Barclays was personally liable to account to the company. His lordship distinguished *Carl-Zeiss Stiftung* v. *Herbert Smith (No. 2)* on the grounds that the clear ratio of that decision was that notice of a doubtful claim does not amount to notice of a trust, holding that that ratio was in no way inconsistent with the ratio of *Selangor United Rubber Estates* v. *Cradock (No. 3)*. Similarly, in *Rowlandson* v. *National Westminster Bank*[32] a settlor had deposited funds at the defendant bank for the benefit of four of her grandchildren without giving any instructions as to how the funds were to be dealt with. The bank placed the funds in a trust account for the grandchildren, the joint signatories of the account and therefore its trustees being two of the settlor's sons.[33] One of the two trustees drew a cheque on this account in favour of his stockbroker and the bank duly honoured this cheque even though it bore his signature alone. Subsequently, the same trustee, again without any signature of the other trustee, transferred the balance of the account to another account held in his sole name. The beneficiaries now claimed that the bank was personally liable to account to them for the sums so paid away. John Mills Q.C.[34] upheld this claim, applying *Karak Rubber Company* v. *Burden (No. 2)*.[35] However, perhaps the most important of this group of cases is *Baden* v. *Société General*,[36] where both Peter Gibson J. and counsel for both parties accepted the correctness of the decisions

---

[31] [1972] 1 W.L.R. 602.

[32] [1978] 3 All E.R. 370.

[33] It seems that the bank dealt with the funds in this way because of the existence in the same branch of another trust account in favour of two of the grandchildren, of which the same two sons were the joint signatories.

[34] Sitting as a Deputy Judge of the High Court.

[35] Given that there were no suspicious surrounding circumstances to place the bank on enquiry, this was in fact a harsher decision than *Selangor United Rubber Estates* v. *Cradock (No. 3)* and *Karak Rubber Company* v. *Burden (No. 2)*. This is not to say that the actual result of the case was wrong since the bank would clearly have been liable for breach of contract had the beneficiaries chosen to proceed in this way (see C. Harpum: *op. cit.* pp. 153–154).

[36] [1983] B.C.L.C. 325.

in *Selangor United Rubber Estates* v. *Cradock (No. 3)* and *Karak Rubber Company* v. *Burden (No. 2)*. In this case, as part of a gigantic financial fraud, funds of the plaintiffs were transferred to a Luxembourg bank who in turn deposited them in a Bahamian bank. The object of the exercise was for the funds to be transferred on to jurisdictions such as Panama from where they would not be able to be recovered. However as a result of the activities of the American Securities Exchange Commission, proceedings were commenced in the Bahamas pending the result of which the Bahamian bank was enjoined from dealing with the funds other than by depositing them in trust funds in certain named banks, including the defendant. The Bahamian bank duly deposited $7,000,000 with the defendant. The Bahamian proceedings were susequently settled on terms embodied in a court order under which the Bahamian bank was required to direct the banks with which the funds were deposited to hold them to the order of the Luxembourg bank. However, as a result of fraud of which the directors of the Bahamian bank were aware, the schedule to the settlement recited that only $3,000,000 was deposited with the defendant. The Bahamian bank subsequently instructed the defendant to transfer the remaining $4,000,000 to Panama. Various contemporaneous circumstances, including a communication from a lawyer representing the plaintiffs, made the officers of the defendant extremely suspicious. However, faced with the Bahamian court order, an assurance from the Luxembourg bank that it had no claim to the $4,000,000 and the absence of any attempt by the plaintiffs to stop the transfer, the defendant eventually transferred the $4,000,000, which disappeared. The plaintiffs now claimed that the defendant was personally liable to account for the sum so transferred. Peter Gibson J. held[37] that an agent of a trust who has assisted in bringing about a disposition of trust property in breach of trust will be personally liable to account if he has any one of the following five types of knowledge: (i) actual knowledge; (ii)

---

[37] *Ibid.* pp. 408–421. His lordship had previously isolated the four elements which together comprise "assistance with knowledge in a dishonest and fraudulent design on the part of the trustees" which were discussed on pp. 91–92. It will be remembered that his lordship rejected the definition of "dishonest and fraudulent" utilised by Ungoed-Thomas J. in *Selangor United Rubber Estates* v. *Cradock (No. 3)*. Mr. Harpum (*op. cit.* pp. 154–157) argues most persuasively that Peter Gibson J. did not appreciate the inconsistency of rejecting Ungoed-Thomas J.'s definition of "dishonest and fraudulent" while accepting his definition of knowledge and concludes that this internal inconsistency together with the concessions of counsel rob his judgment of much of its force.

knowledge that he would have obtained but for wilfully shutting his eyes to the obvious[38]; (iii) knowledge which he would have obtained but for wilfully and recklessly failing to make such inquiries as an honest and a reasonable man would make[39]; (iv) knowledge of circumstances which would indicate the facts to an honest and reasonable man[40]; (v) knowledge of circumstances which would put an honest and reasonable man on inquiry,[41] However, his lordship held that only in exceptional circumstances should the fifth type of knowledge be imputed to an agent acting honestly in accordance with the instructions of his principal. He held that the defendant had twice been put on enquiry: first, on the receipt of the instructions to transfer the $4,000,000 to Panama and, secondly, on receipt of the communication from the lawyer representing the plaintiffs. However, he held that, in the light of the Bahamian court order, the assurance that the Luxembourg bank had no claim to the money and the failure of the plaintiffs to take any steps to stop the transfer, the bank had not failed in its duty. Consequently the bank was not personally liable to account to the plaintiffs for the $4,000,000.[42]

On the other hand, in *Competitive Insurance Company* v. *Davies Investments*,[43] Goff J. clearly preferred the approach taken in the older authorities. The question that arose in this case was whether the liquidator of a company who had received constructive notice of an alleged constructive trust could be personally liable to account for his honest failure to realise the existence of the trust. Goff J. held that he could could not be so liable, applying *Barnes* v. *Addy* and *Carl-Zeiss Stiftung* v. *Herbert Smith (No. 2)*. Subsequently a similar view was expressed by all the members of

---

[38] His lordship described this type of knowledge as "Nelsonian knowledge." Kay L.J. in *Williams* v. *Williams* (1881) 17 Ch.D. 437 at p. 445 (discussed on pp. 92–93) stated that knowledge of this type would render an agent liable.

[39] Buckley L.J. in *Belmont Finance Corporation* v. *Williams Furniture* [1979] 1 All E.R. 118, 130 stated that knowledge of this type would render an agent liable.

[40] Ungoed-Thomas J. in *Selangor United Rubber Estates* v. *Cradock (No. 3)* [1968] 1 W.L.R. 1555, 1590 held that knowledge of this type would render an agent liable. This view was also adopted by all the judges of the Australian High Court in *Consul Development* v. *D.P.C. Estates* (1975) 132 C.L.R. 373 (see in particular *per* Gibbs J. at p. 398.)

[41] Ungoed-Thomas J. in *Selangor United Rubber Estates* v. *Cradock (No. 3)* held that knowledge of this type would render an agent liable. This view was not, however, shared by three of the four judges in *Consul Development* v. *D.P.C. Estates* (1975) 132 C.L.R. 373.

[42] His lordship also dismissed the plaintiffs' alternative claim for damages for negligence. In dismissing the subsequent appeal, the Court of Appeal confined their judgments to the issue of negligence. See Harpum: *op. cit.* p. 156 n. 49.

[43] [1975] 1 W.L.R. 1240.

the Court of Appeal in *Belmont Finance Corporation* v. *Williams Furniture*.[44] This case resulted from yet another successful attempt to purchase a company with its own money, although on this occasion the method employed was rather different. Belmont Finance Corporation was a wholly owned subsidiary of City Industrial Finance, which was in turn a wholly owned subsidiary of Williams Furniture. This group of companies was controlled by one James, who wished to sell Belmont Finance Corporation. He therefore agreed with one Grosscurth, who controlled a company called Maximum Finance, that Belmont Finance Corporation should purchase Maximum Finance from Grosscurth for £500,000 and that Grosscurth should then purchase Belmont Finance Corporation from City Industrial Finance for £489,000. Unknown to James, Maximum Finance was only worth £60,000. Thus Belmont Finance Corporation was to pay £500,000 to Grosscurth for a company worth £60,000. This transaction would provide Grosscurth with the funds necessary to purchase Belmont Finance Corporation so that that company was in effect to be purchased with its own money. The transaction was duly carried through. When Belmont Finance Corporation subsequently went into liquidation with substantial debts, its receiver commenced proceedings in tort for conspiracy against, among others, City Industrial Finance. The case first came before the Court of Appeal on a pleading issue.[45] The plaintiff wished additionally to claim that City Industrial Finance had assisted the directors of Belmont Finance Corporation in a dishonest and fraudulent design. The statement of claim merely alleged that the defendants knew or ought to have known that Maximum Finance had been acquired at an undervalue. The Court of Appeal held that an agent of a trust who assists in bringing about a disposition of trust property in breach of trust will not be personally liable to account unless he has either actual knowledge of the breach of trust, or wilfully shuts his eyes to dishonest, or wilfully or recklessly fails to make such enquiries as an honest and reasonable man would make.[46] An allegation of this type of conduct had to be pleaded specifically so that such an additional claim could not be based on the original statement of claim. Following the necessary amendment to the statement of claim, the case went for trial where it was found as a fact that James had genuinely believed that the purchase of Maximum Finance for £500,000 was a good commercial proposition. Consequently, on

---

[44] [1979] 1 All E.R. 118, (*No. 2*) [1980] 1 All E.R. 393.
[45] [1979] 1 All E.R. 118 (Buckley, Orr and Goff L.JJ.).
[46] *Per* Buckley L.J. at p. 130, *per* Orr L.J. at p. 132, *per* Goff L.J. at p. 134–135.

the appeal against the dismissal of the action,[47] the Court of Appeal held that, although City Industrial Finance was liable as a constructive trustee as a recipient of property disposed of in breach of trust,[48] this honest belief of James meant that none of the defendants had the knowledge necessary for the imposition of any personal liability to account for having assisted in bringing about a disposition of trust property in breach of trust.[49] If the views thus expressed by the Court of Appeal are considered in relation to the five types of knowledge subsequently set out by Peter Gibson J. in *Baden* v. *Société General*,[50] it is clear that, according to the Court of Appeal, only the first three types of knowledge (and not the last two) will lead to the imposition of a personal liability to account for having assisted in bringing about a disposition of trust property in breach of trust. Precisely this view was recently expressed by Megarry V.C. in *Re Montagu's Settlements*,[51] a case which was actually concerned with the liability of recipients of property disposed of in breach of trust, and this opinion of Megarry V.C. was expressly followed and applied by Alliott J. in the most recent case of all, *Lipkin Gorman* v. *Karpnale*,[52] where a personal liability to account was imposed upon a bank who had permitted a solicitor of whose gambling it was aware to withdraw money from his firm's clients' account on the grounds that the bank had either shut its eyes to the obvious source of his gambling money or had wilfully and recklessly failed to make such inquiries as a reasonable and honest man would make.

It seems clear from this review of the authorities that there is general agreement that a personal liability to account will be imposed on an agent who has assisted in bringing about a disposition of trust property in breach of trust if he has any of the first three types of knowledge set out by Peter Gibson J. in *Baden* v. *Société General*. That is to say, such an agent will be liable if he has actual knowledge, knowledge that he would have obtained but for wilfully shutting his eyes to the obvious, or knowledge that he would have obtained but for wilfully and recklessly failing to make such inquiries as an honest and reasonable man would make. However, there is a conflict of authority as to the two remaining

---

[47] [1980] 1 All E.R. 393 (Buckley, Goff and Waller L.JJ.).
[48] This aspect of the decision will be discussed in the next section.
[49] *Per* Buckley L.J. at pp. 405–406, *per* Goff L.J. at pp. 412–413. On this point, Waller L.J agreed with both the other judgments.
[50] [1983] B.C.L.C. 325. These five types of knowledge are set out on pp. 98–99 and in the next paragraph.
[51] March 29, 1985—as yet unreported.
[52] [1986] N.L.J. 659.

types of knowledge, knowledge of circumstances which would indicate the facts to an honest and reasonable man and knowledge of circumstances which would put an honest and reasonable man on inquiry. *Selangor United Rubber Estates* v. *Cradock (No. 3)* and the cases in which that decision has been followed suggest that these two further heads of knowledge also suffice for the imposition of a personal liability to account, the remaining authorities suggest that these last two heads do not suffice. It is suggested that, for the reasons originally adduced by Lord Selborne L.C. in *Barnes* v. *Addy*, the latter view is preferable. On this basis, therefore, an agent who has assisted in bringing about a disposition of trust property in breach of trust will only be personally liable to account if he has either actual knowledge, or knowledge that he would have obtained but for wilfully shutting his eyes to the obvious, or knowledge that he would have obtained but for wilfully and recklessly failing to make such inquiries as an honest and reasonable man would make.

Finally, two subsidiary questions have arisen concerning the liability of agents who have assisted in bringing about a disposition of trust property in breach of trust. First, is the protection conferred by *Barnes* v. *Addy* available to an agent employed by a trustee who has not himself been validly appointed? This issue arose in *Mara* v. *Browne*[53] where it was argued that an agent appointed by such a trustee must act as a principal and so should be deprived of the protection of *Barnes* v. *Addy*—this would mean that the agent in question would be regarded as an intermeddler in the administration of the trust in question and so would inevitably be liable no matter what his state of knowledge. This argument succeeded at first instance before North J.[54] but the Court of Appeal found that the trustee in question had been validly appointed and so the issue did not have to be decided. However, Lord Herschell stated that the protection of *Barnes* v. *Addy* would be available to such an agent. It is suggested that this latter view is preferable since it is unreasonable to expect an agent to carry out a detailed investigation into the precise status of his principal. Secondly, will a personal liability to account be imposed on the partners of an agent who is personally liable to so account? This question had to be decided by Vinelott J. in *Re Bell's Indenture*.[55] A partner in a firm of solicitors assisted the trustees of a settlement and a will, who were also beneficially entitled to life interests thereunder, to dis-

---

[53] [1896] 1 Ch. 199.
[54] [1895] 2 Ch. 69.
[55] [1980] 3 All E.R. 425.

tribute the whole of the trust property to themselves in breach of trust. It was clear that he had had actual knowledge of the facts and it was therefore admitted that he was under a personal liability to account to the remaindermen for the sums so distributed that had passed through his firm's clients' account. However the remaindermen also sought to impose a similar liability on his partner. This claim was based on *Blyth* v. *Fladgate*[56] where, as has already been seen,[57] Stirling J. held that all the partners of a firm of solicitors were liable as constructive trustees of trust funds which had been paid to that firm. This decision had been followed in *Mara* v. *Browne* at first instance, where North J. had held that the partner of the agent upon whom he had imposed a constructive trust was also liable as a constructive trustee. However, in the Court of Appeal in *Mara* v. *Browne* (where the issue did not, of course, have to be decided) all three members of the court had indicated that they would have held the opposite on the grounds that it is no part of the implied authority of a partner to make his co-partners liable to personally account in equity. Vinelott J. followed and applied these statements of the Court of Appeal in *Mara* v. *Browme*, distinguishing *Blyth* v. *Fladgate* on the grounds that in that case the solicitors in question had been intermeddling in the administration of the trust in question and that that had been the basis of the liability of all the partners. It is suggested that this explanation of *Blyth* v. *Fladgate* is clearly correct and that Vinelott J. was therefore right to follow and apply the statements of the Court of Appeal in *Mara* v. *Browne*. It is therefore suggested that the partner of an agent upon whom a personal liability to account is imposed will not himself be so liable.

### Recipients of property disposed of in breach of trust

When property has been disposed of in breach of trust, it is important to distinguish very clearly between, on the one hand, the possibility of following the trust property into the hands of the recipient thereof and, on the other hand, the possibility of the imposition of a constructive trust on the recipient. Where property has been disposed of in breach of trust, the interests of the beneficiaries in that property are, in accordance with the basic principles of property law, enforceable against the whole world unless and until the property in question reaches the hands of someone who takes it free of their equitable proprietary interests therein.

[56] [1891] 1 Q.B. 337.
[57] This case was discussed on p. 86.

Where the property in question is pure personalty or unregistered land, the interests of the beneficiaries will be, according to the equitable doctrine of notice, enforceable against the whole world other than a bona fide purchaser for value of a legal estate in that property without notice actual, constructive or imputed of their equitable interests. Where, on the other hand, the property in question is registered land, the interests of the beneficiaries will be enforceable against the whole world if their interests are overriding interests or have been protected on the Register of Titles as minor interests but otherwise will not be enforceable against any bona fide purchaser for value claiming under a registered disposition of the land in question.[58] Any recipient of property disposed of in breach of trust who is liable to such an equitable tracing claim will of course be a trustee of such property as is in his hands—this is simply because the equitable interests of the beneficiaries therein must necessarily take effect behind a trust of the legal estate. However, the fact that it is thus possible to trace the trust property into its product does not necessarily mean that the recipient will be held to be a constructive trustee of the property transferred to him.[59] Indeed it will only be necessary to seek the imposition of such a constructive trust in certain circumstances. This will be the case where the property in question has depreciated in value or been dissipated while in the hands of the recipient; in such circumstances, an equitable tracing claim will enable the beneficiaries to recover only such property, if any, as remains in the hands of the recipient and the imposition of a constructive trust will thus be necessary in order to make the recipient liable for the reduction in value of the property. Similarly, where the recipient has obtained some incidental profit from the property while it has been in his hands,[60] the imposition of a constructive trust will

[58] The situations in which such an equitable tracing claim will be available are analysed much more fully by Mr. Harpum: *op. cit.* pp. 267–273.

[59] This was stated with great clarity by Megarry V.C. in *Re Montagu's Settlements* (December 21, 1983 (first judgment) and March 29, 1985 (second judgment))—not yet reported. His lordship said this: "It should also be remembered that the doctrines of purchaser without notice and constructive trusts are concerned with matters which differ in important respects. The former is concerned with the question whether a person takes property subject to or free from some equity. The latter is concerned with whether or not a person is to have imposed upon him the personal burdens and obligations of trusteeship. I do not see why one of the touchstones for determining the burdens on property should be the same as that for deciding whether to impose a personal obligation on a man. The cold calculus of constructive and imputed notice does not seem to me to be an appropriate instrument for deciding whether a man's conscience is sufficiently affected for it to be right to bind him by the obligations of a constructive trustee."

[60] Such as one of the types of secret profits discussed in Chapter 3.

be necessary in order to make the recipient liable to account to the beneficiaries for this incidental profit. It is only in these circumstances that there will be any need for the beneficiaries to seek the imposition of a constructive trust upon the recipient of property which has been disposed of in breach of trust. In what circumstances are the courts prepared to impose such a constructive trust?

It is of course apparent that no constructive trust will be able to be imposed on any recipient of property disposed of in breach of trust who has taken that property free of the equitable proprietary interests of the beneficiaries therein. Against such a person, the beneficiaries can have no claim whatsoever. However, the courts have also declined to impose "the heavy obligations of trusteeship"[61] upon recipients of property disposed of in breach of trust who received the property in good faith without any knowledge of the breach of trust in question. This follows from the decision of the Court of Appeal in *Re Diplock*.[62] Under the provisions of a will subsequently declared to be void for uncertainty, executors distributed large sums of money to various charities who received the property in good faith without the slightest idea that the House of Lords would at a later stage hold that the will was void.[63] The next of kin of the testator (who were entitled under the resulting intestacy) brought an action against the charities to recover the money. The Court of Appeal held, *inter alia*, that the charities were not constructive trustees of the money they had received. This did not of course prevent the next of kin from tracing the property in equity into the hands of the charities. But the Court of Appeal held that such sums as could not be recovered by means of this equitable tracing claim[64] could not be recovered by the impo-

---

[61] This was the description utilised by Lord Greene M.R. in *Re Diplock* [1948] Ch. 465.

[62] [1948] Ch. 465.

[63] In *Chichester Diocescan Fund* v. *Simpson* [1944] A.C. 341.

[64] The Court of Appeal in fact greatly reduced the effectiveness of such equitable tracing claims by stating that, where the recipient has no knowledge of the breach of trust, he will be liable only to the extent that those who transferred the property to him cannot compensate the beneficiaries for their loss. (This proposition, which was stated at p. 556, is extremely hard to justify. If such a recipient is holding property which is the subject matter of a trust, the beneficiaries of that trust should be able to claim that property on the grounds that it belongs to them; it is hard to see why the availability of a personal claim against the transferors should deprive them of this right). Further the Court of Appeal also held that, to the extent that such a recipient is liable to an equitable tracing claim, he will be able to resist that claim in so far as he has used the trust property to discharge his debts or improve his property. All these aspects of the decision in *Re Diplock* are reviewed critically in Goff and Jones: *op. cit.* Chap. 2.

sition of a constructive trust upon the charities. It seems entirely appropriate that a recipient of property disposed of in breach of trust who received that property in good faith without any knowledge of the breach of trust in question should not be liable as a constructive trustee thereof.[65]

On the other hand, a recipient of property disposed of in breach of trust who does have knowledge of the trust in question will clearly be liable as a constructive trustee thereof. This obviously raises the question of what types of knowledge will lead to the imposition of such a trust.[66] It is of course clear that a recipient of property disposed of in breach of trust who has actual knowledge of the breach of trust in question will be liable as a constructive trustee thereof. This is illustrated by the decision of the Court of Appeal in *Belmont Finance Corporation* v. *Williams Furniture (No. 2)*.[67] In this case, the facts of which have already been considered,[68] the directors of City Industrial Finance had had actual knowledge of a transaction whereby that company had permitted its wholly owned subsidiary, Belmont Finance Corporation, to be purchased with its own money. This is of course meant that the purchase price paid to City Industrial Finance for Belmont Finance Corporation was in fact the latter company's own money. Consequently City Industrial Finance had received property disposed of in breach of trust[69] with actual knowledge of that breach of trust and so the Court of Appeal had no hesitation in holding that City Industrial Finance was a constructive trustee for Belmont Finance Corporation of the sum received.[70] It is also clear that the imposition of constructive trusts upon recipients of property disposed of in breach of trust is not confined to cases of actual knowledge of the breach of trust in question. In *Nelson* v. *Larholt*[71] one

---

[65] However, once such a recipient acquires the necessary knowledge that the property was transferred to him in breach of trust, he will be liable as a constructive trustee if he subsequently deals with the property in a manner inconsistent with the trust. This point is considered in detail on pp. 109–110.

[66] This question did not have to be considered in *Re Diplock* simply because the charities could not conceivably have known that the House of Lords would subsequently hold that the will in question was void for uncertainty.

[67] [1980] 1 All E.R. 393.

[68] On pp. 100–101.

[69] The directors of a limited company are treated as if they were the trustees of the funds of that company which are in their hands or under their control; consequently if they misapply them, they commit a breach of trust (*Re Lands Allotment Company* [1894] 1 Ch. 616 *per* Lindley L.J. at p. 631, *per* Kay L.J. at p. 638).

[70] *Per* Buckley L.J. at p. 405, *per* Goff L.J. at pp. 410–412. On this point, Waller L.J. agreed with both the other judgments.

[71] [1948] 1 K.B. 339.

of the executors of a will drew eight cheques on the estate's bank
account, all of which were signed by him as executor of the testator, in favour of the defendant who cashed the cheques in good
faith. The other executor and the beneficiaries claimed that the
defendant held the proceeds of the cheques on constructive trust
for the estate. Denning J. held that the defendant must be taken to
know what any reasonable man would have known. Eight successive requests to cash cheques clearly drawn on the bank account of
an estate would have placed a reasonable man upon enquiry. Thus
the defendant must be taken to have known of the executor's
breach of trust and so, although he had obtained the cheques for
value in good faith, he was a constructive trustee of the proceeds.
The type of knowledge thus relied on by Denning J. as the grounds
for the imposition of this constructive trust appears to fall within
the fifth type of knowledge set out by Peter Gibson J. in *Baden* v.
*Société General*[72] (knowledge of circumstances which would put an
honest and reasonable man on inquiry). However, in *Carl-Zeiss
Stiftung* v. *Herbert Smith (No. 2)*,[73] Sachs L.J. described *Nelson* v.
*Larholt* as a case where there had been an obvious shutting of eyes
as opposed to a mere lack of prudence and suggested that a negligent, if innocent, failure to make inquiry was not sufficient to
attract constructive trusteeship. This interpretation of the decision
appears to place the knowledge of the defendant within the second
type of knowledge set out by Peter Gibson J. *Baden* v. *Société
General* (knowledge that he would have obtained but for wilfully
shutting his eyes to the obvious) and it is suggested that it is preferable to interpret *Nelson* v. *Larholt* in this way. This view is con-
firmed by the judgment of Megarry V.C. in *Re Montagu's
Settlements*[74] where his lordship made a definitive review of the
law.

This case concerned a settlement made in 1923 under one of the
clauses of which certain chattels, largely comprising the furniture,
plate, pictures and other heirlooms of the Montagu family, were
assigned to the trustees who, in the events which happened, were
under a fiduciary duty, after the death in 1947 of the Ninth Duke
of Manchester, to select and make an inventory of such of the
chattels as they considered suitable for inclusion in the settlement
and to hold the residue of the chattels on trust for the Tenth Duke
of Manchester absolutely. However, the trustees in fact made no
such selection and inventory but instead treated all the chattels as

---

[72] [1983] B.C.L.C. 325, discussed on pp. 97–99.
[73] [1969] 2 Ch. 276, 298.
[74] (March 29, 1985)—not yet reported.

being the absolute property of the Tenth Duke. Many of the chattels were therefore sold by him in 1949 and the remainder taken by him to Kenya where he was then living. Following his death in 1977, the Eleventh Duke of Manchester sought to recover the chattels or their value from the executrix of the Tenth Duke. Megarry V.C. ordered an inquiry to establish which of the chattels would have been selected had the trustees complied with their obligations in 1947 and held that such of the selected chattels as were still in the hands of the executrix could be traced in equity into her hands. However, so as to enable recovery of such of the selected chattels as had been sold and which therefore would not be able to be recovered by means of such an equitable tracing claim, it was also claimed that the Tenth Duke had received the selected chattels as a result of a disposition of property in breach of trust and that consequently he was a constructive trustee of the selected chattels for the settlement. Megarry V.C. first held that "the equitable doctrine of tracing and the imposition of a constructive trust by reason of the knowing receipt of trust property are governed by different rules and must be kept distinct" and stated that "whether a constructive trust arises in such a case primarily depends on the knowledge of the recipient, and not on notice to him." His lordship then carried out a comprehensive review of the authorities, including all the decisions concerning the liability of persons who have assisted in bringing about a disposition of trust property in breach of trust which were considered in the previous section. His lordship, as has already been seen,[75] expressed the opinion that only the first three of the five types of knowledge set out by Peter Gibson J. in *Baden* v. *Société General*[76] will lead to the imposition of a personal liability to account on a person who has assisted in bringing about a disposition of trust property in breach of trust and held that similar principles should govern the imposition of a constructive trust upon a person who has received property disposed of in breach of trust. Thus, in the opinion of Megarry V.C., a recipient of property disposed of in breach of trust will only be liable as a constructive trustee thereof if he has either actual knowledge, or knowledge that he would have obtained but for wilfully shutting his eyes to the obvious, or knowledge that he would have obtained but for wilfully and recklessly failing to make such enquiries as an honest and reasonable man would make. (On this particular point the view of his lordship was subsequently expressly followed and applied in *Lipkin Gorman* v. *Karpnale*[77]

[75] On p. 101.
[76] [1983] B.C.L.C. 325, discussed on pp. 97–99.
[77] [1986] N.L.J. 659.

where Alliott J. held that a casino where a solicitor had gambled away money which he had withdrawn from his firm's clients' account was not liable as a constructive trustee.) Megarry V.C. then went on to hold that the mistake as to the interpretation of the settlement had occurred as a result of what his lordship described as "an honest muddle." Admittedly the Tenth Duke's solicitor, and possibly also the Tenth Duke himself as one of the settlors of the 1923 settlement, had at one stage been aware of the true position. However, his lordship held that "a person is not to be taken to have knowledge of a fact that he once knew but has genuinely forgotten: the test (or a test) is whether the knowledge continues to operate on that person's mind at the time in question." His lordship also held that, where a person has received property disposed of in breach of trust, any knowledge that may be possessed by his solicitor will not be imputed to him "at all events if the donee or beneficiary has not employed the solicitor to investigate his right to the bounty, and has done nothing else that can be treated as accepting that the solicitor's knowledge should be treated as his own." His lordship consequently held that the Tenth Duke had not been a constructive trustee of the selected chattels.

Although the view expressed by Megarry V.C. in *Re Montagu's Settlements* is, as his lordship expressly admitted, not capable of being reconciled with "all the authorities and dicta," it is suggested that his view achieves a much needed consistency between the circumstances in which a personal liability to account will be imposed on a person who has assisted in bringing about a disposition of trust property in breach of trust and the circumstances in which a constructive trust will be imposed on a person who has received property disposed of in breach of trust. It is therefore suggested that his view should be accepted and that, consequently, a recipient of property disposed of in breach of trust should only be liable as a constructive trustee thereof if he has either actual knowledge, or knowledge that he would have obtained but for wilfilly shutting his eyes to the obvious, or knowledge that he would have obtained but for wilfully and recklessly failing to make such enquiries as an honest and reasonable man would make.

The principles that have just been discussed establish the situations in which a recipient of property disposed of in breach of trust will be liable as a constructive trustee thereof. However, even though such a recipient does not initially know of the breach of trust and is therefore not initially liable as a constructive trustee of the property transferred to him, as soon as he acquires the necessary knowledge that the property was indeed transferred to him in breach of trust, he will nevertheless be liable as a constructive trus-

tee if he subsequently deals with the property in a manner inconsistent with the trust. One of the very few illustrations of the operation of this principle is *Sheridan* v. *Joyce*,[78] a decision of the
Court of Chancery of Ireland. A trustee, acting in breach of trust,
loaned trust money to one Fair. Originally Fair had no knowledge
of the breach of trust and so was initially not a constructive trustee
of the money received. Subsequently, however, he discovered the
true facts and thereafter made all his interest payments to the beneficiary of the trust, rather than to the trustee. In due course, the
trustee sought repayment of part of the loan and, notwithstanding
the contrary requests of the beneficiary, Fair duly made the repayment sought. The money so repaid was lost and Fair was held
liable to repay the sum a second time on the basis that he had
become a constructive trustee of the money as soon as he had
become aware of the true facts and was therefore liable for any
subsequent dealing with the property inconsistent with the trust.
This liability does not of course extend to any act carried out by
the recipient before he acquires the necessary knowledge of the
breach of trust so that his constructive trusteeship is limited to the
property in his hands at the time when he acquires the knowledge
in question. Further, although there does not appear to be any
decided case in which this question has had to be considered, it
seems in accordance with principle that exactly the same types of
knowledge as make a recipient of property disposed of in breach of
trust initially liable as a constructive trustee should determine
whether a recipient of property disposed of in breach of trust who
is not so initially liable as a constructive trustee subsequently
becomes liable as a constructive trustee for dealing with the property in a manner inconsistent with the trust.

### Conclusion

While the rules governing the imposition of constructive trusts
on persons who intermeddle in the administration of a trust are
both clear and in accordance with principle, there is considerable
uncertainty as to what are or indeed should be the rules governing
both the imposition of a personal liability to account on persons
who have assisted on bringing about a disposition of trust property
in breach of trust and the imposition of constructive trusts on
recipients of property disposed of in breach of trust. While it has
been suggested, in accordance with the view expressed by Megarry

---

[78] (1844) 1 Jo. & Lat. 41. This question is discussed in detail by Mr. Harpum: *op.
cit.* pp. 130–141.

V.C. in *Re Montagu's Settlements*, that the imposition of both remedies should require the same knowledge, namely the first three types of knowledge set out by Peter Gibson J. in *Baden* v. *Société General*, it has to be admitted that totally different views of the law have been expressed both by judges and by commentators. Consequently it is unlikely that any view of this area of the law will command general acceptance until the House of Lords has an opportunity to make a definitive ruling on the subject.

## Chapter 5

## SECRET TRUSTS AND MUTUAL WILLS

A secret trust arises when a testator makes a gift of property in his will on the strength of an undertaking by the recipient to hold it on trust for a third party whose identity is not disclosed by the will. In such circumstances the court will enforce performance of the undertaking at the suit of the third party. There are two types of secret trust. Such a trust is said to be either fully secret or half secret. A fully secret trust arises when the legacy which is the subject matter of the trust is, on the face of the will, left to the recipient absolutely. Thus, in such a trust both the existence of the trust and its terms are concealed. A half secret trust, on the other hand, arises when the legacy which is the subject matter of the trust is, on the face of the will, left to the recipient as a trustee. In such a trust only the terms of the trust are concealed.[1] The advantages of a secret trust are that a testator can conceal the true objects of his benevolence from public view—a will is, of course, a public document—and can also, in the case of a fully secret trust, alter those objects at any time before his death simply by communicating with the secret trustee.

Mutual wills arise when two or more persons enter into a legally binding agreement to make wills in a particular form with the intention that the provisions of such wills will be irrevocably binding—the most common example is where two persons agree that each will leave property to the other absolutely with the same substitutionary provisions in the event of non-survival.[2] As soon as the first of the parties dies leaving a will made in accordance with the agreement, equity regards that agreement as irrevocable so far as the survivor is concerned and gives effect to it by the imposition of a trust. Thus if the survivor ultimately leaves his property other than in accordance with the agreement, his personal representatives will be deemed to hold his property on trust for the agreed beneficiary.

---

[1] A secret trust will also arise when a person dies intestate on the strength of an undertaking by the person entitled to his property on his intestacy to hold it on trust for a third party—such a trust is necessarily fully secret.

[2] All the decided cases have concerned wills in substantially similar form so it has never been decided whether this is actually necessary. This point is considered more fully on pp. 132–133.

Both secret trusts and mutual wills depend for their efficacy on the intervention of equity. This intervention is, on the face of things, directly contrary to the important statement of principle contained in section 9 of the Wills Act 1837, which (as amended) provides that:

> "No will shall be valid unless—
>
> (a) it is in writing, and signed by the testator, or by some other person in his presence and by his direction; and
> (b) it appears that the testator intended by his signature to give effect to the will; and
> (c) the signature is made or acknowledged by the testator in the presence of two or more witnesses present at the same time; and
> (d)) each witness either—
>> (i) attests and signs the will; or
>> (ii) acknowledges his signature, in the presence of the testator (but not necessarily in the presence of any other witness),
>
> but no form of attestation shall be necessary."

This provision was enacted for an obvious and important reason of policy—to ensure that false claims cannot be generated after the death of a testator when he is in no position to refute them. Such a policy can undoubtedly operate in an extremely harsh way but the courts, rightly, have always been extremely reluctant to admit as evidence in proceedings concerning the administration of an estate any documents which fail to comply with these formal requirements. It is almost inevitable that the existence of secret trusts and mutual wills will only be able to be proved by evidence which does not comply with these requirements. In the case of a secret trust, the whole object of the exercise is to exclude the identity of the beneficiary from the formally attested documents admitted to probate. Inevitably, therefore, the evidence of the communication, acceptance and terms of the secret trust in question will be either oral or contained in a document which has not been properly signed and attested. In the case of mutual wills, the agreement between the parties is not particularly likely to be found in the will of either[3] and certainly will not be mentioned in any will executed in breach of the agreement. Thus this agreement also will normally

---

[3] There is of course no reason why the agreement should not be recited in one or both of the wills in question, although this will not necessarily be conclusive evidence of its existence.

have to be proved by evidence which does not comply with the Wills Act. Therefore, the existence of secret trusts and mutual wills involves a departure both from the letter and the spirit of the Wills Act and, as might be expected, various justifications for the existence of these doctrines have been suggested by the courts. Many of the rules governing the operation of secret trusts and mutual wills stand or fall depending upon the justification for the particular doctrine which is adopted. Therefore it is necessary to discuss the various justifications for the existence of each before discussing these rules.

### The theoretical justification for the existence of the doctrine of secret trusts

It has often been stated that the justification for the existence of the doctrine of secret trusts is that, if evidence of the terms of the trust were not admitted contrary to the provisions of the Wills Act, the result would be fraud. However, there has been considerable judicial disagreement as to the nature of this fraud. Some judges have pointed to the ability of the legatee to take the property beneficially if evidence of the terms of the trust were not admitted as constituting this fraud. Others have instead pointed to the consequent failure to observe the intentions of the testator and the destruction of the beneficial interests arising under the trust.

The former view is normally expressed in this way: if evidence of the terms of the trust were not admitted contrary to the provisions of the Wills Act, the recipient of the property would be allowed to profit by his own fraud. This is because, if the court did not compel him to honour his undertaking to the testator, he would be able to disregard it and take the property beneficially. This was the argument adopted by the members of the House of Lords in *McCormick* v. *Grogan*.[4] The testator made a will leaving all his property to Grogan. When near to death, he summoned Grogan, told him of the will and said that a letter would be found with it. However, he did not seek to obtain any undertaking from him in respect of the letter, which named various persons to whom the testator wished Grogan to give money and the intended gift to each, concluding with these words:

> "I do not wish you to act strictly to the foregoing instructions, but leave it entirely to your own good judgment to do as you think I would if living and as the parties are deserving, and as

---

[4] (1869) L.R. 4 H.L. 82.

it is not my wish that you should say anything about the document there cannot be any fault found with you by any of the parties should you not act in strict accordance with it."

One of the named persons whom Grogan decided to exclude brought an action claiming that Grogan held the property on secret trust to give effect to the provisions of the letter. This action failed on the grounds that the testator had imposed no legally binding obligation upon Grogan. The members of the House of Lords clearly stated that the doctrine of secret trusts was established so as to prevent any possibility of fraud by the secret trustee. Lord Hatherley L.C. said this[5]:

> "[The doctrine of secret trusts] evidently requires to be carefully restricted within proper limits. It is in itself a doctrine which involves a wide departure from the policy which induced the legislature to pass the Statute of Frauds,[6] and it is only in clear cases of fraud that this doctrine has been applied—cases in which the Court has been persuaded that there has been a fraudulent inducement held out on the part of the apparent beneficiary in order to lead the testator to confide to him the duty which he undertook to perform."

This line of reasoning is a possible justification for the existence of the doctrine when, as in *McCormick* v. *Grogan,* the trust in question is fully secret. In such a case, unless evidence of the trust is admitted contrary to the provisions of the Wills Act, the legatee will be able to take the property beneficially and so will clearly profit from his own misconduct. But this line of reasoning cannot normally justify the existence of half secret trusts. In such a trust, the legatee takes the property as a trustee on the face of the will. Therefore, if the court declined to admit evidence of the terms of the half-secret trust, the legatee would not take the subject matter beneficially but would clearly hold the property in question on trust for the residuary legatee (or, if the legacy in question were the residuary legacy, for those entitled on intestacy).[7] On the face of things, therefore, there is no way in which such a legatee could profit by failing to carry out his promise to the testator, unless of course he were himself the residuary legatee or intestate successor of the testator. It is unclear whether he would in such circumstances be entitled to take the property as residuary legatee or

---

[5] *Ibid.* p. 89.
[6] Prior to the enactment of the Statute of Wills, the formal requirements for wills were contained in the Statute of Frauds.
[7] *Re Pugh's Will Trusts* [1967] 1 W.L.R. 1262.

intestate successor if the half secret trust failed but it is suggested that in principle he should be able to do so on the grounds that in such a situation he would be claiming the property not as a trustee but in a different capacity of which the testator must necessarily have been aware. On this assumption, a legatee holding property under a half secret trust would be enabled to profit by failing to carry out his undertaking to the testator and so the admission of evidence contrary to the terms of the Wills Act could be justified by the fraud argument. But this argument will obviously not apply to the vast majority of half secret trusts simply because the legatee will not normally be the appropriate residuary legatee or intestate successor. Consequently in such circumstances there would be no possibility whatsoever of the legatee taking the subject matter beneficially if evidence of the trust were not admitted contrary to the provisions of the Wills Act. Thus in normal circumstances the fraud argument, while a possible justification for the existence of full secret trusts, cannot justify the existence of half secret trusts.

Thus fraud arising out of the possibility of the secret trustee taking the property beneficially, while a possible justification for the existence of fully secret trusts, cannot normally justify the existence of half secret trusts. Can the existence of both be justified by the alternative view that the fraud in question arises out of the failure to observe the intentions of the testator and the destruction of the beneficial interests arising under the trust?

This view is normally expressed in this way: if evidence of the terms of the trust were not admitted contrary to the provisions of the Wills Act, the testator would be defrauded in that, on the faith of the promise made by the secret trustee, he has either made or left unrevoked a disposition of his property. In the same sort of way, the beneficiaries of the secret trust would be defrauded in that they would be deprived of their beneficial interests. This argument (which of course applies just as much to fully secret trusts as to half secret trusts) emerged as early as 1748 in *Reech* v. *Kennegal*,[8] where Lord Hardwicke L.C. admitted evidence contrary to the Statute of Frauds "in respect of the promise and of the fraud upon the testator in not performing it." This view was expressed even more clearly in the Irish case of *Riordan* v. *Banon*[9] in a passage which was subsequently cited with approval by Hall V.C. in *Re Fleetwood*[10]:

---

[8] (1748) 1 Ves. 123. See also the review of the early authorities by Hargrave in *Jurisconsult Exercitations* (1801) Vol II, p. 91.
[9] (1876) 10 Ir.Eq. 469.
[10] (1880) 15 Ch.D. 594, 606–607.

"The testator, at least when his purpose is communicated to and accepted by the proposed legatee, makes the disposition to him on the faith of his carrying out his promise and it would be a fraud in him to refuse to perform that promise. No doubt the fraud would be of a different kind if he could by means of it retain the benefit of the legacy for himself; but it appears that it would also be a fraud though the result would be to defeat the expressed intention for the benefit of the heir, next of kin, or residuary donees."

While the authorities so far discussed all emphasised the fraud on the testator, Lord Buckmaster emphasised rather the fraud on the beneficiaries in the leading case of *Blackwell* v. *Blackwell.*[11] Blackwell left in his will £12,000 to five persons "upon trust . . . to apply for the purposes indicated by me to them." In fact the money was to be used to maintain the mistress and illegitimate son of the testator. His deceived wife and child brought an action against the five legatees claiming that no valid trust for these purposes existed. Their counsel raised the argument that fraud could not justify the admission of evidence of the terms of a half secret trust contrary to the provisions of the Wills Act because there was no possibility of a half secret trustee taking the property beneficially. Counsel for the legatees relied not on principle but on the previous practice of the courts manifested in cases such as *Re Fleetwood.* The House of Lords upheld the existence of the doctrine of half secret trusts. Lord Buckmaster (with whose speech Lord Hailsham L.C. concurred) said this[12]:

"the personal benefit of the legatee cannot be the sole determining factor in considering the admissibility of the evidence. . . . It is, I think more accurate to say that a testator having been induced to make a gift on trust in his will in reliance on the clear promise by the trustee that such trust will be executed in favour of certain named persons, the trustee is not at liberty to suppress the evidence of the trust and thus destroy the whole object of its creation, in fraud of the beneficiaries."

The emphasis placed in the authorities just discussed on the failure to observe the intentions of the testator and the destruction of the beneficial interests is deceptively simple and is, superficially, quite attractive. In fact, however, such arguments are completely circu-

---

[11] [1929] A.C. 318.
[12] *Ibid.* pp. 328–329.

lar. To refer to the terms of the secret trust as the "wishes of the testator" and to describe those entitled under the secret trust as "beneficiaries" begs the question; only if evidence of the terms of the trust is admitted contrary to the provisions of the Wills Act is it appropriate to describe the terms of the secret trust as the wishes of the testator and to refer to those entitled thereunder as its beneficiaries. It is not possible to use as a justification for admitting evidence contrary to the provisions of the Wills Act facts which can only be proven if such evidence is admitted. Consequently it is impossible to regard this argument as a valid justification for the existence of the doctrine of secret trusts.

Thus far the reliance on the possibility of the secret trustee taking the property beneficially as constituting the necessary fraud appears to justify the existence of fully secret trusts but not the existence of half secret trusts while reliance instead on the failure to observe the wishes of the testator or the destruction of the beneficial interests appears to beg the question and so justify the existence neither of fully secret nor of half secret trusts. Is there any other possible justification for the existence of the doctrine of secret trusts?

Such a possible justification does indeed exist in the totally different approach adopted by Viscount Sumner in *Blackwell* v. *Blackwell*. His lordship stated that the provisions of the Wills Act have nothing whatsoever to do with the doctrine of secret trusts and that it is inappropriate to state that evidence of their existence is adduced contrary to the provisions of the Wills Act. He said this[13]:

> "It is communication of the purpose to the legatee, coupled with acquiescence or promise on his part, that removes the matter from the provisions of the Wills Act and brings it within the law of trusts, as applied in this instance to trustees, who happen also to be legatees."

In other words secret trusts operate wholly outside the will in question and so are governed not by the rules of probate but by the rules of the law of trusts, which in no way prevent the introduction of oral evidence. This argument will obviously apply both to fully secret trusts and to half secret trusts. The notion that secret trusts so operate wholly outside the will, which had in fact been referred to many years earlier by Lord Westbury in *Cullen* v. *Attorney-General for Ireland*,[14] suggests that the enforcement of secret

[13] *Ibid.* p. 339.
[14] (1866) L.R. 1 H.L. 190, 198.

trusts is dependant upon fraud only to the extent that the basic duty of trustees to carry out their obligations as such is dependant on general equitable principles. A similar conclusion may perhaps be drawn from the most recent case on secret trusts, *Re Snowden,*[15] where Megarry V.C. held that the standard of proof necessary to establish the existence of a secret trust is the ordinary civil standard of proof required to establish an ordinary trust, not the higher standard necessary for rectification claims, on the grounds that "the whole basis of secret trusts . . . is that they operate outside the will, changing nothing that is written in it, and allowing it to operate according to its tenor, but then fastening a trust on to the property in the hands of the recipient."[16] Thus, according to these authorities, the justification for the existence of secret trusts, whether fully secret or half secret, is that such trusts operate wholly outside the will in question. This proposition requires close examination.

Clearly, a secret trust cannot operate completely independently of the will in question simply because the will alone can vest the subject matter of the trust in the secret trustee. To take an extreme example, if the will itself is invalid then the secret trust will fail with it for lack of subject matter. Therefore, the rules of probate clearly have some role to play. The crucial question is at what point the rules of probate cease to operate and are superseded by the rules of the law of trusts. This question can only be answered by an examination of the situations where the rules of probate and the rules of the law of trusts are in conflict. It is suggested that this examination shows that the rules of probate govern the vesting of the legacy in the secret trustee, while the rules of the law of trusts govern any matter concerning the operation of the secret trust.

One situation where the rules of probate and the rules of the law of trusts conflict concerns attestation of the will. Section 15 of the Wills Act 1837 provides that a legacy to an attesting witness is ineffective, whereas, as a matter of the law of trusts, there is no reason why the trust deed should not be signed by the trustees or beneficiaries. What happens if the secret trustee or the secret beneficiary attests the will? In *Re Young*[17] one of the beneficiaries under a half secret trust attested the will. Danckwerts J. held that, since the trust arose outside the will, section 15 of the Wills Act 1837 was quite irrelevant and so the beneficiary could take his interest. This conclusion is consistent with the principle suggested

---

[15] [1979] 2 W.L.R. 654.
[16] *Ibid.* p. 660.
[17] [1951] Ch. 344.

above and presumably would apply also to a fully secret trust (there is no authority on this point). What, on the other hand, happens if the secret trustee attests the will? This situation has never arisen but in principle this matter should be governed by the rules of probate since it concerns the vesting of the legacy. A legatee who takes beneficially on the face of the will is clearly caught by section 15. Therefore, if a fully secret trustee attested the will, the legacy to him would be ineffective and so the secret trust would fail for lack of subject matter (unless, presumably, the property nevertheless vested in the secret trustee under the intestacy rules, in which case he would undoubtedly be bound to perform the trust). On the other hand, a legatee who takes as a trustee on the face of the will is not caught by section 15.[18] Therefore, if a half secret trustee attested the will, the legacy to him would be effective and so the half secret trust would not fail by reason of his attestation. This discrepancy between fully secret and half secret trusts is, admittedly, a little odd but, as will be seen, there are many examples of discrepancies of this kind.

A second situation where the rules of probate and the rules of the law of trusts conflict concerns the doctrine of lapse. Section 25 of the Wills Act 1837 provides that, subject to certain exceptions which are not here material, a gift in a will lapses if the recipient predeceases the testator. What happens, therefore, if the secret trustee or secret beneficiary predeceases the testator? If the secret trustee predeceases the testator, the result once again seems to differ depending on whether the trust in question is fully secret or half secret. In *Re Maddock*[19] Cozens-Hardy L.J. stated, by way of dictum, that if a fully secret trustee predeceases the testator the legacy will lapse and the secret trust will fail for lack of subject matter. This conclusion is another example of probate principles being applied to the vesting of the legacy. On the other hand, it has always been clear that a gift to a person who takes as a trustee on the face of a will will not lapse by reason of his predecease.[20] Thus, if a half secret trustee predeceases the testator, this principle will presumably apply and the secret trust will therefore not fail. However, much more controversy surrounds the situation where the secret beneficiary predeceases the testator. This occurred in *Re Gardner (No. 2)*[21] where Romer J. held that a beneficiary under a secret trust acquires an interest in the trust property as soon as the trust is

[18] *Cresswell* v. *Cresswell* (1868) L.R. 6 Eq. 69.
[19] [1902] 2 Ch. 220.
[20] *Re Smirthwaite's Trusts* (1871) L.R. 11 Eq. 251.
[21] [1923] 2 Ch. 230.

communicated to and accepted by the secret trustee. Thus, the beneficiary had acquired an interest before his death and that interest naturally passed to his personal representatives. This decision has been rightly criticised on the grounds that a beneficiary under a trust acquires no interest in the trust property until the trust has been completely constituted.[22] Since this could not possibly have occurred until the trust property vested in the secret trustee at the death of the testatrix, the beneficiary could not have acquired an interest prior to his death. It is therefore generally accepted that this case was wrongly decided.[23] It is of course quite impossible to justify the reasoning which led Romer J. to his conclusion. If, however, it is accepted that the trust became completely constituted at the death of the testator, what has to be considered is the effect of completely constituting a trust in favour of a person who is already dead—that is, after all, what actually happened in *Re Gardner (No. 2)*. If, as the authorities so far discussed suggest, the rules of probate govern the vesting of the legacy in the secret trustee, while the rules of the law of trusts govern any matter concerning the operation of the secret trust, this issue falls to be determined by application of the rules of the law of trusts. Is, therefore, there any rule of the law of trusts which provides that it is not possible to constitute a trust in favour of a dead person? There is no authority which is decisive of this question.[24] If there is indeed such a rule and it is therefore impossible to constitute a trust in favour of a dead person, then *Re Gardner (No. 2)* was indeed wrongly decided. But if on the other hand there is not such a rule and it is consequently possible to constitute a trust in favour of a dead person, then, for this reason rather than the reasoning adopted by Romer J., *Re Gardner (No. 2)* was rightly decided. In principle there seems no reason why it should not be possible to constitute a trust in favour of a dead person and, if this is indeed the case, it is possible to support the result of *Re Gardner (No. 2)*. However, it has to be admitted that the weight of aca-

---

[22] *Milroy* v. *Lord* (1862) 4 De G.F. & J. 264.

[23] See, for example, the views of D.J. Hayton in Hayton & Marshall, *Cases and Commentary on the Law of Trusts* (8th ed.), pp. 103–104.

[24] Prior to the enactment of the Property Legislation of 1925, there was some authority that it was not possible to constitute a trust in favour of a dead person (*Re Tilt* (1896) 74 L.T. 163, applying *Re Corbishley's Trusts* (1880) 14 Ch.D 846). However, it is questionable whether these authorities are still good law. Since 1925, a grantee is presumed to take the greatest interest that his grantor was able to give him (Law of Property Act 1925, s.60(1)) and so arguably will take an interest not only for himself but also for those entitled under his will or intestacy. It is because of this uncertainty that it is stated in the text that there is no authority which is decisive of this question.

demic opinion is against this view[25] so that it is generally accepted that *Re Gardner* (*No. 2*) was indeed wrongly decided. It is at least clear, however, that, no matter which view is taken on this point, that conclusion should in principle apply whether the trust in question is fully secret or, as in *Re Gardner* (*No. 2*), half secret.

A further situation where the rules of probate and the rules of the law of trusts conflict concerns the possibility of a disclaimer of the legacy by the secret trustee. Where a person who is nominated as a trustee declines to act, the court will appoint another to act in his stead.[26] Thus it seems that if a half secret trustee declines to act the court will appoint a replacement trustee and the secret trust will therefore not fail. However, a disclaimer of a legacy by a person who takes beneficially on the face of the will causes the legacy to fail,[27] on which basis a disclaimer by a fully secret trustee will cause the legacy to fail. This will not be a problem if the purpose of the disclaimer is to enable the secret trustee to take not under the disclaimed legacy but rather as residuary legatee or intestate successor of the testator. Such clearly unconscionable conduct will inevitably lead to the imposition of a constructive trust on the basis of the principle enunciated in *Bannister* v. *Bannister*,[28] which was discussed in Chapter 2. Consequently the secret trustee will hold the property which passes to him under the residuary legacy or intestacy on constructive trust to perform the secret trust. But where the disclaiming fully secret trustee takes no other benefit under the will or intestacy of the testator, such a disclaimer will produce a conflict between the rule of probate that a disclaimer of a legacy by a person who takes beneficially on the face of the will causes the legacy to fail and the rule of the law of trusts that equity will not permit a trust to fail for want of a trustee. This conflict has been the subject of opposing dicta: in *Re Maddock*, Cozens-Hardy L.J. suggested that a fully secret trust would fail in such a situation, while in *Blackwell* v. *Blackwell* Lord Buckmaster said that the court would intervene to prevent such a result. There is something to be said for each view: in favour of the view of Cozens-Hardy L.J. is the proposition that probate principles should govern the vesting of the legacy; on the other hand, a court would be most reluctant to permit a trustee who has agreed to act as such to

---

[25] See n. 23, above.

[26] The power of the court to so appoint trustees stems both from statute (Trustee Act 1925, s.41(1)) and from its inherent jurisdiction (see *Dodkin* v. *Brunt* (1868) L.R. 6 Eq. 580).

[27] *Townson* v. *Tickell* (1819) 3 B. & Ald. 31.

[28] [1948] W.N. 261.

destroy a completely constituted trust by disclaiming his office. It remains to be seen which view will be adopted.

The discussion of these three difficult areas shows that it is perfectly possible to decide which rule to apply in situations where there is a conflict between the rules of probate and the rules of the law of trusts. Nearly all the authorities discussed[29] support the view that secret trusts operate wholly outside the will in question. It is therefore suggested that this view, as laid down by Viscount Sumner in *Blackwell* v. *Blackwell,* is both correct and workable. As has already been seen, this view alone is a satisfactory justification for the existence both of fully secret and of half secret trusts. It is therefore suggested that the theoretical justification for the existence of the doctrine of secret trusts is that such trusts operate wholly outside the will in question. The enforceability of such trusts in equity is therefore no more dependant upon fraud than is any other type of trust. For these reasons, it will be later suggested that secret trusts are in fact express trusts.

### Fully secret trusts

The following rules govern the operation of fully secret trusts.

The legatee must take the property as beneficial owner on the face of the will. This requirement is satisfied despite the presence of phrases such as "in the hope that he will use the property for certain purposes which I have communicated to him" or "imposing no trust upon him." Such expressions are insufficiently certain to create a trust on the face of the will and therefore, despite the presence of such expressions, any secret trust that is found to exist will be fully secret.[30]

---

[29] The only decision clearly contrary to this conclusion is *Re Gardner (No.2),* the reasoning of which is on any view clearly incorrect.

[30] An interesting point that has yet to arise in a reported case is whether expressions of this type, although insufficiently certain to create a trust, may nevertheless have an effect upon the rules governing communication of the terms of the trust to the secret trustee. Communication of a fully secret trust may normally be made either before or after the execution of the will provided that it takes place during the lifetime of the testator and may normally be either written or oral. If the will contains some expression such as "in the hope that he will use the property for certain purposes which I have communicated to him in writing," do those words, although imposing no trust upon the face of the will, nevertheless invalidate any communication which is subsequent to the execution of the will and/or any communication which, whether before or after the communication of the will, is oral? (This would undoubtedly be the case if the trust in question were half secret (see *Re Keen* [1937] Ch. 236 and *Re Spence* [1949] W.N. 237, both discussed in the text on p. 127, although such cases are readily distinguishable because in a half secret trust such expressions on the face of the will are

Before his death, the testator must ask the legatee and the legatee must agree to hold the legacy on trust for a third party. The
legatee will be deemed to have agreed unless he positively
refuses—silence constitutes assent for this purpose. It does not
matter whether the communication of the trust to the legatee takes
place before or after the execution of the will provided that it takes
place during the lifetime of the testator—communication by a letter received after the death of the testator is not sufficient since the
legatee then has no opportunity to refuse to act. Nor does it matter
that the legatee does not know the precise terms of the trust—a
testator may hand the legatee a sealed envelope to be opened after
his death or reserve the details of the trusts for future communication provided such communication occurs before his death. These
rules also apply to the case of an intestate who does not make a
will because his intestate successor has agreed to hold his property
on trust for a third party. All these propositions follow from *Moss
v. Cooper*[31] and *Re Boyes*.[32] Problems sometimes arise where the
testator leaves a legacy to two or more persons jointly and fails to
communicate with all of them. Special rules have been developed
to deal with this situation. These rules are generally stated in the
form laid down by Farwell J. in *Re Stead*.[33] If the property is left to
the legatees as tenants in common, only those legatees with whom
the testator has communicated are bound—the others take their
shares in the property beneficially. If the property is left to the
legatees as joint tenants, then if the testator has communicated
with any of the legatees prior to the execution of the will, all the
legatees are bound by the trust; on the other hand, if the testator
does not communicate with any of the legatees until after the
execution of the will, only those with whom he does communicate
are bound—the others take their shares beneficially. The cases

necessarily effective to impose a trust and therefore must inevitably limit the
trust so imposed). It is clear that a court will admit evidence of a fully secret trust
despite the fact that the will in question expressly states that no trust is imposed
on the legatee (*Re Spencer* (1887) 57 L.T. 519, where the will contained the
words "relying but not by way of trust upon their applying the said sum in or
towards the object or objects communicated to them" and a fully secret trust was
upheld). In the light of such authorities and the fact that it has been suggested
that fully secret trusts operate wholly outside the will in question, it is suggested
that in a fully secret trust the presence of such expressions on the face of the will
should not have the effect of limiting the permissible ways of communication of
the terms of the trust. Nevertheless it would be extremely interesting to see how
the courts dealt with this question.

[31] (1861) 1 J. & H. 352.
[32] (1884) 26 Ch. D. 531.
[33] [1900] 1 Ch. 237, 241.

which are alleged to establish these peculiar rules have been examined in detail by Mr. Bryn Perrins.[34] He argues convincingly that this formulation of the rules was based on a misunderstanding of the earlier cases, from which a different rule in fact emerges. In his view, the only question is whether the gift to all the legatees was induced by the agreement to act of any of them; if it was, all are bound but if it was not then only those who have agreed to act are bound—the others take their shares beneficially. In his opinion, neither the type of co-ownership nor the time of communication is decisive in determining whether or not the necessary inducement has occurred, although it will obviously be more difficult to show inducement where the legatees are tenants in common and it will be well-nigh impossible to show it where communication is subsequent to the execution of the will. It is not possible to fault Mr. Perrins' analysis of the authorities. However, it remains to be seen whether the courts will adopt his rule in preference to the more traditional ones.

If the legatee does not hear of the existence of the secret trust until after the death of the testator, he will take the property beneficially even though it can be proved that the testator intended that a secret trust should be imposed upon him. This was held in *Wallgrave* v. *Tebbs*.[35] However, if the legatee agrees during the lifetime of the testator to hold the property on trust but is not informed of the beneficial interests before the death of the testator, then he will hold the property on trust for the residuary legatee (or, if the legacy in question is the residuary legacy, for those entitled on intestacy). This was held in *Re Boyes*. Although the question has never arisen, it is suggested that this would be the case even if the legatee were himself the residuary legatee or intestate successor in question.

Finally, there is no reason why the legatee should not himself be one of the beneficiaries of the secret trust. This was held expressly in *Irvine* v. *Sullivan*,[36] where a legatee who took absolutely on the face of the will was held to be entitled to take whatever surplus remained after observing the testator's instructions to pay various pecuniary legacies. This also follows from *Ottaway* v. *Norman*[37] where the subject matter of the secret trust was left to the secret trustee for life, with remainder over to the testator's son.

The rules relating to attestation of the will by the secret trustee

[34] 88 L.Q.R. (1972) 225.
[35] (1855) 2 K. & J. 313.
[36] (1869) L.R. 8 Eq. 673.
[37] [1972] Ch. 698.

or beneficiary, predecease by the secret trustee or beneficiary and disclaimer of the legacy by the secret trustee have already been dealt with. The question of whether fully secret trusts of land are required to be evidenced in writing and whether fully secret trusts of subsisting equitable interests are required to be created in writing will be considered later on.[38]

### Half secret trusts

It is necessary to distinguish half secret trusts from the cases where the probate doctrine of incorporation by reference arises.[39] If the testator on the face of his will leaves property to a legatee for the purposes set out in a named existing and identifiable document, then that document is deemed to be incorporated into the will and is admitted to probate as part of the will even though it does not itself comply with the formal requirements of the Wills Act.[40] None of the difficulties which surround secret trusts arises in such a case. Where, on the other hand, the testator sets out the details of the trust either orally or in a document which is not sufficiently identified by the will, then a half secret trust will arise provided that the following rules have been satisfied.

The legatee must take the property as a trustee on the face of the will. In other words, the testator must use words which impose upon the legatee an obligation to hold the property upon trust.

Before or contemporaneously with the making of the will, the testator must ask the legatee and the legatee must agree to hold the legacy on trust for a third party. This rule was established by dicta of the members of the House of Lords in *Blackwell* v. *Blackwell*,[41] was reiterated, also by way of dicta, by the Court of Appeal

---

[38] See pp. 129–130.

[39] This doctrine has on occasions been argued to be the theoretical justification for the doctrine of half secret trusts (see Paul Matthews [1979] *Conveyancer*, p. 360). Adoption of this argument would indeed explain the otherwise inexplicable and much criticised rule that in a half secret trust communication of the terms of the trust must be made before or contemporaneously with the making of the will in question. However, apart from the fact that there seems to be no authority whatsoever in support of such an argument, its acceptance would involve either extending the probate doctrine of incorporation by reference to oral communications or alternatively requiring communication of the terms of a half secret trust to be in writing (in which case *Blackwell* v. *Blackwell* was wrongly decided). Neither of these possibilities seems to be consistent either with principle or with precedent ant it is therefore suggested that this argument is not an acceptable justification for the doctrine of half secret trusts.

[40] See *e.g.*, *In the goods of Smart* [1902] P. 238.

[41] [1929] A.C. 318.

in *Re Keen*,[42] and was applied, apparently without any contrary argument from counsel, in *Re Bateman's Will Trusts*.[43] It is difficult to see any justification for making this distinction between half secret trusts and fully secret trusts (where, as has already been seen, communication and acceptance may occur at any time prior to the death of the testator). It is therefore suggested that the rule governing fully secret trusts should be applied also to half secret trusts so as to permit communication and acceptance at any time prior to the death of the testator. This has been done in Ireland[44] and in most of the American jurisdictions.[45] However, at present the rule of English law is quite clear—communication and acceptance must occur before or contemporaneously with the making of the will. As in the case of fully secret trusts, silence constitutes assent and it suffices if the testator hands the legatee a sealed envelope to be opened after his death. However, the communication made must not be contrary to the express provisions of the will. In *Re Keen,* the testator left £10,000 to two persons "to be held upon trust and disposed of by them among such person, persons or charities as may be notified by me to them or either of them during my lifetime." Before the execution of the will, he had handed a sealed envelope containing the name of the intended beneficiary to one of the legatees. The Court of Appeal held that it did not matter that the testator had given the legatee his instructions in a sealed envelope which was not to be opened until after his death. However, the Court held that the express provisions of the will contemplated only a future communication and so the communication before the date of the will was contrary to the express provisions of the will and so was ineffective. (Of course, any communication made after the date of the will in accordance with its provisions would also have been ineffective since communication after the date of the will is impermissible in the case of a half secret trust). Similarly, in *Re Spence,*[46] the testator left property to four persons "to be dealt with in accordance with my wishes which I have made known to them." In fact the testator had communicated only with some of the legatees and this communication was held to be contrary to the express provisions of the will and so was ineffective. Finally, problems can arise where the testator (without having made an express provision as in *Re Spence*) leaves

---

[42] [1937] Ch. 236.
[43] [1970] 1 W.L.R. 1463.
[44] *Re Browne* [1944] Ir.R. 90.
[45] See Scott, *Law of Trusts*, para. 55.8.
[46] [1949] W.N. 237.

a legacy to two or more persons jointly and fails to communicate with all of them. Of course all the legatees will quite clearly be trustees and so the only question that arises is whether those with whom the testator failed to communicate hold their share of the property on trust for the communicated purpose or for the residuary legatee or intestate successor. There seems to be no half secret trust case in which this problem has actually arisen. Presumably the issue would be determined by application of the rules which apply in this situation to fully secret trusts—the nature of these rules is at present uncertain since, as has already been seen, Mr. Perrins has recently challenged the established formulation of the rules.

If for some reason the purposes of the trust cannot be carried out, the legatee will not take the property beneficially but will hold it on trust for the residuary legatee (or, if the legacy in question is the residuary legacy, for those entitled on intestacy). This was held in *Re Pugh's Will Trusts.*[47] It has already been suggested that the half secret trustee should be able to take the property beneficially if he himself is the residuary legatee or intestate successor in question. Further, according to the decision of the Court of Appeal in *Re Rees' Will Trusts,*[48] a half secret trustee cannot be one of the secret beneficiaries since such a beneficial interest would be contrary to the express provision of the will that he takes the property as a trustee.[49] On the basis that secret trusts operate outside the will, it is not easy to justify this harsh rule, which must undoubtedly lead to the frustration of the intentions of the testator. Considerable doubts as to the validity of this rule were expressed by Pennycuick J. in *Re Tyler's Fund Trusts,*[50] although his lordship conceded that he would have been bound by *Re Rees' Will Trusts* if the point had arisen for decision. Finally, if the testator asks the legatee to hold a particular sum on trust and in fact leaves him a larger sum, only the sum in respect of which the legatee undertook to act will be subject to the secret trust and the legatee will hold the balance on trust for the residuary legatee or intestate successor. This was decided in *Re Colin Cooper.*[51]

The rules relating to attestation of the will by the secret trustee

---

[47] [1967] 1 W.L.R. 1262.
[48] [1950] Ch. 204.
[49] This rule was also stated by way of dicta in *Irvine* v. *Sullivan* (1869) L.R. 8 Eq. 673, which actually concerned a fully secret trust.
[50] [1967] 3 All E.R. 389, 394.
[51] [1939] Ch. 580.

or beneficiary, predecease by the secret trustee or beneficiary and disclaimer of the legacy by the secret trustee have already been discussed. The question of whether half secret trusts of land are required to be evidenced in writing and whether half secret trusts of subsisting equitable interests are required to be created in writing will be considered in the next section.

### The nature of secret trusts

The final question that arises in relation to secret trusts is whether such trusts are express trusts or constructive trusts. This is not purely an academic issue. Section 53(1) of the Law of Property Act 1925 lays down certain formal requirements for the valid creation of trusts, from which section 53(2) exempts implied, resulting, and constructive trusts. Thus, if secret trusts are express trusts, a secret trust of land will be required to be evidenced in writing under section 53(1)(*b*) and a secret trust of a subsisting equitable interest will be required to be created in writing under section 53(1)(*c*). On the other hand, if secret trusts are constructive trusts, no such formalities will be necessary. The cases are inconclusive. In *Re Baillie*,[52] a half secret trust of land was held to be ineffective because of the absence of the necessary writing. That decision suggests that half secret trusts, at least, are express trusts. On the other hand, fully secret trusts of land have been upheld in the absence of the necessary writing—most recently in *Ottaway* v. *Norman*,[53] although neither in this nor in any other of the reported cases has the absence of this writing actually been raised. At first sight, this might be thought to suggest, if only by virtue of the silence of the courts, that fully secret trusts are not express trusts. Any such conclusion would, however, be unsound. The absence of evidentiary writing must be specifically pleaded; if it is not so pleaded, then the absence of the writing will not be a bar to the success of the action.[54] Consequently the fact that fully secret trusts have been upheld in the absence of the evidentiary writing required by section 53(1)(*b*) is totally irrelevant to the question of whether such writing is actually necessary. What then

---

[52] (1886) 2 T.L.R. 660 (this was of course a decision on the pre-existing provision, Statute of Frauds 1677, s.7).

[53] [1972] Ch. 698.

[54] *North* v. *Loomes* [1919] 1 Ch. 378 (actually a decision on Statute of Frauds 1677, s.4 (now Law of Property Act 1925, s.40); however both provisions require only evidentiary writing and are generally thought to be governed by the same principles).

is the nature of secret trusts? Most commentators, on the strength of *Re Baillie* and the fact that half secret trusts, unlike fully secret trusts, appear on the face of the will, seem to accept that half secret trusts are express trusts. However, the general view seems to be that no fully secret trust can ever fail for lack of writing, simply because of the maxim that a statute cannot be used as an instrument of fraud; for this reason, most commentators seem to classify fully secret trusts as constructive trusts.[55] Apart from the fact that it seems contrary to principle to distinguish in this way between fully secret and half secret trusts, the proposition that no fully secret trust can ever fail for lack of writing is in fact unsound. Obviously no fully secret trustee will be allowed to profit by upholding the absence of the necessary writing as the basis of a claim to take the property beneficially—the clearly unconscionable conduct involved in any attempt to do this will inevitably lead to the imposition of a constructive trust on a quite different ground— the principle enunciated in *Bannister* v. *Bannister*.[56] But there remains the possibility that a fully secret trustee who admits that he is holding the subject matter of his legacy on a secret trust but cannot point to the writing required by section 53(1) will find himself confronted by opposing claims from the beneficiaries of the secret trust and from the residuary legatees or intestate successors of the testator. In this situation, the maxim that a statute cannot be used as an instrument of fraud will be of no assistance whatsoever and the result will turn on whether fully secret trusts are constructive trusts, in which case the property will go to the beneficiaries of the secret trust, or express trusts, in which case because of the absence of the necessary writing the property will go to the residuary legatees or intestate successors. It is therefore necessary to decide as a matter of principle whether secret trusts are express trusts or constructive trusts. Obviously in the case of both fully secret and half secret trusts the testator clearly intends to create a relationship of trustee and beneficiary. This suggests that, as a matter of definition, both fully secret and half secret trusts should be classified as express trusts. It is accordingly suggested that all secret trusts are express trusts and so must comply with section 53(1) of the Law of Property Act 1925. However, it must be admitted that there is no general agreement on this question, which must therefore await a definitive resolution by the courts.

---

[55] See, for example, the views of D.J. Hayton in Hayton & Marshall, *Cases and Commentary on the Law of Trusts* (8th ed.), pp. 106–107.
[56] [1948] W.N. 261.

### The theoretical justification for the existence of the doctrine of mutual wills

Mutual wills arise where two or more persons enter into a legally binding agreement to make wills in a particular form with the intention that the provisions of such wills will be irrevocably binding.[57] As soon as the first of the parties dies leaving a will made in accordance with the agreement, equity regards that agreement as irrevocable so far as the survivor is concerned and gives effect to it by the imposition of a trust. Thus if the survivor ultimately leaves his property other than in accordance with the agreement, his personal representatives will be deemed to hold it on trust for the agreed beneficiary. The theoretical justification for this intervention of equity is quite clearly the fact that, but for this intervention, the survivor would be enabled to benefit by his own fraud. This was stated particularly clearly by Lord Camden L.C. in *Dufour* v. *Pereira*.[58] During the joint lifetime of the parties, the relationship between them is purely contractual. Breach of the agreement by revocation of the mutual will during this period is therefore purely a matter of contract—if the other party can show loss (which is extremely unlikely), he will be able to recover compensation by way of damages. The situation will be the same if the first party to die does not leave a will made in accordance with the agreement. But as soon as one of the parties dies leaving a will which is made in accordance with the agreement, he will irrevocably have disposed of his property in reliance upon the agreement. Therefore, any revocation of the mutual will at this stage will be not only a breach of contract but also a blatant fraud. Any such revocation will enable the survivor to take the benefit for which he contracted—the disposition by the other party of his property in accordance with that agreement—without the corresponding burden. Thus the survivor, by delaying his revocation until after the death of the other party, will have fraudulently obtained the benefit of the contract. This will be the case not only where the survivor takes some material benefit under the will but also where he disclaims any such benefit and where the agreement gave him no such benefit since in all three situations he will have obtained the benefit he sought—the disposition of the property under the will. Thus equity admits evidence contrary to the provisions of the Wills

---

[57] All the decided cases have concerned wills in substantially similar form so it has never been decided whether this is actually necessary. The point is considered more fully on pp. 132–133.

[58] (1769) Dick. 419, 421 (better reported in 2 Hargrave, *Jurisconsult Exercitations* 100, 104).

Act in order to prevent the survivor benefiting his own fraudulent conduct. Therefore, the theoretical justification for the existence of the doctrine of mutual wills is that, but for this doctrine, the survivor would be enabled to benefit by his own fraud.

## Mutual wills

Mutual wills will only be held to have been created where a legally binding agreement between the parties can be shown to exist. Before equity will intervene, it must be shown not only that the parties agreed to execute wills in a particular form but also that they intended that the provisions of those wills should be irrevocably binding.

It is often said that the doctrine of mutual wills requires the parties to agree to make wills in substantially similar form. It is undoubtedly true that all the reported cases have concerned agreements of this type. The most common example of mutual wills is where two persons agree that each will leave property to the other absolutely with the same substitutionary provisions in the event of non-survival. The property in question is most commonly the residuary estate of each but there is obviously no necessity for this—the agreement can take any form that the parties desire. Thus there is no reason why the agreement should not be for each to leave a specific sum or specific assets in this way with no restriction whatsoever on the disposition of the residue. Even where the agreement in question is for each person to dispose of his residue in this manner, it is common for each party to make individual specific bequests or pecuniary legacies. Thus in the most recent case to come before the courts, *Re Cleaver*,[59] the agreement held to be irrevocably binding was that each party should leave quite distinct pecuniary legacies but, subject thereto, should leave his residue to the other absolutely with identical substitutionary gifts in the event of non-survival. Because all the reported cases have concerned agreements to make wills in such substantially similar form, it has never actually had to be decided whether this is necessary—whether, in other words, the doctrine of mutual wills is limited to agreements to make wills in substantially similar form. Suppose that two parties enter into an agreement that, if the first party devises his freehold land Blackacre to the second party, the latter will devise Blackacre and his own freehold land Whiteacre to a third party. Obviously this agreement is subject to two con-

---

[59] [1981] 1 W.L.R. 939.

ditions precedent; the first party must die before the second party and must devise Blackacre to him. Equally obviously, in the event that either of these pre-conditions is not fulfilled, the second party with clearly be under no obligation whatsoever to devise White-acre to the third party. On the assumption that it can be proved that the parties intended that, in the event that both pre-conditions were satisfied, their obligations thereunder should be irrevocably binding, is there any reason why this should not be regarded as falling within the doctrine of mutual wills so that, once the pre-conditions have been fulfilled, any disposition of Blackacre and Whiteacre by the second party other than to the third party will give rise to the intervention of equity? There is no authority what-soever on this point but it is suggested that, assuming that the necessary evidence can be produced, the doctrine of mutual wills should be capable of applying to such a case.[60]

What evidence must be adduced that the parties intended that the provisions of their wills should be irrevocably binding? The best conceivable evidence will obviously be recitals in the wills themselves. In *Re Hagger,*[61] a husband and wife made a joint will (such a document takes effect not as one will but as the separate wills of each party and is admitted to probate successively as the will of each testator.) This joint will expressly stated that the par-ties had agreed to dispose of their property by that will and that there was to be no alteration or revocation except by agreement. Although the mere fact that the parties had made a joint will did not necessarily make it a mutual will, this recital clearly showed that the parties had agreed to bind themselves to make a mutual will. Equally convincing proof will be recitals of this type in the separate wills of the parties to the agreement. However, cases only tend to reach the courts where the survivor has revoked his mutual will in breach of the agreement and in such a situation his will will obviously contain no such recital. A recital in the sole will of the first party to die obviously will be no more than prima facie evi-

---

[60] If this conclusion were not adopted and the doctrine of mutual wills were held to be inapplicable to such a case, there would in any event be a secret trust of the property left by the first party to the second party (this would be of Blackacre in the example given) but such a secret trust could not of course affect the second party's ability to dispose of his own property (Whiteacre in the example given). Such a secret trust would be similar to that upheld in *Ottaway* v. *Norman* [1972] Ch. 698 and would presumably be a fully secret trust (unless of course the agree-ment was recited in the will of the first party in such a way as to make the second party a trustee on the face of the will).

[61] [1930] 2 Ch. 190.

dence of an agreement.[62] In such a case and also in situations where there is no mention of any agreement in either will, the agreement will have to be proved by other forms of evidence. No agreement will be inferred merely because two parties make wills in substantially similar forms. In *Re Oldham*,[63] a husband and wife both made wills leaving their property to the other absolutely with the same alternative provisions in the event of the other's predecease. Although it was clear that they had agreed to make substantially identical wills, no evidence could be adduced of any agreement not to revoke them and so Astbury J. declined to infer such an agreement, particularly since both had left their property to the other absolutely. (Of course, although this will be a factor against the implication of such an agreement, there is nothing to prevent parties expressly agreeing to make mutual wills in this form.[64]) Thus, the agreement not to revoke must be clearly proved.

Where such an agreement has been made, the position before either of the parties dies will be governed by contractual prin-

---

[62] Where there is a recital in the sole will of the first party to die containing the terms of the alleged agreement and it is finally found that there is no evidence to prove the existence of any legally binding agreement, it is possible that the equitable doctrine of election may apply. This doctrine operates where a testator not only gives his own property to a beneficiary but also purports to give some of that beneficiary's own property to a third party. In this case, on the principle that a person cannot take under a will without conforming to all its provisions, the beneficiary has to make a choice: he may either disclaim the property left to him in the will; or elect in favour of the will—this means that he will receive the property left to him in the will but will have to comply with the terms of the will and dispose of his own property to the third party; or elect against the will—this means that he will receive the property left to him in the will and out of it will have to pay to the third party the value of the property of his own disposed of by the testator to the third party. (See generally Snell *Principles of Equity* (28th Ed.), p. 495.) If this doctrine does indeed apply in the situation mentioned above, the survivor would have the following choice: disclaiming all benefit under the will of the first to die and retaining free disposition of his own existing property; electing in favour of the will by taking the property left to him and subsequently making the dispositions envisaged in the will of the first to die: or electing against the will by taking the property left to him and subsequently disposing just of the value of that property in the manner envisaged in the will of the first to die. There has as yet been no reported case in which this situation has arisen—it is of course relatively unlikely that there will be found to be no evidence of a legally binding agreement where the will of the first to die recites one! However, if such a situation ever arises (as might occur where the first to die made a will reciting an agreement which he hoped to make with the survivor and either failed to secure his agreement and subsequently died without changing his will or died before he had discussed the matter with the survivor) it is suggested that the result should be as above.

[63] [1925] Ch. 75.

[64] Such was the case both in *Re Green* [1951] Ch. 148 and the most recent case to come before the courts, *Re Cleaver* [1981] 1 W.L.R. 939.

ciples. If one party revokes his mutual will in breach of the agreement during the lifetime of the other, the latter will be able to recover damages for breach of contract. However, since the only possible loss is loss of the right to receive an unascertained amount at an unascertained time in the future and since the other party still has unrestricted powers to dispose of his own property, it is relatively unlikely that any substantial damages could be recovered. Similarly if the first party to die does not leave a will made in accordance with the agreement, the other party will be able to claim damages from his estate. However, although the loss suffered could be quantified in such a case, the other party will not have relinquished his powers over his own property and so may still find difficulty in obtaining substantial damages. A further bar to any successful action for damages is the fact that it seems that no such action will be available if the mutual will was revoked not by the act of the party but by operation of law (for example by his remarriage or divorce).[65] Thus, while it is clear that revocation of the mutual will during the joint lives of the parties will determine the agreement and release the other party from his obligations thereunder,[66] no effective remedy is likely to result to the other party.

However, once one of the parties has died leaving a will made in accordance with the agreement, the situation changes completely. Equity intervenes to ensure performance of the agreement by the survivor and imposes a trust upon him for the benefit of those entitled under the agreement. It is quite clear from the authorities that this trust arises as soon as one of the parties dies leaving a will made in accordance with the agreement.[67] This emerges most clearly from *Re Hagger,* where one of the ultimate beneficiaries under the joint mutual will of a husband and wife survived the wife but predeceased the husband. Clauson J. held that her interest under the trust imposed by equity arose on the death of the wife and therefore did not lapse when she predeceased the husband. It is less clear whether this trust is imposed irrespective of whether or not the survivor takes any benefit under the will of the first to die. The English courts have never had to consider a case where the survivor has disclaimed his beneficial interest or where no such interest was given to the survivor by the agreement. However, dicta in *Dufour* v. *Pereira* and *Re Oldham* suggest that it is immaterial whether or not the survivor takes any benefit. This view is

---

[65] *Robinson* v. *Ommanney* (1883) 23 Ch.D. 285.
[66] *Stone* v. *Hoskins* [1905] P. 194.
[67] See J.D.B. Mitchell (1951) 14 M.L.R. 137.

undoubtedly in accordance with principle since whenever the first party to die leaves a will made in accordance with the agreement the survivor will have obtained the benefit for which he contracted (the disposition of the property under the will) whether or not he obtains any material benefit. However, it must be admitted that other jurisdictions have taken the opposite view and regarded a benefit under the will of the first to die as essential,[68] It is to be hoped that this view is not adopted here.

The purpose of the imposition of the trust is to prevent the survivor revoking his will in breach of the agreement. However, equity does not interfere with the fundamental probate principle that no will is irrevocable. If the survivor revokes his mutual will in breach of the agreement, his property will pass under his new will or intestacy to his personal representatives, who will hold it on trust to give effect to the agreement.[69] This will be the case even if the will is revoked by operation of law upon a subsequent remarriage.[70] But whether or not the survivor revokes his will, difficulties arise in determining precisely what property is subject to the trust.[71] Of course this will primarily be determined by the agreement. In *Re Green*,[72] the agreement specifically provided that each party would leave his property to the other absolutely and, at the death of the survivor, half his residuary estate was to be treated as his property and the other half as the property received from the first to die. Vaisey J. held that only the property received under the will of the first to die (and not the survivor's own property) was subject to the trust. This decision is justifiable as a matter of construction of the agreement in question but certainly cannot apply where an agreement contains no such provision. In such a case, there is relatively little difficulty about any property received by the survivor under the mutual will. If he receives a limited interest, such as a life interest, the property will already be held on an express trust and so there is no scope for the trust imposed by equity. If, on the other hand, he receives an absolute interest, a trust will clearly be imposed. However the precise nature of this trust is far from clear. In one sense, the survivor will be holding the property on trust for himself for his lifetime and then for the benefit of the ultimate beneficiary of the mutual will. But it is most unclear whether the interest of the survivor is a life interest in the technical sense (in which

---

[68] *Denyssen* v. *Mostert* (1872) L.R. 4 P.C. 236 (Colony of the Cape of Good Hope), *Minakshi Ammal* v. *Viswanath Aiyar* (1909) I.L.R. 33 Mad. 406 (India).
[69] *In the Estate of Heys* [1914] P. 192.
[70] *Re Green* [1951] Ch. 148.
[71] See J.D.B. Mitchell (1981) 14 M.L.R. 137.
[72] See n. 70, above.

case he would have no right to resort to the capital) or whether the survivor has the right to dispose of the capital for his own benefit. This problem becomes even more acute when the survivor's own property is considered. Is this property subject to a trust from the time the first party dies and, if so, what is the nature of this trust?

It seems fairly clear from the decision in *Re Hagger* that the survivor's own property is subject to a trust from the death of the first party since in that case the beneficiary was held to have an interest in property which was quite clearly vested in the survivor until his death. But if all the property owned by the survivor at the death of the first party becomes subject to a trust in favour of himself for life and thereafter for the ultimate beneficiary of the mutual will, the survivor will not be able to dispose of his own property for his own benefit without committing a breach of trust. Further, what happens to any property acquired by the survivor after the death of the first party? Does it immediately become subject to the same trust? If so, the effect of the death of the first party will be to make the survivor a life tenant both of the property he receives under the will and of his own property. All after-acquired property will be subject to the same trust and so the survivor will have no power during the rest of his life to apply any capital for his own benefit. On the other hand, it could be argued that the intention of the parties could reasonably be assumed to be that the survivor has the right to deal as he wishes with his own property and perhaps also with the property left to him absolutely under the terms of the agreement. The difficulty about this view is that the trust imposed by equity then becomes so uncertain as to be virtually useless since the survivor can destroy the subject matter of the agreement by alienation or dissipation. The English courts have been spared the task of considering this problem because most litigation involving mutual wills does not commence until after the death of the survivor and so can only be concerned with the property owned by him at his death. Thus English courts have generally been content to apply the terms of the agreement to this property. However, in the Australian case of *Birmingham* v. *Renfrew*,[73] Dixon J. considered this issue and said this[74]:

> "The purpose of an arrangement for corresponding wills must often be, as in this case, to enable the survivor during his life to deal as absolute owner with the property passing under the will of the party first dying. That is to say, the object of the transaction is to put the survivor in a position to enjoy for his

[73] (1937) 57 C.L.R. 666.
[74] *Ibid.* p. 689.

own benefit the full ownership so that, for instance, he may convert it and expend the proceeds if he choose. But when he dies he is to bequeath what is left in the manner agreed upon. It is only by the special doctrines of equity that such a floating obligation, suspended, so to speak, during the lifetime of the survivor can descend upon the assets at his death and crystallise into a trust. No doubt gifts and settlements, *inter vivos*, if calculated to defeat the intention of the compact, could not be made by the survivor and his right of disposition, *inter vivos,* is, therefore, not unqualified. But, substantially, the purpose of the arrangement will often be to allow full enjoyment for the survivor's own benefit and advantage upon condition that at his death the residue shall pass as arranged."

This view undoubtedly recognises what actually happens in most mutual will cases. But it seems hardly satisfactory to describe the floating obligation referred to by Dixon J. as a trust, since such an obligation lacks the element of certainty of subject matter which is one of the principal requirements of a trust. Perhaps the only answer is to regard the trust imposed to give effect to mutual wills as an entrenched anomaly.

### The nature of the trust imposed to give effect to mutual wills

It is quite clear that the trust imposed to give effect to mutual wills is not an express trust. However, there is a division of academic opinion as to whether this trust is an implied or resulting trust or a constructive trust. Nothing turns on the classification adopted but it is suggested that, since this trust is imposed to prevent the survivor obtaining a benefit by his own fraudulent conduct, it is akin to the types of constructive trust described in Chapter 2 and so should be classified as a constructive trust.

### A comparison between secret trusts and mutual wills

Secret trusts and mutual wills alike can only take effect because equity is prepared to accept evidence of their existence which does not comply with the provisions of the Wills Act. Both therefore owe their existence to the intervention of equity and exemplify the "long-established principle that if the owner of property makes a gift of it on the faith of a promise by the donee that he will deal with the property in a particular way, an obligation so to deal with it is placed upon the donee and can be enforced in the courts."[75] Indeed at times there is considerable factual similarity between the

---

[75] Romer J. in *Re Gardner (No. 2)* [1923] 2 Ch. 230, 232.

two. In *Ottaway* v. *Norman*,[76] a testator devised his bungalow to his housekeeper and bequeathed her £1,500 and half his residuary estate. Before the death of the testator, she had agreed to leave the bungalow and whatever money was left at her own death to the testator's son. However, in the event she left all her property away from the son, who brought an action against her executor for a declaration that her estate was subject to a trust in his favour. At first sight this situation seems more akin to a mutual will than to a secret trust. The testator has given property to one person to enjoy for her lifetime and then to leave it by her will to another. However, the whole case was argued and decided on the basis that a fully secret trust had been created. This was due to the fact that, since there was no evidence of any contractual agreement between the testator and his housekeeper, any attempt to raise mutual wills would clearly have failed. The voluntary undertaking by the housekeeper, therefore, could only give rise to a secret trust. Brightman J. duly held that the bungalow was subject to a fully secret trust in favour of the son. However, he held that there was no valid secret trust of the residue of the money. His lordship was prepared to assume, without deciding, that it was possible to impose a secret trust under which the secret trustee could deal as he liked with the subject matter during his lifetime and then leave anything that was left to a third party. However, even on that assumption, he held that the terms of the alleged trust were far too unclear. The housekeeper had not been placed under any obligation to keep the money subject to the alleged trust separate from her own funds and, in any event, it was unclear precisely what was meant by money in this context. This decision has several novel features. It is unusual to find a secret trust where the obligation imposed on the trustee is to enjoy the property for his lifetime and then leave it to a third party. There is no particular objection to this provided that the property is clearly ascertainable (as the bungalow clearly was). However, if a secret trust is feasible (as Brightman J. was prepared to assume without deciding) where the secret trustee is entitled to dispose of the property at will and need only leave anything that is left to a third party, then secret trusts will have moved into the murky area that causes such conceptual difficulties in the case of mutual wills. It is much to be hoped that no such secret trusts will ever be upheld so that the doctrine of secret trusts can be spared this sort of conceptual confusion. However the possibility of such a trust being upheld shows the interrelation between the two doctrines.

[76] [1972] Ch. 698.

Thus, despite the similarities between secret trusts and mutual wills, one clear distinction emerges: mutual wills arise as a result of contractual agreement whereas secret trusts arise as a result of a voluntary undertaking. At present there is also one further distinction: no secret trust has yet been upheld where the trust property is of a changeable nature, whereas such a situation often occurs in the case of mutual wills. It is much to be hoped that this distinction will be retained and thus save secret trusts from the conceptual difficulties of mutual wills.

## Conclusion

The existence of the doctrines of secret trusts and mutual wills is clearly justifiable. However, while the ramifications of the doctrine of secret trusts have generally been worked out logically and satisfactorily within the trust concept, many of the ramifications of the doctrine of mutual wills have not been worked out at all so that the doctrine appears anomalous and inconsistent with basic trust concepts. It is therefore much to be hoped that the confusion which surrounds the operation of the doctrine of mutual wills will not be transferred to the doctrine of secret trusts.

## Chapter 6

## CONSTRUCTIVE TRUSTS IMPOSED UPON A VENDOR WHO HAS ENTERED INTO A CONTRACT OF SALE WHICH IS CAPABLE OF BEING SPECIFICALLY ENFORCED

The constructive trust which is imposed upon a vendor who has entered into a contract of sale which is capable of being specifically enforced is one of the oldest types of constructive trust, having been well established by 1651.[1] When such a contract is valid, equity in accordance with one of its earliest maxims regards as done that which ought to be done. Therefore, the equitable doctrine of conversion operates and equity regards the purchaser as owner of the subject matter of the contract and the vendor as owner of the purchase money. The operation of this equitable doctrine does not, of course, affect the legal title to the subject matter of the contract, which remains in the vendor pending performance of the contract. Thus, the effect of the operation of the doctrine is to separate the legal and beneficial ownership of the property and it is only to be expected that equity therefore regards the vendor as a trustee of the property for the purchaser pending performance of the contract. No corresponding trust of the purchase money will arise simply because such a trust would lack the necessary certainty of subject matter. However, the vendor acquires a lien or charge on the property for the unpaid purchase money. But where such a contract is a contract of barter (where, for example, two persons agree to exchange landholdings), then reciprocal trusts will arise and each will hold the property which is to be exchanged on trust for the other.

The operation of the equitable doctrine of conversion and the consequent constructive trust are important because of the effect that can be produced both upon the devolution of property and upon the liabilities of the parties. Where a party to a contract dies after the equitable doctrine has operated, his property will devolve as if the contract has been performed. Thus, if a vendor or purchaser of freehold land dies after the doctrine of conversion has operated, the interest of the vendor devolves with his personalty

---

[1] *Lady Foliamb's Case* cited in *Davie* v. *Beversham* (1661) which is reported under various names in 3 Chan.Rep 4, Nels. 76 and 1 Chan.Cas. 39.

141

and the interest of the purchaser devolves with his realty.[2] Today this is important only when a testator leaves his realty and personalty (or his land and pure personalty) to different persons. However, this aspect of the operation of the doctrine of conversion was formerly much more important. Before 1926 realty and personalty devolved in different ways upon intestacy with the result that the operation of the doctrine of conversion affected the devolution of property whenever a vendor or purchaser of freehold land died after the doctrine had operated. Further, until the enactment of the Real Estate Charges Act 1854,[3] if a purchaser of freehold land died after the equitable doctrine of conversion had operated and his realty and personalty devolved in different ways upon his death, the person on whom the realty devolved was not only entitled to the benefit of the contract but was also entitled to have the purchase price paid out of the personalty. Thus in effect the person on whom the personalty devolved had to pay for property which was going to someone else—this is undoubtedly one of the reasons why so many of the decided cases on the operation of the equitable doctrine of conversion arose in this period. Since 1854, however, the person on whom the realty devolves must himself furnish any unpaid balance of the purchase money if he wishes to take the benefit of the contract—the present provision to this effect is section 35(1) of the Administration of Estates Act 1925. Thus in such circumstances his inheritance is limited to the value of such deposit or instalments as have already been paid, plus of course the actual benefit of the transaction.[4] While it is thus apparent that the operation of the doctrine of conversion will today only rarely affect the devolution of property, its effect on the liabilities of the parties remains today as important as it has ever been. Since the effect of the doctrine is to make the vendor a trustee of the subject matter of the contract for the purchaser, the vendor becomes liable to deal with the property as a trustee and the purchaser becomes liable for all the risks attendant upon ownership.

---

[2] The operation of the doctrine of conversion does not of course produce this result where the subject matter of the sale and purchase is leasehold land or pure personalty since the interests of both vendor and purchaser will be interests in personalty both before and after the operation of the doctrine and so will at all times devolve with their personalty.

[3] Generally known as Locke-King's Act.

[4] If the person on whom the realty devolves is not prepared to furnish the unpaid balance of the purchase money and so disclaims his right to take the benefit of the contract, the personal representatives of the purchaser will have to complete the contract in the course of their administration of the estate and will almost certainly then have to resell the subject matter in order to recoup the funds thus expended.

Of course, this trusteeship of the vendor is of an extremely unusual nature in that he himself retains a substantial interest in the property for the simple reason that, in the event that the contract is not in the end completed, he will once again become absolute legal and beneficial owner. Be that as it may, however, these effects of the operation of the doctrine of conversion mean that it is essential to know in what circumstances and at precisely what moment the doctrine will operate and also to know the precise nature of the trust imposed upon the parties. These questions will be considered in turn.

### The circumstances in which the doctrine of conversion will operate

Only when a contract of sale is capable of being specifically enforced will the doctrine of conversion operate and give rise to a constructive trust. It is therefore important to ascertain the circumstances in which equity will order specific performance of a contract of sale. Specific performance is a discretionary remedy but the discretion of the court is exercised according to fixed and settled principles of equity—this was stated particularly clearly by Romilly M.R. in *Haywood* v. *Cope*.[5] Three basic requirements must be satisfied before an order for specific performance will issue: first, there must be an enforceable contract between the parties; secondly, the claimant must have furnished actual consideration in that he has either performed or is ready and able to perform his part of the bargain; thirdly, damages for breach of contract must be an inadequate remedy. It is this third requirement that is most significant for present purposes. Equity will not order specific performance of a contract of sale unless the failure of the vendor to transfer the subject matter of the contract to the purchaser is incapable of being adequately compensated by an award of damages. Thus, specific performance will never be ordered where the subject matter of the contract of sale is an item which is readily available on the open market. So a contract to sell a vehicle which is in current production, a book which is in print, or shares in a public company will not be capable of being specifically enforced. On the other hand, a contract to sell something which is unique or, for some other reason, not readily available will be capable of being specifically enforced. Therefore, a contract to sell a rare antique, a rare book or shares in a private company generally will be specifically enforced since the purchaser would not be able to purchase an acceptable substitute with his damages.

[5] (1858) 25 Beav. 140, 151.

Further, equity regards every piece of land as unique and so damages are never regarded as adequate compensation for the loss of an interest in land. Therefore, every contract for the sale of an interest in land is capable of being specifically enforced.

Thus the doctrine of conversion will only operate where the contract of sale in question is capable of satisfying these requirements. However, Professor D.W.M. Waters has argued that there is one further limitation. He suggests that only where the subject matter of the contract of sale is a legal interest will the doctrine of conversion operate to give rise to a constructive trust. He states that "the constructive trust, assuming as it does a division of legal and equitable interests, is irreconcileable with the sale of an equitable interest."[6] It is, in principle, difficult to accept this view. Equity has long accepted that an equitable interest is capable of being the subject matter of an express trust, taking effect by way of sub-trust.[7] As a matter of principle there seems no reason why a constructive trust should not operate by way of sub-trust. However, the issue is not devoid of authority. In *Oughtred* v. *I.R.C.*[8] shares in a private company were settled on trust for a mother for life, remainder to her son. The mother was also entitled absolutely to certain other shares in the same company. Mother and son therefore agreed to exchange the shares to which she was absolutely entitled for his equitable remainder—thus her life interest would be enlarged into absolute ownership. Such an exchange prima facie attracted a heavy liability to stamp duty, which is payable *ad valorem* on any "instrument . . . whereby any property, or any estate or interest in any property, upon the sale thereof is transferred to or vested in a purchaser."[9] Under section 53(1)(c) of the Law of Property Act 1925, a disposition of a subsisting equitable interest must be made in writing. Thus, on the face of things, the assignment of the son's equitable remainder had to be made in a written document, which would attract *ad valorem* stamp duty. However, section 53(2) excepts from the provisions of section 53(1) implied, resulting and constructive trusts. The mother and son therefore argued that their oral contract for the exchange of the shares was specifically enforceable (clearly the case) and so gave rise to a constructive trust (or more strictly sub-trust) under which the son held his equitable remainder on constructive trust for his mother. No writing was necessary for the creation of this constructive sub-trust and

---

[6] *The Constructive Trust*, p. 116.
[7] See *Re Lashmar* [1891] 1 Ch. 258.
[8] [1960] A.C. 206.
[9] Stamp Act 1891, s.54.

the mother had therefore acquired an interest in the shares without the use of any instrument on which stamp duty could be levied. The subsequent transfer of the legal title to the shares from the trustees to her had transferred only the bare legal title which was worthless and therefore liable only to a nominal duty of 50p.

At first instance,[10] Upjohn J. accepted this argument and held that only 50p stamp duty was payable. Thus his lordship clearly thought that a constructive trust does arise under a contract for the sale of an equitable interest which is capable of being specifically enforced. However, in the Court of Appeal,[11] it was held that the transfer by the trustees to the mother was the contemplated completion of the oral contract. Hence it was a transfer upon sale and was therefore within the wording of the Stamp Act. On this approach (which is not without its problems as a matter of construction of the agreement), the constructive trust argument did not have to be considered. However, Lord Evershed M.R. (who gave the judgment of the court) commented that the court was not prepared to accept the conclusion of Upjohn J. as to the effect of section 53. In the House of Lords, the judgment of the Court of Appeal was affirmed by a majority. Lord Jenkins (with whose judgment Lord Keith of Avonholm concurred) held that, if the subject matter of a sale is such that the full title to it can only be transferred by an instrument, then any instrument executed by way of transfer ranks for the purposes of stamp duty as a conveyance upon sale. This conclusion was sufficient to dispose of the appeal and so Lord Jenkins did not reach any decision as to whether a constructive trust arose on conclusion of the oral contract. Nor did the other member of the majority, Lord Denning, who delivered a brief speech adopting the same view as the Court of Appeal. However, both the dissentients clearly accepted that the effect of the oral contract was that the son held his equitable remainder on constructive trust for his mother. Viscount Radcliffe followed the reasoning of Upjohn J. Lord Cohen, on the other hand, held that the existence of the constructive trust did not remove the need for a written assignment of the equitable remainder. However, he held that the transfer by the trustees could not have constituted such an assignment since they had only a bare legal title to transfer. Thus, the only two members of the House of Lords who considered the point (both admittedly dissenting on the main issue) clearly agreed with Upjohn J. that a constructive trust arose as a result of the oral contract. No contrary statement occurs

---

[10] [1958] Ch. 383.
[11] [1958] Ch. 678.

in any of the majority judgments—indeed the point was conceded by counsel for the Revenue. Further confirmation for the view that a constructive trust will arise as a result of a specifically enforceable contract to sell an equitable interest may be found in *Re Holt's Settlement*,[12] where Megarry J. held that, when beneficiaries of a trust agree, for valuable consideration, to a variation of the beneficial interests, their existing interests (which are necessarily equitable) become subject to a constructive trust. These authorities do not provide any support for the view of Professor Waters. Therefore, neither precedent nor principle suggests that a constructive trust does not arise under a specifically enforceable contract for the sale of an equitable interest. It is therefore suggested that a constructive trust does arise under such a contract. Thus the doctrine of conversion will operate whether the subject matter of the contract of sale in question is a legal interest or an equitable interest.

A somewhat analogous question arises in the case of a sub-sale (where before completion a purchaser himself enters into a contract to sell the whole or part of the subject matter to a third party sub-purchaser). Clearly in such a situation once the equitable doctrine of conversion has operated, the original vendor will hold the subject matter of the contract on constructive trust for the purchaser and the purchaser in his turn will hold his equitable interest in the subject matter of the contract of sub-sale on constructive sub-trust for the sub-purchaser. Equally clearly, in such a situation the sub-purchaser can in effect obtain specific performance of both contracts by compelling the purchaser to seek specific performance of his contract with the vendor—such an action is feasible because the sub-purchaser is the beneficiary of a completely constituted trust of the benefit of the original contract.[13] However, in certain circumstances the much more difficult question arises as to whether the sub-purchaser can maintain a direct action against the original vendor for breach of his duty of trusteeship. This problem had to be considered in *Berkley* v. *Poulett*.[14] The defendant, Lord Poulett, entered into a contract for the sale of his ancestral estate to a third party who simultaneously contracted to sub-sell to the plaintiff a part of that estate, including the principal house. Before either contract had been completed, Lord Poulett auctioned off the contents of the house, including several items which the plaintiff contended were fixtures and so should eventually have passed

---

[12] [1969] 1 Ch. 100.
[13] See *Fletcher* v. *Fletcher* (1844) 4 Hare 67.
[14] [1977] *Estates Gazette Digest* 754.

to him under his contract of sub-sale. Both contracts were subsequently completed and in this action the plaintiff sought delivery up of the alleged fixtures or damages for their loss. Of course, his most obvious means of bringing this about would have been to have compelled his immediate vendor, the third party, to bring an action for breach of trust against Lord Poulett. However, the third party was not in a position to bring such an action in respect of the alleged fixtures because he had completed his contract with Lord Poulett without reserving any rights in respect of them. Thus the plaintiff had to bring a direct action against Lord Poulett. This claim was dismissed by the Court of Appeal. Scarman L.J. merely held that none of the chattels in question was a fixture. This of course meant that the plaintiff had never been entitled to the chattels at all and so was not in a position to sue anyone. His lordship thus did not have to consider whether a sub-purchaser is able to maintain a direct action for breach of trust against the original vendor. Stamp L.J. held that a vendor does not become a constructive trustee for a sub-purchaser, even one of whose rights he is aware. Consequently a sub-purchaser can never maintain a direct action for breach of trust against the original vendor. His lordship then went on to agree with Scarman L.J. that in any event none of the chattels claimed was a fixture. The third member of the court, Goff L.J., however, dissented, holding that several of the chattels claimed were indeed fixtures and that the plaintiff sub-purchaser was entitled to maintain a direct action against Lord Poulett in respect of them. Thus, given that the only two members of the Court of Appeal to consider the matter disagreed, there is at present a conflict of authority as to whether a sub-purchaser can maintain a direct action for breach of trust against the original vendor. What is crucial to this issue is the presence or absence of mutuality. One of the defences to an action for specific performance is the absence of mutuality—the fact that, if the defendant rather than the plaintiff were claiming specific performance, no decree would be able to be granted. In other words, specific performance will not be ordered in favour of one party to a contract unless the other party would have been equally capable of obtaining specific performance against the claimant. Since the constructive trusteeship of a vendor only arises where the contract in question is capable of being specifically enforced, it is apparent that the ability of the sub-purchaser to bring a direct action for breach of trust against the original vendor is dependant upon each being able to obtain specific performance against the other. While the sub-purchaser is, as has already been mentioned, able to obtain specific performance against the original vendor indirectly by compell-

ing the purchaser to seek specific performance of his contract with
the vendor, there is no possibility whatever of the original vendor
being able to maintain an action for specific performance against
the sub-purchaser—how could the original vendor conceivably
maintain an action for specific performance against a person who
was not a party to any contract with him? Consequently, since
there is no mutuality as between the original vendor and the sub-
purchaser, there is no specifically enforceable obligation between
them and so the vendor cannot be a constructive trustee for the
sub-purchaser. It is therefore suggested that the view expressed by
Stamp L.J. is correct and that consequently it is not possible for a
sub-purchaser to maintain a direct action for breach of trust
against the original vendor. However, it must be emphasised that
this is only important where the original purchaser has put it out of
his power to maintain an action for breach of trust against the original vendor. Other than in this situation, the sub-purchaser will
always be able to sue the original vendor for breach of trust
indirectly by means of his own rights against his immediate vendor, the original purchaser.

### The moment of time at which the doctrine of conversion will operate

In principle the doctrine of conversion will operate as soon as a
valid and enforceable contract of the requisite type has been
formed. From that moment the vendor will hold the subject matter
of the contract on trust for the purchaser. Little difficulty arises in
the case of a contract for the sale of pure personalty. In normal circumstances, such a contract will be valid and enforceable as soon
as the parties agree to buy and sell the property in question. Thus,
the vendor will hold the subject matter of the contract on trust for
the purchaser from the moment of contract. However, as has
already been seen, comparatively few contracts for the sale of pure
personalty are capable of being specifically enforced. The vast
majority of cases to which the doctrine of conversion is relevant
concern contracts for the sale of land. Such contracts, in addition
to complying with the requirements of the ordinary law of contract, are only valid if the vendor is in a position to make title in
accordance with the contract or the purchaser agrees to accept
such title as the vendor has, notwithstanding that it is not in
accordance with the contract. The general law governing contracts
for the sale of land does not oblige the vendor to establish his title
until after the parties have entered into a binding contract. This is
for a very good reason—only an ill-advised purchaser would be

prepared to incur the very considerable expense of investigating title before the vendor was bound. Thus a contract for the sale of land will not normally become enforceable until some considerable time after the parties have entered into a binding contract. Thus, in the case of such contracts it is not immediately obvious at what stage the doctrine of conversion operates.

Initially the courts seem to have adopted the view that, as in the case of a contract for the sale of pure personalty, conversion occurs at the moment of contract.[15] However, during the eighteenth and nineteenth centuries this view came to be questioned and various other possibilities were suggested.[16] The law thus reached a state of confusion, from which it was rescued by the classic judgment of Jessel M.R. in *Lysaght* v. *Edwards*.[17] His lordship said this[18]:

> "the moment you have a valid contract for sale the vendor becomes in equity a trustee for the purchaser of the estate sold, and the beneficial ownership passes to the purchaser, the vendor having a right to the purchase-money, a charge or lien on the estate for the security of that purchase-money, and a right to retain possession of the estate until the purchase-money is paid, in the absence of express contract as to the time of delivering possession. . . . Now, what is the meaning of the term 'valid contract?' 'Valid contract' means in every case a contract sufficient in form and in substance, so that there is no ground whatever for setting it aside as between the vendor and purchaser—a contract binding on both parties. As regards real estate, however, another element of validity is required. The vendor must be in a position to make a title according to the contract, and the contract will not be a valid contract unless he has either made out his title according to the contract or the purchaser has accepted the title, for however bad the title may be the purchaser has a right to accept it, and the moment he has accepted the title, the contract is fully binding upon the vendor. Consequently, if the title is accepted in the lifetime of the vendor, and there is no reason for setting aside the contract, then, although the purchase-money is unpaid, the contract is valid and binding; and being a valid contract, it has this remarkable effect, that it converts

---

[15] *White* v. *Nutts* (1702) 1 P.Wms. 61, *per* Wright L.K. at p. 62.
[16] The various views are fully discussed and analysed by Professor D.W.M. Waters in *The Constructive Trust*, pp. 76–87.
[17] (1876) 2 Ch.D. 499.
[18] *Ibid.* pp. 506–507.

the estate, so to say, in equity; it makes the purchase-money a part of the personal estate of the vendor, and it makes the land a part of the real estate of the vendee; and therefore all those cases on the doctrine of constructive conversion are founded simply on this, that a valid contract actually changes the ownership of the estate in equity."

Thus, conversion occurs at the moment when the vendor makes title in accordance with the contract or, if he cannot do so, if and when the purchaser agrees to accept such title as the vendor has. However, his lordship went on to say that, once a contract was so valid, conversion took effect from the moment of contract.[19] This is generally taken to mean that once conversion has occurred it has retrospective effect from the moment of contract. In other words, once the vendor has made title in accordance with the contract or the purchaser has agreed to accept such title as the vendor has, conversion is deemed to have occurred from the moment at which the parties entered into a binding contract. If on the other hand the vendor cannot make title in accordance with the contract and the purchaser does not agree to accept such title as the vendor has, no conversion will occur at all.

The notion that the operation of the doctrine of conversion has a retrospective effect has considerable practical advantages. No difficulty is likely to be encountered in ascertaining the date upon which the parties enter into a binding contract. On the other hand, the precise moment at which the vendor makes title or the purchaser agrees to accept what title the vendor has is likely to be extremely unclear. The retrospective nature of conversion therefore enables the commencement of the vendor's trusteeship to be clearly established. This may be the reason why the principle enunciated in *Lysaght* v. *Edwards* has been adopted ever since. On the other hand, as Professor P.H. Pettit has demonstrated,[20] the notion of retrospective effect is not without its difficulties and it has been argued that conversion should be retrospective only where the vendor is in fact able to make title in accordance with the contract and not when the purchaser agrees to accept a title which is not in accordance with the contract. There is no case in which it has had to be decided whether conversion is or is not retrospective in effect when the purchaser agrees to accept a title which is not in accordance with the contract. A number of cases have arisen, however, where one of the parties to a binding contract has died before the purchaser has agreed to accept a title not

[19] At pp. 510 and 518.
[20] In (1960) 24 *Conveyancer* (N.S.) 47.

in accordance with the contract. In such a situation, the interest of the vendor has been held to devolve with his realty[21] and the interest of the purchaser has been held to devolve with his personalty.[22] But in these cases the title was never subsequently accepted and so there was never any conversion at all—thus the issue of retrospectivity did not arise. The point would have to be decided if a vendor who could not make title in accordance with the contract died leaving his realty and personalty to different persons and the purchaser subsequently agreed to accept such title as the vendor had. The point would also arise for decision if a purchaser who had agreed to accept a title not in accordance with the contract sought to impeach the vendor for a failure to look after the property between the date of the contract and the date of the acceptance of title—in such a case, the vendor would only be liable if his trusteeship predated the acceptance of title, in other words, only if conversion was retrospective to the date of contract. It is suggested that in this latter situation it would be unfortunate if it was decided that the trusteeship of the vendor did not arise until acceptance of title by the purchaser—such a rule would, in effect, oblige the purchaser to carry out a further inspection of the property before accepting the title. Therefore, it is suggested that conversion should be regarded as retrospective both where the vendor is able to make title in accordance with the contract and where the purchaser agrees to accept such title as the vendor has.

Thus in the case of contracts for the sale of land, the doctrine of conversion will not operate until the vendor has made title in accordance with the contract or the purchaser has agreed to accept a title not in accordance with the contract; however, once conversion has so occurred, its operation has retrospective effect from the moment at which the parties entered into a binding contract. How do these basic principles operate in relation to two particular types of contracts for the sale of land, compulsory purchases and options?

Where a contract for the sale of land arises as the result of a compulsory purchase by a Local Authority or by the Secretary of State for the Environment under the provisions of the Compulsory Purchase Act 1965, it is clear that there is no enforceable contract between the parties until the price has been ascertained, whether by agreement or by determination by the Lands Tribunal[23]—no

---

[21] *Re Thomas* (1886) 34 Ch.D. 166.
[22] *Broome* v. *Monck* (1805) 10 Ves. Jun. 597.
[23] *Re Manchester and Southport Railway Company* (1854) 19 Beav. 365, *Watts* v. *Watts* (1873) L.R. 17 Eq. 217.

contract for the sale of land is formed by the mere service of a notice to treat by the acquiring authority.[24] Consequently, when the vendor makes title to the land in question, the operation of the doctrine of conversion is retrospective only to the moment at which the price was ascertained, not to the moment when the notice to treat was served. Thus it is apparent that compulsory purchases comply with the basic principles governing contracts for the sale of land. This cannot be said, however, in the case of options, where the retrospective nature of conversion has caused some difficulties.

When the owner of property grants an option to purchase that property, there is obviously no binding contract of sale. Such a contract only exists when the option is exercised by the holder. When the subject matter of the option is land, the contract of sale will become valid only when the vendor makes title in accordance with the contract or the purchaser agrees to accept a title which is not in accordance with the contract. Conversion will clearly occur, therefore, at this stage. The question that therefore arises is to what point conversion will become retrospective—to grant of the option or to the exercise of the option. In principle, conversion should be retrospective only to the exercise of the option since there is no binding contract of sale until that moment. However, as a result of the decision in *Lawes* v. *Bennett*,[25] English law has long adopted a different view.

In *Lawes* v. *Bennett* a freeholder granted a lease which included an option to purchase the freehold. In a subsequent will, the freeholder left his realty and personalty to different persons. After the death of the freeholder, an assignee of the lease exercised the option and the question then arose as to whether the proceeds of sale were to devolve with the realty or the personalty. Kenyon M.R. held that the proceeds of sale were to devolve with the personalty—in other words, conversion operated retrospectively to the grant of the option, not to its exercise. This decision is extremely hard to justify and has been universally condemned. Nevertheless, it was followed by Lord Eldon L.C. in *Townley* v. *Bedwell*[26] and by Page-Wood V.C. in *Weeding* v. *Weeding*[27] and thus is clearly English law. Only statute, or perhaps the House of Lords, could now reverse this rule. However, it is important to note that the rule does not affect the enjoyment of the property

---

[24] *Re Shrewsbury and Hereford Railway* (1853) 1 Drew 508.
[25] (1785) 1 Cox. Eq. 167.
[26] (1808) 14 Ves.Jun. 591.
[27] (1861) 1 J. & H. 424.

pending exercise of the option, for the doctrine of conversion will not operate unless and until a valid and binding contract of sale is formed. Thus, upon the death of the grantor of the option, the property will devolve as realty and will continue to devolve as realty unless and until the option is exercised. Thus the person entitled to the realty takes an estate which is defeasible upon exercise of the option and the subsequent formation of a valid and binding contract of sale. Consequently, he is entitled to all the income from the property until that point—this was expressly held in *Townley* v. *Bedwell*.[28] Further, in the event that the option determines without having been exercised, his estate will become indefeasible.

Although the basic rule in *Lawes* v. *Bennett* thus remains English law, the judges have restricted its operation by a series of distinctions which are, if anything, more anomalous than the rule itself. It has been repeatedly held that, where the property in question is the subject of a specific devise after the grant of the option, the rule will not apply. This, as Page-Wood V.C. stated by way of dicta in *Weeding* v. *Weeding*[29] (where, as has already been mentioned, the rule in *Lawes* v. *Bennett* was actually applied), is because the testator, by making a specific devise of the property at a time when he was aware of the existence of the option, must have intended to pass to the devisee the entire interest therein, no matter what its nature. This rule has been applied not only where the will followed the grant of the option,[30] but also where a prior will was republished by codicil after the grant of the option[31] and where the will and the option were executed on the same day even though it was uncertain which was executed first.[32] Further, the courts have restricted the operation of the basic rule in *Lawes* v. *Bennett* to those interested in the estate of the grantor of the option. Therefore it does not apply as between those interested in the estate of the holder of the option[33] nor between the grantor and the holder of the option so as to make the former liable as a trustee of the subject matter between the grant and exercise of the option.[34] These latter restrictions do indeed reduce the ambit of the rule and limit the effects of its operation to volunteers. Nevertheless it is extremely difficult to see why the doctrine of conver-

---

[28] (1808) 14 Ves.Jun. 591.
[29] (1861) 1 J. & H. 424.
[30] *Drant* v *Vause* (1842) 1 Y. & C. 580.
[31] *Emuss* v. *Smith* (1848) 2 De G. & S. 722.
[32] *Re Pyle* [1895] 1 Ch. 724.
[33] *Re Adams and Kensington Vestry* (1884) 27 Ch.D. 394.
[34] *Edwards* v. *West* (1878) 7 Ch.D. 858.

sion should operate retrospectively to the grant of the option only for the purposes of the estate of the grantor. It is of course impossible to justify the rule in *Lawes* v. *Bennett* itself. However, given its undoubted existence, the law would be more satisfactory if it operated for all rather than merely for some purposes.[35]

Once a contract is valid in accordance with the rules that have just been discussed and the doctrine of conversion has consequently operated, the question may arise as to what is to happen if the contract is not in the end completed. It seems that in this situation the property that has been converted nevertheless devolves in its converted state quite irrespective of the reason why the contract has not been completed. In *Curre* v. *Bowyer*,[36] the vendor under a contract for the sale of freehold land died after the doctrine of conversion had operated and an action by the purchaser for specific performance against his personal representative subsequently failed because of delay, or laches, by the purchaser. The interest of the vendor was held to devolve with his personalty. Thus although the property in the estate was obviously realty, it devolved upon whoever was entitled to the personal property of the deceased vendor. Similarly, in *Whittaker* v. *Whittaker*,[37] the purchaser under a contract for the sale of land died after the equitable doctrine of conversion had operated. Owing to difficulties in the administration of his estate, there was a very long delay which led in the end to the vendor being released from the contract, which was therefore never completed. The estate of the purchaser was held to devolve in its converted state. This means in practice that in such circumstances any returned deposit or sum paid by way of damages will devolve upon whoever is entitled to the real property of the deceased purchaser. These two authorities both resulted from a failure to complete by one of the parties. However, the result is the same even if the contract is not completed for some other reason. In *Hudson* v. *Cook*[38] the purchaser under a contract for the sale of freehold land died after the doctrine of conversion had operated and the vendor subsequently exercised a contractual right to rescind the contract. The estate of the purchaser was held to devolve in its converted estate. Similarly, where a contract is rescinded *ab initio* for some reason such as misrepresentation after the doctrine of conversion has operated, the interests of the parties will nevertheless devolve in their converted

---

[35] The authorities are fully analysed by Professor D.W.M. Waters, *op. cit.* pp. 136–141.

[36] (1818) 5 Beav. 6n.

[37] (1792) 4 Bro.C.C. 31.

[38] (1872) 13 Eq. 417.

state. This follows from *Rose* v. *Watson*.[39] These authorities establish that non-completion of the contract, for whatever reason, after the doctrine of conversion has operated does not affect the converted state of the subject matter of the contract. This conclusion is perhaps at first sight somewhat surprising, particularly in the case of a contract which has been rescinded *ab initio* because the normal attitude of the courts when a contract is rescinded *ab initio* is to deem that there has never been such a contract. However, the attitude adopted by the courts can in fact be justified since, in the event that a failure to complete a contract brought about a reconversion of the property, the person with the right to determine whether or not the contract was completed would by his decision also be determining how the property in question was to devolve. Having said this, however, it must be admitted that similar arguments do not prevent a purchaser exercising an option or accepting a title not in accordance with the contract after the death of his vendor and thus determining by means of the resulting conversion how the latter's property will devolve. The distinction, presumably, is that anyone who has granted an option or entered into a contract of sale must have contemplated the possibility of the transaction being completed whereas it cannot be assumed that contracting parties will necessarily have contemplated the possibility of non-completion of their contract. Whether or not the attitude of the authorities can be justified, however, their approach is at least clear—non-completion of a contract, for whatever reason, after the doctrine of conversion has operated, does not affect the converted state of the property which is the subject matter of the contract.

**The position of the vendor**

It has already been seen that the effect of the operation of the doctrine of conversion is that the vendor will be deemed to hold the subject matter of the contract on constructive trust for the purchaser. However this trusteeship is clearly of a highly unusual nature. As Lord Cairns remarked in *Shaw* v. *Foster*[40]:

> " . . . the vendor, whom I have called the trustee, was not a mere dormant trustee, he was a trustee having a personal and substantial interest in the property, a right to protect that interest, and an active right to assert that interest if anything should be done in derogation of it. The relationship, there-

[39] (1864) 10 H.L.C. 672.
[40] (1872) L.R. 5 H.L. 321, 338.

fore, of trustee and *cestui que trust* subsisted, but subsisted subject to the paramount right of the vendor and trustee to protect his own interest as vendor of the property."

What then are the rights of the vendor during his trusteeship? He is clearly entitled to remain in possession of the property until completion and acquires an equitable lien on the property for payment of the purchase money.[41] Further, he is entitled to receive and retain all benefits of an income nature which accrue to the subject matter of the contract—thus a vendor of land may retain any rent which becomes due before completion.[42] However, as a necessary corollary the vendor must discharge all outgoings (such as rates and taxes) which become payable in respect of the property. Benefits of a capital nature, on the other hand, accrue prima facie for the benefit of the purchaser but, as will be seen later, the vendor is entitled to retain any benefits of a capital nature which are unconnected with the subject matter of the contract. Further, once the vendor has received the purchase money, the qualified nature of his trusteeship will disappear since the vendor no longer has any interest to protect. From that moment, pending transfer of the legal title, he will be a bare trustee and will therefore have to hand over all benefits to the purchaser. All these rules may be varied in any individual case by the express provisions of the contract.

The duties of the vendor, on the other hand, cannot be stated so precisely. The basic rule was stated by Lord Coleridge C.J. in *Clarke* v. *Ramuz*[43]: the vendor must "use reasonable care to preserve the property in a reasonable state of preservation, and, so far as maybe, as it was when the contract was made." Thus the vendor must keep the subject matter of the contract in repair—this was established in *Royal Bristol Permanent Building Society* v. *Bomash*[44] where damage was caused to the property by an outgoing tenant. Thus the vendor must repair broken windows and broken slates and must take reasonable steps to ensure that the property does not freeze up in wintertime.[45] He must not himself damage the property either intentionally or negligently—such intentional damage occurred in *Phillips* v. *Lamdin*,[46] where a vendor who replaced an ornate Adam door by a plain white wooden door was held liable to return and replace the door he had

---

[41] *Re Birmingham* [1959] Ch. 523.
[42] *Cuddon* v. *Tite* (1858) 1 Giff. 395.
[43] [1891] 2 Q.B. 456, 459–460.
[44] (1887) 35 Ch.D. 390.
[45] *Lucie-Smith* v. *Goreman* [1981] S.C.L. 286.
[46] [1949] 2 K.B. 33.

removed, and in *Cumberland Consolidated Holdings* v. *Ireland*,[47] where a vendor who left the cellars of the property two-thirds filled with bags of solidified cement was held liable for the costs of their removal, while an example of negligent damage would be the results of a fire caused by a vendor's carelessness. Nor must the vendor through lack of reasonable precautions permit others to damage the property—thus in *Clarke* v. *Ramuz* the vendor was held liable for failing to take reasonable precautions to prevent unknown strangers from removing several hundred cartloads of earth from the land. Nor must the vendor prejudice the future ability of the purchaser to deal with the land by, for example, withdrawing an application for planning permission—it was held in *Sinclair-Hill* v. *Southcott*[48] that if the vendor withdraws such an application without consulting his purchaser, he will be liable in damages if the withdrawal causes the purchaser loss or delay. All these principles are entirely straightforward.

However, particular difficulties can arise when land is sold subject to existing tenancies which come to an end before the contract is completed. In *Earl of Egmont* v. *Smith*[49] the vendors, at the request of the purchaser, gave their tenants notice to quit. Completion was delayed and so the vendors informed the purchaser that they intended to relet for a further yearly term on expiry of the notice. The purchaser did not reply so the vendors duly relet. The purchaser now claimed that the vendors were liable for the losses he suffered by virtue of their reletting. Jessel M.R. held that, where properties fall vacant before completion, it is the duty of the vendor to notify the purchaser. Subject thereto, the vendor must relet the premises unless the purchaser indicates otherwise and undertakes to indemnify the vendor (who is of course entitled to the rents) for any loss suffered thereby. Thus the claim failed. On the other hand, in *Abdulla* v. *Shah*,[50] the vendors had relet part of the premises without notifying the purchasers. Since the premises were subject to rent control, they were more valuable unlet and the purchasers therefore claimed that the vendors were liable for the loss of this extra value. The Privy Council upheld this claim. From these authorities it may be deduced that, in these days of universal rent control, a vendor who relets without notifying his purchaser will be liable for any loss suffered thereby. On the other hand, if the purchaser does not reply to this notification, the ven-

---

[47] [1946] K.B. 264.
[48] (1973) 226 E.G. 1399.
[49] (1877) 6 Ch.D. 469.
[50] [1959] A.C. 124.

dor is under a duty to relet—this is as much in his interest as that of the purchaser since he will normally be entitled to the rent. If, however, the purchaser directs the vendor not to relet and undertakes to reimburse him for any loss suffered thereby, the vendor will be quite safe in not reletting. All these duties of the vendor continue for as long as he remains in possession. This is the case even if the vendor remains in possession after the contractual completion date only because the purchaser has failed to complete on time.[51] Completion of the contract does not constitute waiver of any breach and so the purchaser can sue for such a breach even after completion. Further, since performance of these duties is as much in the interest of the vendor as the purchaser (because of the possibility of the sale falling through), the vendor is not entitled to be reimbursed for any expense he has thereby incurred.[52]

**The position of the purchaser**

The effect of the operation of the doctrine of conversion is that the purchaser is regarded in equity as the owner of the subject matter of the contract. Therefore it is often said that he becomes liable for all the risks attendant upon such ownership. While this is indeed the basic rule, in contracts for the sale of land a distinction has to be drawn between, on the one hand, defects in title that arise after the operation of the doctrine of conversion and, on the other hand, other events that occur after the doctrine has operated.

In a contract for the sale of land, the vendor is under a duty to make title in accordance with the contract by the contractual completion date. Consequently, if a defect in title arises after contract but before the contractual completion date (or, in the event that the vendor is not in a position to complete on the contractual completion date, before such later date as the vendor is first in a position to complete), this is entirely the responsibility of the vendor—the purchaser does not assume the risk of such a defect in title arising merely by entering into the contract. Even if a vendor makes title in accordance with the contract and thus brings about the operation of the doctrine of conversion, the subsequent appearance of a defect in title before the contractual completion date will place the vendor in breach of contract and the purchaser will thus be entitled to withdraw from the contract, recover his deposit and claim damages for breach of contract. Thus in *James*

---

[51] *Phillips* v. *Silvester* (1872) L.R. 8 Ch. 173.
[52] *Re Watford Corporation and Ware's Contract* [1943] Ch. 82.

*Macara* v. *Barclay*[53] the subject matter of the contract was requisitioned between the exchange of contracts and the contractual completion date and the Court of Appeal held that the purchaser was entitled to repudiate the contract and recover his deposit. Similarly in *Wroth* v. *Tyler*[54] the fact that the vendor's wife registered a charge under what is now the Matrimonial Homes Act 1983 only on the day after contracts for the sale of the property had been exchanged did not prevent the vendor from being liable for damages for breach of contract when he was unable to persuade her to remove the charge and so failed to make title on the contractual completion date. Of course in this case the fact that the defect arose so soon after the exchange of contracts meant that the vendor never actually made title in accordance with the contract and so the doctrine of conversion never in fact operated. But the result would have been identical if the vendor had made title in accordance with the contract (or, for that matter, if the purchaser had accepted such title as the vendor had) so that the doctrine of conversion had operated and his wife had subsequently registered her charge. However, it must be emphasised that the risk of a defect in title arising is only on the vendor until the contractual completion date or, in the event that the vendor is not in a position to complete on the contractual completion date, until such later date as the vendor is first in a position to complete. Where the vendor has made title in accordance with the contract (or, for that matter, the purchaser has accepted such title as the vendor has) by the contractual completion date, completion is delayed otherwise than through the fault of the vendor and a defect in title then arises during the period of delay, the vendor will not be in breach of contract and will be able to compel the purchaser to complete the contract. Thus in *Hillingdon Estates Co.* v. *Stonefield Estates*[55] the vendor had made title in accordance with the contract by the contractual completion date but, during a period of delay for which the vendor was not responsible, the Local Authority issued a compulsory purchase order in respect of the subject matter of the contract. The court emphasised that had this defect arisen before the contractual completion date the vendor would have been in breach of contract. However, since on the contractual completion date the vendor had been in a position to give the purchaser title in accordance with the contract, the court held that the vendor had complied with his contractual obligations

[53] [1945] 1 K.B. 148.
[54] [1974] Ch. 30.
[55] [1952] Ch. 627.

and consequently the risk of any subsequent compulsory purchase was on the purchaser. Any other conclusion would have been unjustifiable; had the purchaser completed on time, he would have been absolute owner of the subject matter by the time the compulsory order was issued—thus there was no reason why a delay in completion for which the vendor was not responsible should place the purchaser in a more favourable position.

Apart from such defects in title as are the responsibility of the vendor, however, the purchaser will indeed, once the doctrine of conversion has operated, become liable for all the risks attendant upon his equitable ownership of the subject matter of the contract. In the case of a contract for the sale of specific goods, accidental destruction of the subject matter before the risk has passed to the purchaser will of course avoid the contract.[56] It is also possible for any contract of sale to be frustrated by such occurrences as a subsequent change in the law, supervening illegality or the outbreak of war. But once the risk has actually passed to the purchaser by virtue of the operation of the doctrine of conversion, accidental destruction of the subject matter of the contract will not normally bring the doctrine of frustration into play. Consequently the purchaser will generally be liable to complete the contract and pay the purchase price in full no matter what happens to the subject matter of the contract. Further, although it has long been accepted that a contract for the hire of premises will be frustrated by their accidental destruction by fire[57] and although the House of Lords has now decided that there is no reason in principle why the doctrine of frustration should not, in appropriate circumstances, be equally applicable to an executed lease,[58] no English court has ever actually held that a contract for the sale of land has been frustrated. Admittedly in *Amalgamated Investment and Property Co.* v. *John Walker & Sons*[59] all three members of the Court of Appeal were prepared to assume that the doctrine of frustration did apply to contracts for the sale of land. However, they actually held that a contract for the sale of land was not frustrated by the fact that the buildings thereon had subsequently been listed as of special architectural or historic interest under the Town and Country Planning legislation (such a listing apparently does not constitute a defect in title). Similarly, in *Universal Corporation* v. *Five Ways Proper-*

---

[56] Sale of Goods Act 1979, s.7.
[57] *Taylor* v. *Caldwell* (1863) 3 B. & S. 826.
[58] *National Carriers* v. *Panalpina* (*Northern*) [1981] A.C. 675.
[59] [1977] 1 W.L.R. 164.

*ties*[60] the same Court, while again prepared to assume the said applicability of the doctrine to contracts for the sale of land, actually held that a change in Nigerian exchange control regulations which prevented a purchaser from withdrawing from that country the funds with which to complete his purchase did not frustrate the contract. These decisions were in accordance with earlier authorities which establish that a contract for the sale of land is not frustrated either by reason of an earthquake[61] or by the destruction of its buildings by fire[62] or by bomb damage[63] or by the imposition of a compulsory purchase order.[64] However, given that the object of the purchase in *Amalgamated Investment and Property Co.* v. *John Walker & Sons*—the redevelopment of the site in question—was rendered completely impossible by the listing, it is rather hard to see what will be held to constitute frustration of a contract for the sale of land short of the land in question actually disappearing (by, for example, falling into the sea). It has admittedly been held in Canada that a contract for the sale of land has been discharged by frustration. In *Capital Quality Homes* v. *Colwyn Construction*[65] the vendor had contracted to sell 26 lots of building land by separate conveyances to the purchaser. Shortly before the contractual completion date, the area in question became subject to sub-division control—this meant that very restrictive conditions had to be fulfilled before the land could be subdivided. This in practice meant that the vendor could not execute the 26 separate conveyances and, even though he could have conveyed the land to the purchaser in one conveyance, the legislation would then have prevented any sub-division by the purchaser. The Ontario Court of Appeal had no hesitation in holding that this intervention by the legislature had frustrated the contract. This decision has been accepted, although not actually applied, in several subsequent Canadian decisions; however, at least one of these decisions[66] has confined the doctrine to situations where the parties are engaged in a "common venture," this requirement presumably being satisfied in *Capital Quality Homes* v. *Colwyn Construction* by the fact that the vendor was participating in the purchaser's plans by agreeing to convey by 26 separate deeds. This

[60] [1979] 1 All E.R. 552.
[61] *Cass* v. *Rudele* (1693) 2 Vern. 280.
[62] *Paine* v. *Mellor* (1801) 6 Ves. 349.
[63] *Killner* v. *France* [1946] 2 All E.R. 83.
[64] *Hillingdon Estates Co.* v. *Stonefield Estates* [1952] Ch. 627.
[65] (1975) 61 D.L.R.(3d.) 385.
[66] *Victoria Wood Development Corporation* v. *Ondrey* (1978) 22 O.R.(2d.) 1

explanation of the decision is, presumably, how it would be reconciled with *Amalgamated Investment and Property Co.* v. *John Walker & Sons,* where the vendor was in no sense a participant in the purchaser's redevelopment plans. Thus, whether or not the Canadian approach is ever adopted here, it is clear that in a contract of sale where the doctrine of conversion has operated the doctrine of frustration is unlikely to be of any significant assistance to the purchaser.

The fact that the purchaser will generally be liable to complete the contract and pay the purchase price in full no matter what happens to the subject matter of the contract (even though he may be able to claim some abatement if, under the rules which have already been discussed, the vendor is in some way responsible for what has happened) generally causes him to safeguard himself against this risk by taking out insurance as from the date of contract. It is the normal practice for the solicitors retained by the purchaser in a contract for the sale of land to do this as a matter of course. However, in the event that no such insurance cover is taken out, the question will arise as to whether the purchaser is able to obtain the benefits of any insurance taken out by his vendor (the latter retains an insurable interest until he has received payment of the purchase price in full[67]). This question arose in *Rayner* v. *Preston*[68] and the Court of Appeal held that the purchaser was not entitled to recover the insurance money from the vendor on the grounds that a contract for the sale of land does not, without more, include the benefit of insurance policies thereon. (This does not mean that the vendor can obtain both the insurance money and the purchase price—if he claims under the policy, the insurance company will be subrogated to his claim for the purchase price. This issue arose as the direct result of the decision in *Rayner* v. *Preston* and was so resolved in *Castellain* v. *Preston*).[69] However, the basic rule established in *Rayner* v. *Preston* is now subject to section 47 of the Law of Property Act 1925, which enables a purchaser, on or after completion, to recover from the vendor any insurance money paid in respect of any damage to or destruction of property included in the contract. The apparent reversal of *Rayner* v. *Preston* contained in this provision is however qualified by the fact that the right so conferred is subject to any contrary stipulation in the contract of sale, any requisite consent of the insurance company, and the payment by the purchaser of the pro-

---

[67] *Collingridge* v. *Royal Exchange Assurance Corp.* (1877) 3 Q.B.D. 173.
[68] (1881) 18 Ch.D. 1.
[69] (1883) 11 Q.B.D. 380.

portionate amount of the premium from the date of contract. Many household insurance policies contain the necessary consent in general terms, thus rendering any express request unnecessary, although it is not clear whether the purchaser is able to take advantage of this provision if he pays the proportionate amount of the premium only after the loss has occurred. Further, while some standard form contracts for the sale of land do indeed expressly envisage the use of this provision,[70] others choose instead to expressly exclude it.[71] However, a purchaser under a contract for the sale of land, even if unable to take advantage of this statutory attempt to reverse *Rayner* v. *Preston,* may nevertheless not be without remedy where buildings on the land have been destroyed or damaged by fire. Section 83 of the Fire Prevention (Metropolis) Act 1774 (a provision which, despite the title of the Act, applies to all land in England and Wales[72]) provides that, where buildings have been so destroyed or damaged by fire, any person interested may require the insurance company to lay out the insurance money towards rebuilding or reinstating the building in question provided, of course, that the money has not already been paid out to the assured. There seems in principle no reason why the interest of a purchaser under a contract for the sale of land should not be sufficient to enable him to take advantage of this provision. However, for no very convincing reason, this possibility is discounted by many conveyancers.[73] However, even if a purchaser is able to bring himself within the scope of one or other of these statutory provisions, their existence is in no sense a full protection for the somewhat obvious reason that the vendor is under no obligation to insure at all. Consequently, every purchaser should always take pains to insure the subject matter of the contract.

So far as benefits are concerned, the basic rule is that the purchaser is entitled to all benefits of a capital nature which accrue to the actual subject matter of the contract subsequent to the operation of the doctrine of conversion. Thus if land which is the subject matter of a specifically enforceable contract of sale is improved between contract and conveyance, the purchaser will be entitled to that improvement even if the improvement is financed by the vendor.[74] However, the benefit in question must actually

---

[70] See Condition 7 of the current (20th) edition of the National Conditions of Sale.
[71] See Condition 11 of the current edition of The Law Society's General Conditions of Sale (1984 Revision).
[72] *Sinnott* v. *Bowden* [1912] 2 Ch. 414.
[73] Gibson, *Conveyancing* (20th ed.), p. 150, although *Williams on Vendor and Purchaser* (4th ed.), Vol. I, pp. 549–552 takes the opposite view.
[74] *Monro* v. *Taylor* (1848) 8 Hare 51 *per* Wigram V.C. at p. 60.

accrue to the property contracted to be sold—the vendor may retain any benefits of a capital nature which are unconnected with the contract of sale. It has already been seen that the vendor is at common law entitled to retain any insurance money that becomes payable to him after the doctrine of conversion has operated.[75] In *Re Lyne-Stephens and Scott-Miller's Contract,*[76] a vendor contracted to sell with vacant possession property which was subject to a lease due to determine between contract and conveyance. Under the terms of the lease, the vendor became entitled to a sum in respect of delapidations. Sargant J. and the Court of Appeal held that the vendor was entitled to retain this sum on the grounds that the subject matter of the contract was the house, not the house subject to the lease. Similarly, in *Re Hamilton-Snowball's Conveyance,*[77] the respondent was in occupation of a house which had been requisitioned by a local authority. He contracted to purchase the house from the then owners subject to the requisition and on the same day contracted to resell the house at a much higher price. This second contract contained no mention of the requisition simply because the sale and conveyance to the respondent would cause the property to be derequisitioned. The house was duly conveyed to the respondent and derequisitioned and then conveyed on under the contract of resale. The owner of the property on the date of derequisition was entitled to a payment by way of compensation. The purchaser under the contract of resale claimed this sum as an accrual to the property between contract and conveyance. However, Upjohn J. held that the contract of sale included only the house not the compensation money. Thus, the right of the purchaser to capital benefits is clearly limited to accruals to the actual subject matter of the contract. So far as benefits of an income nature are concerned, it has already been seen that these are the property of the vendor until payment of the purchase price but thereafter belong to the purchaser. Once again, however, all these rules may be varied in any individual case by the express provisions of the contract.

Further, once the purchaser has become owner of the property in equity as a result of the operation of the doctrine of conversion, he is entitled to rely on his equitable ownership of the property in any way he pleases. Thus, a purchaser under a contract for the sale of land is entitled, once the doctrine of conversion has operated, to enter into contracts of sub-sale and to carry out such activities as making applications for planning permission to develop the sub-

---

[75] *Rayner* v. *Preston* (1881) 18 Ch.D. 1.
[76] [1920] 1 Ch. 472.
[77] [1959] Ch. 308.

ject matter of the contract—this was expressly stated by Slade J. in *English* v. *Dedham Vale Properties.*[78] However, the purchaser must take care not to purport to exercise his rights as equitable owner until he has actually acquired the necessary equitable ownership of the subject matter. This is illustrated by the facts of *English* v. *Dedham Vale Properties* where, seven days before the parties entered into formal contracts, the prospective purchaser, purporting without authority to act as agent for the prospective vendors, submitted an application for planning permission in respect of part of the subject matter of the proposed sale. Outline planning permission was duly granted between exchange of contracts and completion but the vendors did not learn of the successful planning application that had been made in their names until some months after completion. They now successfully sought an account of the profits accruing to the defendant by reason of the grant of the planning permission. Slade J. held that where in the course of negotiations for a contract of sale and purchase of land the proposed purchaser, in the name of and purporting to act as agent of the proposed vendor but in fact without his knowledge or consent, takes some action in regard to the subject matter of the proposed contract, such as entering into a contract of sub-sale or making an application for planning permission, which if disclosed to the proposed vendor might reasonably be supposed to have been likely to have influenced his decision as to whether to enter into a contract, a fiduciary relationship arises between the two parties; consequently if the self-appointed agent fails, before the contracts are actually entered into, to disclose to the proposed vendor what he has done, he will be obliged to account to the vendor for any profit he has made as a result of the purported agency. Consequently, his lordship ordered an account of the profits made by the defendant as a result of the non-disclosure to the vendors of the application for and subsequent grant of planning permission in the vendors' name. This decision is of course entirely consistent with the authorities on intermeddlers discussed in Chapter Four— see for example *Lyell* v. *Kennedy*[79] where the House of Lords imposed a constructive trust on a self-appointed agent who had for twenty-two years collected the rents of property which he knew to belong to another. However, it is equally clear that had the defendant waited a further seven days before submitting the application, the vendors would have had no claim whatsoever. Conse-

---

[78] [1978] 1 W.L.R. 93.
[79] (1889) 14 App.Cas. 437, discussed on pp. 86–87.

quently the result of the case, while wholly justifiable, produced a wholly unexpected and somewhat fortuitous benefit for the vendors. It is certainly not probable that many other cases of this kind will arise.

Finally, the existence of a constructive trust may be of assistance to a purchaser where the vendor in breach of contract transfers the subject matter of the sale to a third party who takes free of the interest of the purchaser. In such a situation the purchaser will obviously be able to claim damages for breach of contract from the vendor. However, the existence of the trust will enable him alternatively to claim the purchase money paid to the vendor by the third party. Since the vendor has sold property which formed the subject matter of a trust in breach of that trust, the purchaser is able to trace that property into its product—the purchase money. This type of claim succeeded in *Lake* v. *Bayliss,*[80] where a vendor agreed to sell land in exchange for the abatement of certain writs. The purchaser failed to protect his estate contract by the necessary registration and the vendor subsequently sold the land for £50,000 to a third party who of course took free of the interest of the purchaser. The purchaser now claimed that he was entitled to obtain the £50,000 in exchange for the abatement of the writs. This entirely novel claim succeeded before Walton J. This remedy will normally be of no particular assistance to a purchaser. He will have to account to the vendor for the purchase price and so will only recover the difference between the contract price and the price paid by the third party—exactly the same as the measure of damages for breach of contract where the third party paid the market price. However, in three situations this remedy will be advantageous to a purchaser. Where, as in *Lake* v. *Bayliss,* the consideration for the purchase is other than monetary, the measure of damages for breach of contract will be more or less nil since the consideration on each side will normally have been subject to identical inflation. The existence of the trust, however, will enable the purchaser to recover in exchange for the agreed consideration the entire sum paid by the third party. Secondly, where the third party pays more than the market price, damages for breach of contract will be only the difference between the contract price and the market price. The existence of the trust will enable the purchaser to recover the difference between the contract price and the price actually paid by the third party. Finally, where the vendor is bankrupt, the existence of the trust will enable the purchaser to take priority over the

[80] [1974] 1 W.L.R. 1073.

general creditors of the vendor—a priority which a claim for damages for breach of contract would not obtain. In these three situations, this rather unexpected extension of the trusteeship of the vendor will be most advantageous to a purchaser.

## The nature of the trust imposed on the vendor

The judges have traditionally described the trust imposed upon the vendor under a contract of sale which is capable of being specifically enforced as a constructive trust. It is clear that such a trust will arise whenever a valid contract of sale is capable of being specifically enforced. Since the availability of specific performance is governed by fixed and settled principles, it is clear that the trust arises by operation of law quite independently of the intentions of the parties. Therefore, it is suggested that it is correct to classify this trust as a constructive trust.

## Conclusion

Professor Waters has claimed that the existence of the constructive trust between vendor and purchaser "has led to no conceptual development in the law of sale and . . . has in fact created problems which otherwise would not have existed."[81] He therefore argues that "the vendor/purchaser relationship is one which could always have been contained adequately within the law of contract."[81] It is certainly possible to argue that anomalous rules such as that enunciated in *Lawes* v. *Bennett* would not have arisen had the relationship between vendor and purchaser been governed entirely by the law of contract. On the other hand, the practice of implying terms into contracts to govern situations to which the parties have clearly given not the slightest thought has not always been a particularly happy one and it is by no means certain that different anomalies might not have resulted from basing the relationship entirely on the law of contract. Historically, the relationship was based upon the law of trusts because the special nature of the relationship was recognised only by equity and the trust was the concept with which equity was most familiar. Generally speaking, apart from the totally unjustifiable rule in *Lawes* v. *Bennet,* the courts have managed to apply the trust concept consistently to the different problems that have arisen—there seems little objec-

---

[81] *Op. cit.* pp. 141–142, summarising the previous argument on pp. 87–141.

tion to the vast majority of the rules which have been formulated. Therefore, there seems little justification for or likelihood of any attempt to recast the relationship between vendor and purchaser on a purely contractual basis. It is therefore suggested that the constructive trust provides an acceptable basis for the relationship between vendor and purchaser.

## Chapter 7

## CONSTRUCTIVE TRUSTS IMPOSED
## UPON MORTGAGEES

Before the enactment of the Property Legislation of 1925, the vast
majority of mortgages of land were effected by means of transfer
of the subject matter of the mortgage to the mortgagee subject to a
proviso for retransfer upon discharge of the mortgage debt. The
mortgagee thus became legal owner of the subject matter of the
mortgage but his rights of ownership were clearly fettered by
reason of his obligations to the mortgagor. The precise nature of
the ownership of the mortgagee was called into question in a large
number of cases and many judges saw fit to describe the mortgagee
as a constructive trustee of the mortgaged property. Professor
D.W.M. Waters has carried out an exhaustive investigation of the
development of this concept and has illustrated that, by the end of
the nineteenth century, the courts had come to recognise that the
mortgagee, as such, was not a trustee at all.[1] However, it had
become clearly established that a mortgagee might be held to have
become a constructive trustee as a result of the exercise of his
powers under the mortgage and that, once the mortgage debt had
been fully repaid, the mortgagee became a constructive trustee of
the mortgaged property pending its retransfer to the mortgagor.
Most of this body of law has been swept away as a result of the
enactment of the Law of Property Act 1925, which prohibited the
creation of mortgages of land by way of transfer of the subject
matter. The mortgaged property must now remain vested in the
mortgagor and so the mortgagee may only obtain a lesser interest
therein. Hence, a mortgagee cannot possibly become a trustee of
the mortgaged property since the property cannot now be vested
in him. Therefore, a mortgagee can now become a constructive
trustee only in respect of property which reaches his hands as a
result of the exercise of his powers under the mortgage. Only to
this extent does the earlier law retain any significance. Therefore
this chapter will merely consider the two situations in which the
constructive trust remains relevant, namely where a mortgagee

---

[1] See *The Constructive Trust*, pp. 144–224. The change in attitude referred to
seems to stem from the classic judgment of Plumer M.R. in *Marquis Cholmon-
deley* v. *Lord Clinton* (1820) 2 Jac. & W. 1, pp. 182 *et seq.*

exercises his power of sale and where he exercises his right to enter into possession of the mortgaged property.

## The exercise by a mortgagee of his power of sale

At common law a mortgagee had no effective power of sale, merely a right to transfer the mortgaged property subject to the equitable right of the mortgagor to redeem the mortgage. Thus, the practice arose of inserting an express power of sale of the mortgaged property in the mortgage deed (this power is now implied by s.101(1)(i) of the Law of Property Act 1925 provided that the mortgage is by deed). After some initial uncertainty, it became clear that the mortgagee was not a trustee of his power of sale and therefore could exercise his contractual right quite irrespective of the interests of the mortgagor.[2] However, it was equally clear that, if the exercise of power of sale produced more than was necessary for the discharge of the liability of the mortgagor, the surplus was held by the mortgagee upon a constructive trust for the mortgagor.[3] The reforms of 1925 are in no way inconsistent with the continued existence of this trust. However, in 1881, the legislature had intervened to provide that the mortgagee held any surplus arising from the exercise of his power of sale upon a statutory trust for those entitled to the equity of redemption.[4] This provision was reproduced in section 105 of the Law of Property Act 1925 as follows:

> "The money which is received by the mortgagee, arising from the sale, after discharge of prior incumbrances to which the sale is not made subject, if any, or after payment into court under this Act of a sum to meet any prior incumbrance, shall be held by him in trust to be applied by him, first, in payment of all costs, charges, and expenses properly incurred by him as incident to the sale or any attempted sale, or otherwise; and, secondly, in the discharge of the mortgage money, interest, and costs, and other money, if any, due under the mortgage; and the residue of the money so received shall be paid to the person entitled to the mortgaged property, or authorised to give receipts for the proceeds of the sale thereof."

This section obliges the mortgagee to apply the purchase money in the following order: first, in the discharge of prior incumbrances to which the sale is not made subject; secondly, in the discharge of

---

[2] *Warner* v. *Jacob* (1882) 20 Ch.D. 220.
[3] *Banner* v. *Berridge* (1881) 18 Ch.D. 254.
[4] Conveyancing Act 1881, s.21(3).

the costs of sale and thirdly in the discharge of the mortgage debt. Any surplus must then be paid to the person entitled to the mortgaged property or authorised to give receipts for the proceeds of sale. This includes subsequent mortgagees and therefore the mortgagee must pay any surplus to any subsequent mortgagees of whose rights he has notice rather than to the mortgagor.[5] Whether this statutory trust has superseded the old constructive trust is far from clear—in *Re Thomson's Mortgage Trusts*[6] counsel quite clearly took the view that the constructive trust continues to exist alongside the statutory trust. Since no attempt has been made to abolish the constructive trust, this argument is technically justifiable but it seems highly artificial. Further, the judges have been content to apply the pre-1881 decisions to the statutory trust[7] which seems to suggest that they regard the statutory trust as a codified form of the old constructive trust rather than as a new trust existing alongside it. It is therefore suggested that the old constructive trust of the proceeds of sale should be regarded as having been totally superseded by the statutory trust.

**The exercise by a mortgagee of his right to enter into possession**

As between the parties to a mortgage it has always been the law that the mortgagee has the right to possession of the mortgaged property. This right, which before 1926 arose by virtue of the fact that the mortgagee held the legal title, was expressly preserved by section 95(4) of the Law of Property Act 1925. Thus, as Harman J. remarked in *Four-Maids* v. *Dudley Marshall (Properties)*,[8] "[t]he mortgagee may go into possession before the ink is dry on the mortgage unless there is something in the contract, express or by implication, whereby he has contracted himself out of that right." Thus, in the absence of such a provision and subject to various restrictions imposed by statute where the subject matter of the mortgage is a dwellinghouse,[9] a mortgagee has an unassailable right to take possession of the mortgaged property.

Once in possession however, the mortgagee becomes liable to account to the mortgagor on what is described as "a footing of wilful default." This means that a mortgagee in possession has to account not merely for benefits actually obtained from his pos-

---

[5] *Re Thomson's Mortgage Trusts* [1920] Ch. 508.
[6] [1920] Ch. 508.
[7] See *Young* v. *Clarey* [1948] Ch. 191.
[8] [1957] Ch. 317 at p. 320.
[9] Administration of Justice Act 1970, s.36, Administration of Justice Act 1973, s.8.

session but also for all benefits that could have been obtained therefrom. Thus a mortgagee who himself remains in possession will have to account for a full occupation rent and a mortgagee who takes advantage of his statutory power to lease the mortgaged property will have to account for the maximum rent that could conceivably have been obtained. For example, in *White* v. *City of London Brewery*,[10] a brewery, having entered into possession of a mortgaged public house, let it as a tied house and were held liable to account not only for the rent actually received but also for the additional rent that would have been obtained by letting it as a free house. The extreme nature of this liability does not exactly encourage mortgagees to enter into possession. However, a mortgagee who wishes to exercise a power of sale will often be obliged to enter into possession for at least a short period in order to be able to give vacant possession to the purchaser.

The precise nature of this liability to account is not free from controversy. Until the middle of the nineteenth century, many judges saw fit to describe all mortgagees as constructive trustees of the mortgaged property. This terminology was obviously particularly appropriate when the mortgagee was in possession under an obligation to account and so there are a number of decisions dating from this period in which mortgagees in possession were described as constructive trustees of the rents and profits.[11] However, as has already been seen, by the end of the nineteenth century the courts had come to recognise that a mortgagee, as such, was not a trustee at all. It therefore came to be accepted that a mortgagee was no more a trustee when he was in possession than at any other time.[12] Consequently, the obligation of a mortgagee in possession in respect of rents and profits became no more than an obligation to account for such sums to the mortgagor. This view seems to be entirely in accordance with principle. How can a constructive trust effectively be imposed upon sums which the mortgagee should have but in fact has not received? An obligation to account for such sums seems far more appropriate in every way. Nevertheless, at least one leading text[13] still describes a mortgagee in possession as a constructive trustee of the rents and profits, citing as authority the same five cases, all decided in or before 1821.[14] These

---

[10] (1889) 42 Ch.D. 237.

[11] *The Constructive Trust*, pp. 189–197.

[12] *Kirkwood* v. *Thompson* (1865) 2 De G.J. & S. 613.

[13] *Lewin on Trusts* (16th ed.), p. 149.

[14] *Copping* v. *Cooke* (1684) 1 Vern. 270, *Bentham* v. *Haincourt* (1691) Prec.Ch. 30, *Parker* v. *Calcroft* (1821) 6 Madd. 11, *Hughes* v. *Williams* (1806) 12 Ves. 493, *Maddocks* v. *Wren* (1680) 2 Ch.Rep. 209.

decisions (and other authorities dating from the same period)[15] provide support for this proposition but this is hardly surprising since at this stage the judges regarded mortgagees as constructive trustees for almost all purposes. It is suggested that the view put forward in *Lewin* does not take sufficient account of the later developments which have already been discussed. In any event it is clear that, for at least the last hundred years, the judges have described the liability of the mortgagee in possession merely as a liability to account for rents and profits. It is therefore suggested that a mortgagee in possession is not a constructive trustee of rents and profits.

**Conclusion**

Professor Waters has stated that "the constructive trust between mortgagor and mortgagee is nothing else today, and particularly since 1925, than an arid debating point."[16] This view seems entirely justified. The reforms of 1925 remove any possibility of regarding the mortgagee as a constructive trustee of the subject matter of the mortgage. It has already been suggested that the old constructive trust of the proceeds of sale has been superseded by the statutory trust now contained in section 105 of the Law of Property Act 1925 and it has been clear for more than a hundred years that the liability of a mortgagee in possession to account for rents and profits does not arise under a constructive trust. Therefore, it is suggested that, so far as the mortgagee is concerned, the constructive trust no longer has any role to play.

---

[15] *Amhurst* v. *Dawling* (1700) 2 Vern. 401, *Chambers* v. *Goldwin* (1804) 9 Ves.Jun. 254 at p. 272.
[16] *Op. cit.* p. 227.

Chapter 8

# CONSTRUCTIVE TRUSTS IMPOSED TO GIVE EFFECT TO INCOMPLETE TRANSFERS

No transfer of the legal title to property is effective until all the necessary formalities have been completed. Where the parties to a transfer are themselves capable of carrying out all the appropriate formalities, any failure to comply with any necessary formal requirement will inevitably make the transfer in question wholly ineffective both at law and in equity. However, the formalities necessary for the transfer of the legal title to certain kinds of property cannot all be carried out by the parties themselves. A transfer of registered land is not effective to pass the legal title to that land until the duly executed transfer form is presented to the Land Registry and registered in the Register of Titles. Similarly a transfer of shares is not effective to pass the legal title to those shares until the transferor has complied with the procedure required by the Articles of Association of the company in question and the transfer is duly registered in the Register of Shareholders. In both these cases, the intervention of a third party is necessary to enable legal title to pass; consequently the transfer will not be effective at law until the third party in question acts. However, it has been held that once the parties have complied with all the formal requirements capable of being carried out by themselves, the transfer will become effective in equity and the transferor will hold the property in question on trust for the transferee pending the intervention of the third party. This rule was established by the Court of Appeal in *Re Rose*[1] and for this reason is generally known as the Rule in *Re Rose*.

**The rule in Re Rose**

In *Re Rose*, the registered owner of shares executed two share transfers, one in favour of his wife absolutely and the other in favour of his wife and a third party on certain trusts. These transfers were duly registered exactly three months later. The transferor subsequently died more than five years after the execution of the transfers but less than five years after their regis-

[1] [1952] Ch. 499.

174

tration. At this time no estate duty was payable on property disposed of more than five years before death.[2] Were the transfers effective upon execution or upon registration? The Court of Appeal held that, although the legal title to the shares had not passed until the transfers had been registered, from the moment of their execution the transferor had held the legal title to the shares on trust for the transferees. The beneficial interest in the shares had thus passed to them on the execution of the transfers more than five years before the death of the transferor so that no estate duty was payable thereon. The Court of Appeal held that this trust arose simply because the transferor, once he had executed the transfers in the appropriate form, had done all in his power to vest the legal interest in the property in the transferee.

This conclusion is not easy to reconcile with the classic judgment of Turner L.J. in *Milroy* v. *Lord*[3] where the Court of Appeal in Chancery laid down the general rule that any failure to comply with any necessary formal requirement will make the transfer wholly ineffective both at law and in equity. Turner L.J. expounded the law in the following justifiably famous passage[4]:

> "I take the law of this court to be well settled, that, in order to render a voluntary settlement valid and effectual, the settlor must have done everything which, according to the nature of the property comprised in the settlement, was necessary to be done in order to transfer the property and render the settlement binding upon him. He may, of course, do this by actually transferring the property to the persons for whom he intends to provide, and the provision will then be effectual, and it will be equally effectual if he transfers the property to a trustee for the purposes of the settlement, or declares that he himself holds it in trust for these purposes; and if the property be personal, the trust may, as I apprehend, be declared either in writing or by parol; but, in order to render the settlement binding, one or other of these modes must, as I understand the law of this court, be resorted to, for there is no equity in this court to perfect an imperfect gift. The cases, I think, go

---

[2] The necessary period was subsequently increased to seven years but this particular exemption disappeared with the abolition of Estate Duty and the introduction of Capital Transfer Tax in 1974. However the replacement of Capital Transfer Tax by Inheritance Tax in 1986 has brought about the return of this exemption; consequently the Rule in *Re Rose* has once again become extremely significant.

[3] (1862) 4 De G.F. & J. 264.

[4] *Ibid*. pp. 274–275.

further to this extent: that if the settlement is intended to be effectuated by one of the modes to which I have referred, the court will not give effect to it by applying another of those modes. If it is intended to take effect by transfer, the court will not hold the intended transfer to operate as a declaration of trust, for then every imperfect instrument would be made effectual by being converted into a perfect trust. These are the principles by which, as I conceive, this case must be tried."

The final section of this passage clearly appears to negate any possibility of the court interpreting an ineffective transfer as a declaration of trust. However in *Re Rose* the Court of Appeal held that the statement of Turner L.J. to this effect applied only where the transfer in question had not been carried out in the appropriate way (admittedly this was the situation under consideration in *Milroy* v. *Lord* since no document in the appropriate form had ever been executed[5]). Sir Raymond Evershed M.R. said this[6]:

"I agree that if a man purporting to transfer property executes documents which are not apt to effect that purpose, the court cannot then extract from those documents some quite different transaction and say that they were intended merely to operate as a declaration of trust which *ex facie* they were not; but if a document is apt and proper to transfer the property— is, in truth, the appropriate way in which the property must be transferred—then it does not seem to me to follow from the statement of Turner L.J. that, as a result, either during some limited period or otherwise, a trust may not arise, for the purpose of giving effect to the transfer. The simplest case will, perhaps, provide an illustration. If a man executes a document transferring all his equitable interest, say, in shares, that document, operating and intended to operate as a transfer, will give rise to and take effect as a trust, for the assignor will then be a trustee of the legal estate in the shares for the person in whose favour he has made an assignment of his ben-

---

[5] A settlor convenanted to transfer certain bank shares to the defendant on trust for the plaintiffs. The defendant already held a general power of attorney to transfer shares of the settlor so the settlor merely handed over the share certificates to the defendant and gave him a further power of attorney authorising him to receive the dividends. During the next three years the defendant duly received the dividends but neither he nor the settlor ever procured the entry in the books of the bank which was necessary for the transfer of the legal title. Following the death of the settlor, the plaintiffs were held to be unable to enforce the trust of the shares.

[6] [1952] Ch. 499, 510.

eficial interest. And for my part I do not think that *Milroy* v.
*Lord* is an authority which compels this court to hold that in
this case, where, in the terms of Turner L.J.'s judgment, the
settlor did everything which, according to the nature of the
property comprised in the settlement, was necessary to be
done by him in order to transfer the property, the result
necessarily negatives the conclusion that, pending registration, the settlor was a trustee of the legal interest for the transferee.''

In reaching this conclusion his lordship emphasised that, if in
spite of having executed the transfers the transferor had remained
beneficially entitled to the shares, he would have been entitled, as
against the transferees, to any dividends declared between
execution and registration. His lordship doubted whether such a
result would even be comprehensible to anyone other than a law-
yer. Thus the Court of Appeal held that, as soon as a transferor
has correctly complied with all the formal requirements that have
to be carried out by him, he will hold the subject matter of the
transfer on trust for the transferor pending performance of such
remaining formalities as have to be carried out by third parties.

On the assumption that the decision in *Re Rose* can thus be
reconciled with *Milroy* v. *Lord*, can the rule so established be supported? This obviously depends on whether it is possible to say
with certainty when a transferor has done all in his power to vest
the legal interest in the property in question in the transferee. It is
of course possible to establish whether the transferor has executed
all the necessary documents in the appropriate form. Where difficulties arise is in relation to the rôle of the third party. Some third
parties have a merely formal rôle in that they have no effective discretion to refuse to act—those responsible for registering a
transfer of registered land or the transfer of shares in a public company presumably fall within this category. Is the Rule in *Re Rose*
limited to situations such as these or does it also operate where the
third party in question is able to decline to act? In *Re Rose* itself,
because of the nature of the company in question, its directors had
the right to refuse to register the share transfers. This suggests that
the rule will indeed operate even where the third party in question
is entitled to decline to act. However on this point it is difficult to
reconcile *Re Rose* with the decision in *Re Fry*.[7] In this case, which
was admittedly decided before *Re Rose*, a gift by an American
donor required exchange control consent from the Treasury. The

---

[7] [1946] Ch. 312.

donor executed all the necessary documents, including the necessary application forms to the Treasury but the gift was held to be wholly ineffective unless and until the consent was obtained. In *Re Rose* the Court of Appeal regarded *Re Fry* as a case in which the donor had not done all in his power to vest the property in the donee but it is not easy to see what more he could actually have done. Further, if the absence of the Treasury consent made the gift in *Re Fry* imperfect, why was the gift in *Re Rose* not imperfect until the directors had given their consent? However, the only conclusion that can be drawn from *Re Rose* is that the rule enunciated by the Court of Appeal in that case will operate no matter what the rôle of the third party.

Despite the doubts expressed in the previous paragraph the Rule in *Re Rose* is clearly English law at the present time. The rule was applied by Lord Wilberforce in *Vandervell* v. *I.R.C.*[8] in order to justify his conclusion as to the scope of section 53(1)(*c*) of the Law of Property Act 1925[9] and more recently in *Mascall* v. *Mascall*[10] it was held that delivery by the transferor of registered land to the transferee of a duly executed transfer form and the land certificate will bring the rule into operation. What then is the nature of the trust that arises as a result of the operation of the Rule in *Re Rose*? It is clear that this trust does not arise out of any intention of the parties thereto; it must therefore necessarily be brought into existence by operation of law. It is therefore suggested that the trust brought into existence by the operation of the Rule in *Re Rose* is a constructive trust.

### Conclusion

While some of the aspects of the Rule in *Re Rose* have yet to be fully clarified, there is no doubt whatever that that rule is English law at the present time. Any trust that arises as a result of the operation of the rule clearly arises by operation of law and therefore should be classified as a constructive trust.

---

[8] [1967] 2 A.C. 291.
[9] In fact the argument used by Lord Wilberforce was circular (see Hayton and Marshall, *Cases and Commentary on the Law of Trusts* (8th Ed.), p. 74) but that does not alter the fact that he applied the Rule in *Re Rose*.
[10] (1984) 50 P. & C.R. 119.

# INDEX